ECOHOLIC HOME

THE GREENEST,

CLEANEST AND

MOST ENERGY-EFFICIENT

INFORMATION

UNDER ONE (CANADIAN) ROOF

# ADRIA VASIL

BASED ON THE POPULAR NOW COLUMN

# ECOHOLIC HOME

VINTAGE CANADA

VINTAGE CANADA EDITION, 2009

Adapted from the "Ecoholic" columns previously published in
NOW *Magazine*, Toronto, Canada.

Published by Vintage Canada, a division of Random House of Canada Limited, in 2009. Distributed in Canada by Random House of Canada Limited, Toronto.

Vintage Canada with colophon is a registered trademark.

www.randomhouse.ca

Library and Archives Canada Cataloguing in Publication

Vasil, Adria
Ecoholic home : the greenest, cleanest and most energy-efficient information under one (Canadian) roof / Adria Vasil.

Includes bibliographical references and index.

ISBN 978-0-307-35714-4

1. Sustainable living—Handbooks, manuals, etc. 2. Household ecology. 3. Green products—Canada—Handbooks, manuals, etc. I. Title.

QH541.5.H67 V38 2009      640      C2009-900381-3

© **Mixed Sources**
Product group from well-managed forests, controlled sources and recycled wood or fiber
FSC   www.fsc.org  Cert no. SCS-COC-00648
© 1996 Forest Stewardship Council

Book design by Kelly Hill

Printed and bound in the United States of America

2    4    6    8    9    7    5    3    1

# CONTENTS

# INTRODUCTION

Peel away the layers and one thing most Canadians have in common is a roof over our heads (the pelting snow that whacks us in January kind of necessitates that). Now, whether that shelter takes the form of a tiny apartment on the 20th floor of a drafty old building, a 5,000-square-foot McMansion in the burbs or a remote wooden cabin with bears for neighbours, we all know we can do a little more to green up this country. In fact, we have to. Canadian households are responsible for a whopping 46% of the nation's total climate-cooking emissions (ha, and you thought your a/c cranking could go unnoticed). A large chunk of those greenhouse gases comes from obvious sources like the car you have parked outside, the fuel in your furnace and the electricity you pull from the wall, but a surprising percentage of emissions comes buried in all the things we buy (from flatscreen TVs to imported lettuce). No matter where those greenhouse gases come from, one thing's clear: we're getting more and more bloated with every passing decade.

But here in Ecoholicland, we like our eggs sunny side up. Which means we should take a moment to commend ourselves for the fact that a whopping 90% of us have already made some moves to ease our impact. We're changing our light bulbs, buying low-flow shower heads and turning down the thermostat in record numbers. And all this stuff makes especially good sense when times are tight and our wallets are a little slimmer. Keeping our bank accounts *and* the planet green are zen-ly one and the same. Just ask your grandparents: saving energy, saving resources—hell, saving rubber bands—saves you money. And if we're smart about where we put our cash and we make sure that what we bring into our kitchens, bathrooms, bedrooms and basements is truly earth-friendly, we can all help guarantee that our address on the third rock from the sun stays peachy green.

We just have to remember that we can't buy our way out of this mess. Putting organic curtains on the credit card isn't what's going to save the planet from ourselves. Of course, if you have to make a purchase, then, yes, put your money on the most environmentally sound option you can—and make sure that it's really as earth-friendly as it claims to be. That's what *Ecoholic Home* is all about, really—helping you make those choices. But at the end of the day, you and everyone in your household will be the biggest superheroes if you make "reduce" and "reuse" your two favourite words, and along the way turn your gassy, energy-gulping home into a lean, green, planet-rescuing sanctuary. Hell, I'll even sew you a big lime-coloured cape if you do.

Follow this birdy and you'll find more money in your wallet.

Sniff out questionable green marketing claims (a.k.a. greenwash) by tracking down this symbol.

# CLEANING

## You're not fully clean until you're zestfully green

# When I was growing up, my family's

home was so clean I swear I could see a bald man winking at me from the kitchen tiles. Still, that was nothing compared to the frenzy of daily spritzing, sterilizing and disposable-mop tossing going on in the world today. We might be trying to keep our families safe from germs, but (wait, let me get my pipe and sweater vest out) today's young 'uns are growing up too clean. The hygiene hypothesis says children's bodies don't learn how to duke it out with germs, and in the end they get knocked down by allergies, asthma and eczema—more than kids in much poorer countries ever do. Not only that, but we're also misting the air with so many chemicals that pollution levels inside our homes can be 100 (sometimes up to 1,000) times worse than they are outdoors. It's time to air the dirty laundry, kids, and breathe in a new type of clean.

# CONVENTIONAL CLEANERS

How could products we casually clean our homes with end up contaminating our bodies and the environment so? Easy—no one's stopping their use. I could give you a list of toxic cleaning chemicals to avoid, but what's the point? The government hasn't made it mandatory for companies to list their ingredients (see the Your Right to Know sidebar, page 7). Although, if you need a quick rundown of the toxins in conventional products to win the green cleaning argument with your partner/roommate/mother, here's a small taste of what you're bringing into your home on cleaning day: asthma-triggering volatile organic compounds (in degreasers,

> How could products we casually clean our homes with end up contaminating our bodies and the environment so? Easy—no one's stopping their use

disinfectors and virtually every air freshener), endocrine-disruptors like DEGME (in floor cleaners), neurotoxins like toluene (in all-purpose cleaners), liver-damaging and lung-irritating phenols (in all-purpose cleaners), nerve-damaging butyl cellosolve, a.k.a. 2-butoxyethanol (in most oven and auto cleaners and all-purpose cleaners such as Simple Green), as well as estrogen-mimickers like nonylphenol ethoxylate (the chemical found in some degreasers, disinfectants and stain removers such as Clorox's Stain Out, which is gender-bending rainbow trout). Sure, that last one, nonylphenol ethoxylate, was officially declared toxic by Canadian federal officials back in 2001, but that doesn't mean it was banned from shelves. Companies were told they had till 2010 (a whole nine years) to reduce their use of the toxin by 95% below 1998 levels. The battle of the mops rages on, particularly south of the border, as enviros and fishermen's groups demand a full-on ban.

In early 2009, it looked like Canadians had new reason to get excited when the feds announced they'd be targeting a few more major health hazards found in cleaning products. But once again, they didn't quite go far enough. For instance, tumour-inducing thiourea, found in tarnish and silver polishes, will be restricted in new products but will still be allowed in existing consumer products

5

(gee, thanks). Endocrine-disrupting DEGME is being banned from cosmetics, but the feds are still mulling over whether it should be banned from floor cleaners, too. Still waiting to hear whether diethyl sulphate, a former chemical warfare agent (no kidding), will definitely be banned from existing fabric softeners. In the meantime, I'm not sure how comforting it is to know these toxins have been hiding in common household products for years and might still be on shelves, though at least some are on their way out.

At long last, Canada is officially banning phosphates from dishwashing detergent by 2010. The ingredient was largely phased out of laundry detergent way back in Wham!'s heyday, but for some reason dish detergents got to keep it (maybe because some big-brand dishwashing detergents are said to contain up to 40% phosphates). Why the big fuss? Phosphates are an important plant nutrient (that just so happens to be good at removing fatty grime and preventing dirt from settling back onto your dishes during the wash cycle), but too much of it in the environment is definitely a bad thing. The heavy presence of phosphates in water feeds blooms of toxic blue-green algae that have invaded lakes and rivers across the country, causing serious health scares. Drinking water contaminated with these algae, known as cyanobacteria (a.k.a. pond scum), will make you nauseous, headachy and feverish. It also builds up in fish and can kill your dog if Scruffy drinks from an affected lake.

Until they phase out every other ingredient of concern, here's a few ways to keep clean 'n' green:

- Make your own cleaning products with simple, natural ingredients. You'll save yourself the $200 to $300 a year on cleaning supplies otherwise forked out by the average household, according to Industry Canada.
- Reach for 100% natural, plant-based cleaners that tell you they're free of bleach, phosphates, ammonia, phenols, triclosan and more.
- Pick products that list all their ingredients on the back.

- If there are no ingredients listed, look for trusted third-party certified logos like the EcoLogo Environmental Choice stamp.

EcoLogo®

- Snag scent-free options or brands scented with essential oils to avoid hormone-disrupting phthalates in conventional perfumes. And don't be a sucker. It may smell like green apples or have a flower on the label, but that doesn't mean it's natural.
- Look for natural concentrated cleaners you can dilute at home (this saves on packaging over time).

**Antibacterial Chemicals:** If I were Dr. Phil, I'd give all you antibacterial addicts a good whuppin'. Exposure to household germs isn't a

---

### YOUR RIGHT TO KNOW: TIME TO COME CLEAN ABOUT INGREDIENTS

You gotta wonder why we have no right to know what ingredients we're dousing our homes with, especially when the feds have already forced beauty-care companies to cough up their contents. Sure, they have to put a warning label on products with any hazardous ingredient that might, you know, burn you or poison you. But what about long-term risks like cancer or asthma? In California, companies are actually forced to tell consumers right on the packaging "Warning: this product contains chemicals known to cause cancer, birth defects or other reproductive harm." It's time we see that here. Contact your Member of Parliament and demand that companies disclose their ingredient lists and put warning labels on products that contain carcinogens or hormone disruptors. You can find your MP by punching in your postal code at **parl.gc.ca**. Or email your thoughts to the current Health Minister at minister_ministre@hc-sc.gc.ca. See Toxic Free Canada for more on their campaign to bring in a federal Toxic Substances Labelling Act (**toxicfreecanada.ca**). In the meantime, some mainstream companies are starting to wake up to public demands for more transparency. In 2009, SC Johnson released a new website: **whatsinsidescjohnson.com**. Too bad it only comes clean on a minuscule handful of products, but hey, it's a beginning.

bad thing. In fact, it bolsters our immunity. But what is bad is when bug-fighting chemicals, namely triclosan and triclocarbon, in dishwashing detergent, toothpaste and hand soap make their way past sewage treatment plants and into 58% of our streams. Along the road they can create bioaccumulative and carcinogenic dioxins when mixed with sunlight and/or chlorinated water. The industry stands by their safety, but do you really want to risk it when these chemicals are already turning up in breast milk? British food retailers such as Marks & Spencer decided to ban triclosan from their products in 2003. No word yet from Canadian officials on this. Bottom line: stay away from anything synthetic that's labelled antibacterial, including household items treated with Microban—triclosan is its main ingredient. If the product

## SEE THESE? STAY AWAY

If you spot these symbols on a product, it's a sign you're dealing with serious chemical hazards. Best to stay away. And send any half-used products with these symbols to your household hazardous waste depot—don't just dump them down the drain.

 **Corrosive:** The product can burn your skin or eyes. If swallowed, it will damage your throat and stomach.

 **Flammable:** The product or its fumes will catch fire easily if it is near heat, flames or sparks. Rags used with this product may begin to burn on their own.

 **Explosive:** The container can explode if heated or punctured. Flying pieces of metal or plastic from the container can cause serious injury, especially to eyes.

 **Poisonous:** If you swallow, lick or, in some cases, breathe in the chemical, you could become very sick or die.

(Courtesy of Health Canada)

doesn't get its germ-fighting powers from triclosan it's commonly made with quaternary ammonium compounds (like dimethyl benzyl ammonium chloride and benzalkonium chloride), which have been found in soil samples and municipal sewage sludge, as well as hospital effluent and, like triclosan, have been linked to super germs. Disinfecting lines by Lysol, Clorox, Fantastik and Scrubbing Bubbles all contain the stuff.

If you must banish bacteria, Toronto-made **Benefect** makes a 100% plant-based product line that kills 99.99% of germs naturally with thyme oil. In fact, Benefect makes the only botanical hospital disinfectant and fungicide registered with Health Canada and used everywhere from hospitals to eco-conscious hotel chains like the Fairmont, on everything from ducts to kitchen cupboards (benefect.com/canada). Benefect is largely an industrial brand, but the good news is that Benefect happens to be the maker of two natural disinfectants available to Canadian shoppers—**Nature Clean Household Disinfectant** (available at health stores and grocers) and **Natura Disinfectant** (available at Home Hardware locations). Quebec's **Attitude** also makes a thyme oil disinfectant (certified by EcoLogo).

## BRIGHT 'N SHINY: SILVER POLISH

Stay away from toxic store-bought silver polish and make your own by adding a mix of salt and baking soda (two tablespoons of each) to a sink full of really hot water. Slip a sheet of aluminum foil in, then go ahead and dip your tarnish away (soak for a few minutes if need be). Rinse, dry with a soft cloth, and watch your silver sparkle. For smaller jobs, you could also use a damp cloth to rub toothpaste on the tarnished item, and rinse.

# CLEANING TOOLS

It all started with a disposable mop. Seemed so ingenious, seeing as no one likes wringing out a dirty old mop head, and those clever marketers had finally figured out a way to get us buying cleaning tools indefinitely. As we snapped them up from store shelves, we never really thought about the ecological burden of an entire continent throwing away mop heads, toilet wands, cleaning cloths, each and every single week. Sure, they claim to be biodegradable, but that doesn't mean they actually are (even decades-old hot dogs and newspapers have been found perfectly preserved in our dark, airless landfills). It's time to put an end to the madness. Stop Swiffering and start cleaning with a pledge to go disposable-free.

**Mops, Cloths and Sponges:** Even if you're not willing to go back to the mop of latter days, there are plenty of great **washable microfibre mops** (available in every cleaning aisle) that actually dust and clean without the need for chemical soaps. Canadian company **Blue Wonder**, the champion of the chemically sensitive, makes a great Microfiber Mopping System with a dry/dust mop head and damp/wet mop head that can be used on floors, windows, ceilings, you name it (online only via bluewonder.net). In conventional cleaning aisles, you'll find the Hero floor duster, which picks up the dust really well, but can't be used wet (and I've heard a lot of complaints about parts breaking quickly). Better to get a wet/dry model like **Vileda's Fibro Contact** or **Ultramax Mop**. Or just get yourself a good quick-wring pail, so at least you don't have to hunch and get your hands wet.

Stay away from conventional antibacterial sponges and cloths (J Cloths, for instance, are embedded with Microban, a.k.a. triclosan, see page 8). Invest in a decent **e-cloth** instead (see page 26 for review), and you'll also cut back dramatically on your need for cleaners. You can even buy totally natural **kitchen sponges** now! Free of artificial colours, plastics and chemical dyes, **Twist's Loofah Sponge** is unbleached, undyed white cellulose (the spongy side), backed with a scrubby loofah. Twist also makes a **Dish Dumpling** (made from natural sponge), a **Ravioli Scrubby** (abrasive hemp burlap stuffed with biodegradable sponge) and more (twistclean.com).

**Paper Towels:** True story: when the economy suffers, so does paper towel usage. People start tearing them in half or straight-up abandoning them for—gasp—dish towels. While it's nice that Bounty is marketing its half-size paper towels as "future friendly," it would be nicer to see them be genuinely future friendly and go the recycled route.

- If every household in North America replaced just one roll of virgin-fibre paper towels (70 sheets) with 100% recycled ones,

**IT'S BIODEGRADABLE, BUT IS IT GREEN?**

Biodegradable products sound oh so green, but, to be honest, there's no one policing what it all means. Does it take six weeks to biodegrade into elements found in nature or six years? Will it break down in dark, airless landfills or does it need UV light and oxygen to disappear? Will it biodegrade in lakes and streams or only in sewage treatment plants? And what does it break down into exactly? DDT biodegrades into two compounds that are more toxic than DDT itself, according to *Consumer Reports'* Eco-Labels centre. It's anyone's guess unless the company coughs up specifics. And don't assume a biodegradable ingredient is all-natural or non-toxic in any way. "Natural," "non-toxic" and "biodegradable" aren't necessarily one and the same.

- Look for products that are certified biodegradable by Scientific Certification Systems or certified to meet the standards of the Organization for Economic Co-operation and Development (OECD).
- Look for specifics: 99% biodegradable within 28 days is good.
- Don't be duped by tricky wording. Many mainstream cleaning products say they contain "biodegradable surfactants" (surfactants make things sudsy and rinse "clean"). But what about the rest of the ingredients?
- Remember that even super-biodegradable products such as Sierra Dawn's **Campsuds** should never be used directly in rivers or lakes, where they could harm fish.

11

we'd save about 550,000 trees, according to New York–based Natural Resources Defense Council.

- Look for 100% post-consumer recycled paper towels by companies like **Cascades** or **Seventh Generation**. Weirdly, White Swan's paper towels made in eastern Canada are 100% recycled, while those made in western Canada come from tree farms.

 - Use old rags to get the job done for free and pocket the $2.99 per two-pack you would have spent on disposable paper towels.

Napkins: Don't you start telling me that wiping your greasy hands on a paper napkin is more eco-friendly than reusing a cloth over and over and over again. Although truth is, if you're starting a hot-water wash just for napkins, you're making matters worse.

- If you're stuck on disposables, stock up on unbleached 100% post-consumer recycled napkins. If every household in North America replaced just one 250-pack of virgin-fibre napkins with 100% recycled ones, we could save over 1 million trees (says the Natural Resources Defense Council).

- Better still, get **reusable cloth napkins**. Who says you have to wash them after every use? Get a different napkin ring for every member of the family, so you can keep track of whose is whose. Toss them in with your regular wash at the end of the week and hang dry. You'll find organic napkins at the green home stores nearest you (see Resources: Green Home Storefronts) or from online shops like ziaandtia.com, which sells organic fair-trade napkins and tablecloths made with natural dyes.

## HOUSEHOLD CLEANERS PRODUCT TESTING GUIDE

I know what you're thinking. You want to ditch your old chemical cleaners, but you're nervous about losing scrubbing power. I get it. Not every green cleaner is all that effective. Who wants to waste $5 a bottle on

something that works about as well as spit on a rag? That's why I've taken it upon myself to test as many green cleaners as possible over the years (I've also enlisted a few friends to partake in the experiment). For the sake of research, I'd let stains dry up on my stovetop overnight and gunk build up on my bathroom sink. Oh, who am I kidding? My partner and I are naturally, well, chaotic, so making the mess was the easy part! FYI, we couldn't cover all the green cleaners available from coast to coast, but we did try to stick to brands available across the country (though there may be some great indy brands available in your home town, like Live for Tomorrow out of Vancouver, www.live-for-tomorrow.com). Of course, these products might perform differently on different surfaces (my friend Victoria hates Nature Clean Tile & Bath spray, for instance, but I love the stuff), but most of the products here were tried by several households (you know, for backup opinion).

**All-Purpose Cleaning:** Want the ease of the ready-to-spray types? Health stores are stocked with a variety of largely natural cleaners, but which ones are worth spending your money on? FYI, these were tried on both kitchen and bathroom surfaces, but by and large, all-purpose branded cleaners seem to do a much better job cleaning kitchens than soap-scum-riddled bathrooms.

| | | |
|---|---|---|
| **SEVENTH GENERATION KITCHEN CLEANER** | Smells lovely, but I used it on my sink and it felt like I was just spreading dirty water around with a cloth. Good for light cleaning of smudged walls, counters, cabinets. That's it. |  |
| **ECOVER ALL PURPOSE CLEANER** | Removed muck beneath burners well enough with some elbow grease. But the matte, filmy finish it leaves on everything isn't great for shiny kitchen surfaces. Pretty good on sinks; foams well. |  |

**CITRA-SOLV NATURAL CLEANER AND DEGREASER**

Orange extract easily cuts through post-meal messes left on stovetops and sinks (with nice residue-free finish), but not as great on the dirty ring around the tub. (Note that the orange peel oil, a.k.a. d-Limonene, that makes it a good grease cutter is also a volatile organic compound [VOC] that can irritate asthmatics.)

**EARTH FRIENDLY CREAMY CLEANSER**

Super scouring cream is well suited to tackling embedded dirt in porous surfaces like old tubs and counters. I still prefer Nature Clean in the bath, though. Nonetheless, it did the job with relative ease and only slightly more elbow grease.

**❦ SIMPLY CLEAN PROFESSIONAL STRENGTH SUPER-CLEANER**

Much better than feeble regular-strength Simply Clean at baked-on, caked-on grime. Pretty generic at cleaning the sink or toilet. I'm not a fan of its non-lather format in the tub (which took more muscle), but it's easier to wipe up on counters and sinks.

**CLOROX GREEN WORKS ALL-PURPOSE CLEANER**

Made wiping up caked-on BBQ sauces and crusty globs as effortless as kicking back in a La-Z-Boy (okay, slight exaggeration). Good if you like mild citrus scents, though scent isn't all natural.

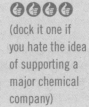

(dock it one if you hate the idea of supporting a major chemical company)

**♣ BIO-VERT ALL PURPOSE CLEANER** — I use this Quebec-made cleaner on stovetops, counters and sinks all the time. The only downside is it's slightly more sudsy for kitchen surfaces than need be, but it doesn't require rinsing. 👍👍👍👍

**♣ NATURE CLEAN ALL PURPOSE CLEANING LOTION** — This one goes from washing dirty dishes to smudged surfaces, no problem. But it sucked on my kitchen sink. I'd give it 3 thumbs up, but it gets extra points for versatility (including cleaning pesticides off fruit). 👍👍👍👍

**♣ BIOSOURCE KITCHEN & BATH SPRAY CLEANER** — This east-coast original may have left Nova Scotia, but it hasn't lost its spunk. It cut through some nasty caked-on gunk on my organics bin with one quick stroke and took on grimy kitchen messes with impressive ease. Also beat out bathroom soap scum no problem. 👍👍👍👍

👍 GREEN THUMB LEGEND   5 = A clean freak's dream   4 = Mr. Clean's green brother
3 = Decent grime fighter   2 = Ouch, my elbow hurts   1 = You'd be better off with spit on a rag

**DIY ALL-PURPOSE CLEANER**

$$ If you're looking for a solid, all-natural, truly eco-friendly all-purpose cleaner, that's easy: just combine one part vinegar and one part water in a spray bottle. You can add a few drops of essential oil if you want to mask the vinegar scent. In tandem, a vinegar-dampened sponge and a sprinkle of baking soda or salt make a good all-purpose grease-cutting scouring agent. Or toss ¼ cup (50 mL) of castile soap and 2 tablespoons (25 mL) of lemon juice in 8 cups (2 L) of hot water, shake and use at will. Stores for years. Seriously.

**Window Cleaners:** You might not want birds crashing into them, but you do want your windows to be see-through. Stay away from the big boys that pump your air full of lung-irritating ammonia, chemical detergents, surfactants and perfumes (don't be fooled by newer pseudo-natural lavender types). How do environmentally squeaky-clean health store varieties hold up? That's where our handy-dandy testing comes in.

| | | |
|---|---|---|
| **ECOVER GLASS & SURFACE CLEANER** | If you yearn for the scent of chemical cleaners, this product's for you! How can natural ingredients smell so synthetic? Very concentrated and effective indoors, but it did smear outdoor windows and stovetop grease. |  |
| **CITRA-CLEAR WINDOW AND GLASS CLEANER** | Perfectly fine on the bathroom mirror, but I had to rub outdoor windows a few times to get rid of smears. Still, it's not bad considering that even Windex leaves smears outdoors unless you wash with soap first. |  |
| ❦ **NATURE CLEAN GLASS & WINDOW CLEANER** | Got rid of greasy stovetop streaks left by Ecover, and made appliances sparkle. Also made my dirty outdoor windows 99% streak-free. Lack of scent is refreshing. |  |
| ❦ **ATTITUDE WINDOW & MIRROR CLEANER** | Misted this lovely lime- and lavender-scented spray on a winter's worth of outdoor window grime and it got the job done. Did a Windex-worthy job on indoor glass and mirrors too. Only downside is it's kind of lathery, so you have to wipe it up well. |  |

🌿 **GREEN THUMB LEGEND**   5 = A clean freak's dream   4 = Mr. Clean's green brother
3 = Decent grime fighter   2 = Ouch, my elbow hurts   1 = You'd be better off with spit on a rag

Combine ¼ cup (50 mL) vinegar, ½ teaspoon (2 mL) natural dish soap (any of the ones listed on pages 21–23), and 2 cups (500 mL) water in a spray bottle and go to town. Works as well as or better than almost anything you can find in stores. It just dries more slowly. Same ingredients with a bucket and rag will wash up filth on outdoor windows nicely.

**Bathroom Cleaners:** Bathroom cleaners are some of the harshest around. Whatever you do, stay away from the cleaning power of chlorine bleach. It gives off harmful vapours that trigger wheezing and headaches and can produce carcinogenic, bioaccumulative dioxins, as well as trihalomethanes, including carcinogenic chloroform, when it mixes with organic matter like dirt and poop in our sewer systems. Combine that with sodium hydroxide (which nearly every bathroom

## BYOJ: GREEN CLEANING PARTIES

So what's BYOJ exactly? Why, that's bring your own jar, of course. It's the mantra of a whole slew of cleaning parties sprouting up across the country. You don't actually have to scrub your host's floors, you just bring a few jars (preferably glass) to fill with DIY cleaning recipes, from homemade furniture polish to toilet bowl cleaners. Think of them as new-wave Tupperware parties where guests don't have to cough up any cash (and the cleaners they take  home won't leave their families coughing either). Download a Green Cleaning Party Kit from **Women's Voices for the Earth** and you'll get a short educational DVD to show at your shindig on the health risks of conventional household cleaners, as well as recipe cards, container labels, advocacy tips and ideas for gag cocktails like blue Window Cleaner Martinis (**womenandenvironment.org**).

cleaning product has in various concentrations), and you're misting your shower stalls and squirting your toilets with chemicals that can burn your skin and irritate your eyes, nose, throat and lungs. Totally unnecessary, really.

## Tub and Tile Cleaners

| | | |
|---|---|---|
| **SEVENTH GENERATION BATHROOM CLEANER** | I've had better luck with plain hot water. No cling power, no bubbles, and I had to scrub like hell. No thanks. Fine for light jobs like bathroom counters since it doesn't suds up. |  |
| ✹**ATTITUDE BATHROOM SURFACE CLEANER** | Got rid of black soap scum no problem (remind me never to buy black bar soap again). Creamy cleanser frothed up nicely and didn't need buffing to bring ceramic surfaces to high shine. This squeeze-gel format lathered up better than mist-format of Attitude's Mold & Mildew Bathroom Cleaner. |  |
| **ECO MIST TUB & TILE** (exclusive to Home Depot) | Love the wide reach of its mister. It doesn't froth up as much as others, but after I let it sit for 5 minutes before getting to work (as recommended), black soap scum is effortlessly whisked away with one stroke. |  |
| ✹**NATURE CLEAN TUB & TILE CREAM CLEANSER OR SPRAY** | Love this stuff! Both spray and cream format lather up into a frenzy of bubbles and zap ring around tub in seconds. Creamy version has extra scouring power equal to Vim. I usually pass on tub duty, but this changes everything. Almost. |  |

| CLOROX GREEN WORKS BATHROOM CLEANER | I gotta admit this is in my top two (despite its dirty corporate affiliations). Sudsy spray lifted off dark tub ring with a quick wipe. No sweating or cursing involved. | 👍👍👍👍👍 (dock it one if you hate the idea of supporting a major chemical company) |

👍 GREEN THUMB LEGEND  5 = A clean freak's dream  4 = Mr. Clean's green brother
3 = Decent grime fighter  2 = Ouch, my elbow hurts  1 = You'd be better off with spit on a rag

**DIY BATHROOM CLEANER**

$$ It requires more elbow grease, but nothing beats a sprinkle of baking soda and/or salt on the tub for affordability and minimal packaging. It's like the poor man's Comet! Straight heated-up vinegar is amazing at lifting built-up soap scum on shower doors if you let it sit a few minutes before wiping.

## GOT MILDEW PROBLEMS?

Pull out an old toothbrush, dip it in a paste of borax and water, give 'er. You can also try putting 2 teaspoons (10 mL) of antifungal **tea tree oil** in 2 cups (500 mL) of water; spray and walk away without wiping. A spritz of hydrogen peroxide cut with water is a great preventative my mom swears by (especially good on shower ceilings).

**Toilet Bowl Cleaners:** Why is blue toilet water the international signal for cleanliness? I've stumbled into roadside outhouses in rural Central America and found blue water, for god's sake. I know we're ashamed of what happens in there, but really, corrosive chemicals such as lye and hydrochloric and sulphuric acid aren't necessary to get that bowl clean. It's not as though someone's going to be drinking out of it (though, hey, if you happen to have a cat or dog that does, the last thing they should be slurping on is the toxic soup swirling around in there).

| Product | Description | Rating |
|---|---|---|
| ✿ NATURE CLEAN TOILET BOWL CLEANER | Odourless and all Canadian. Fine for frequent cleaners but not the greatest on really stained bowls. Had a hard time seeing how much I was squirting, and overpoured every time. | ☘☘ |
| ECOVER TOILET BOWL CLEANER | Potent pine scent, not for everyone (one colleague likened it to cheap air freshener in a Camaro). Toilet was spic 'n' span, though. | ☘☘☘ |
| SEVENTH GENERATION TOILET BOWL CLEANER | Like to see where you squirt? This effective gel comes in a blue hue, which may not be natural, but the rest of the ingredients are. Love the refreshing peppermint scent. Would buy again. | ☘☘☘☘ |
| CLOROX GREEN WORKS NATURAL TOILET BOWL CLEANER | White creamy lotion easily clings to bowl and takes down stains with one flick of the toilet wand. | ☘☘☘☘ (dock it one if you hate the idea of supporting a major chemical company) |
| GREENER CHOICE TOILET BOWL CLEANER | Accidentally left this naturally scented Oxi Brite product in bowl for a couple hours and came back to find the bowl whiter than it had been in years! That's never happened with other forgotten toilet cleaners. | ☘☘☘☘☘ |

☘ GREEN THUMB LEGEND    5 = A clean freak's dream    4 = Mr. Clean's green brother
3 = Decent grime fighter    2 = Ouch, my elbow hurts    1 = You'd be better off with spit on a rag

**DIY TOILET CLEANER**

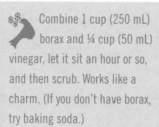 Combine 1 cup (250 mL) borax and ¼ cup (50 mL) vinegar, let it sit an hour or so, and then scrub. Works like a charm. (If you don't have borax, try baking soda.)

**Dish Detergents—Handwashing:** No one likes washing dishes, but a sink full of bubbles seems to make the whole thing more pleasant. Too bad the petrochemical process used to make some plant-based sudsers (as well as chemical ones) creates carcinogenic 1,4-dioxane. Keep in mind that even cleaners advertised as organic have been found to contain troubling levels of the contaminant. It's not on ingredient lists because it's not added intentionally. However, it's the by-product of a process called ethoxylation, used to make certain sudsers (including plant oils) milder. Dish soaps are the worst offender. Citrus Magic dish soap's levels were the highest when the Organic Consumers Association tested dozens of products in 2008. **Seventh Generation** and **Whole Foods' 365** brand had close to the lowest levels, followed by **Ecover**; all had trace amounts. Check out organicconsumers.org/bodycare for more details. Note that some original poor scorers, like Earth Friendly Dishmate and Citrus Magic, have since been reformulated.

**CLOROX GREEN WORKS NATURAL DISHWASHING LIQUID** — Artificial scent clings to dishes, requiring more rinsing. Way too many suds makes me, correctly, suspect sodium laurel sulphate. Also, can someone tell me why this has to be so Palmolive green? Too fake all around.

 (dock it one if you hate the idea of supporting a major chemical company)

### ❦ ATTITUDE DISHWASHING LIQUID

This one's nowhere near as good as its fellow Quebec brand, Bio-Vert. Kept pouring more onto my sponge every minute because it just didn't feel brawny enough, and it left a gritty residue on wineglasses even after I scrubbed them for ages.

### EARTH FRIENDLY ULTRA DISHMATE

Smells like an almond cookie, which is kind of a weird scent for dishes. Sudses well. Didn't clean greasy burnt-up wok at all, but maybe that's unfair, since the wok needed serious soaking.

### SEVENTH GENERATION NATURAL DISH LIQUID

I gave this a 4 at first, as it seemed to clean dirty coffee mugs, greasy wok and glasses well, with tons of bubbles, but it leaves a foggy film on stuff as it dries if you don't rinse excessively. Scent-free.

### ECOVER DISHWASHING LIQUID

Plenty o' bubbles, spreads and rinses easily, lasts long. It just plain works. Too bad it contains sodium laureth sulphate.

### ❦ NATURE CLEAN DISHWASHING LIQUID

I used this before and hated it because it had almost no suds and I had to use a ton. But it's since been reformulated and now cuts through last night's grease well, with lots of bubbles. It's also tested to be 1,4-dioxane-free!

### ULTRA CITRA-DISH

I didn't find it foamed so well, though it cleaned perfectly fine. Left zero film on glasses. Boyfriend liked the citrusy smell so much he gave it a 5, but he's biased for lemon scents.

🍁 **NATURE CLEAN ALL PURPOSE CLEANING LOTION**  All purpose, but label says it can do dishes. Sudses really well. Rinses clean. Cuts through muck easily. Used it to clean fridge, fingerprint-covered doors, even washed fruit! No smell. Would buy it again any day.

🍁 **BIO-VERT DISHWASHING LIQUID**  My dad is my family's No. 1 dishwasher (he even has an apron declaring him as such) and he recently confessed to sneaking in a bottle of Palmolive for super-greasy jobs—until he found Bio-Vert. If he's a convert, this stuff will win everyone over.

👍 **GREEN THUMB LEGEND**   5 = A clean freak's dream   4 = Mr. Clean's green brother
3 = Decent grime fighter   2 = Ouch, my elbow hurts   1 = You'd be better off with spit on a rag

## WATER-SAVING HAND DISHWASHING TIPS

Washing dishes by hand can be a surprisingly water-wasting affair (see Dishwashers, page 72). Avoid tap-running like the plague. Fill one plugged basin half-full with warm water and add a quick squirt of natural dish soap as it's filling. Let dirty dishes soak for a minute or two before you pull out the sponge and start scrubbing. Fill the second basin with clean warm water and add ¼ cup (50 mL) of vinegar as a rinsing agent. If you don't have a second basin, you could use a countertop plastic basin. Okay, now get to work! And when washing single items like a pan or pot, conserve as much as you can by turning off the water as you lather.

**Dish Detergents—Machine Washing:** Let's be honest here, (almost) none of these will work quite as well as your old phosphate-heavy dish soap, but suck it up. You're not choking our rivers and lakes with destructive phosphates. You can try adding a tablespoon or two (15 to 25 mL) of white vinegar as a rinse aid to help some of these along in your dishwasher.

| ❋ NATURE CLEAN AUTO DISHWASHER GEL | Not a fan. It left wineglasses slightly grimy or cloudy. Unless you're a pre-rinser, forget it. Powder format isn't much better. | 👎👎 |
| SEVENTH GENERATION AUTOMATIC DISHWASHER GEL | Lemony smell is reminiscent of Cascade. Greasy wineglasses came out clear enough. But overall it's soft on grime and won't fight baked-on grub. | 👍👍 |
| ❋ ATTITUDE DISHWASHING LIQUID | What can I tell you; once you've gone Bio-Vert (see opposite) it's hard to go back. While I have to say this one did a great job on caked-on bowls and greasy plates, it left a cloud on glasses, demoting it to a 3. | 👍👍👍 |
| ULTRA CITRA-DISH AUTOMATIC DISHWASHING POWDER | In newer dishwashers, dishes seem to come out nearly spotless (less so in older machines). My editor vouches that it cleared away tough, baked-on batter from her Hello Dolly squares. Not individually packaged, which is a bonus. | 👍👍👍👍 |
| ECOVER AUTOMATIC DISHWASHING POWDER | My fave until I found Bio-Vert. Removed crusted-on pizza sauce and peanut butter. Film-free. I made my Cascade-using parents try it, and they were fans. Just make sure to use the loose powder version—the tabs come individually wrapped in plastic, tsk, tsk. | 👍👍👍👍 |

**⚜ BIO-VERT AUTOMATIC DISHWASHER TABS** The hands-down winner. Erased all signs of yesterday's caked-on pancake batter on bowls, as well as crusty seaweed shake on glasses. Potent stuff. Must be the enzymes. The crazy excess packaging on tabs is a major downer, though improved packaging is expected by fall of 2009. (Score some through Shoppers Drug Mart, Whole Foods, Planet Organic, Capers, Wal-Mart, Costco.) 👍👍👍👍👍

👍 GREEN THUMB LEGEND 5 = A clean freak's dream 4 = Mr. Clean's green brother 3 = Decent grime fighter 2 = Ouch, my elbow hurts 1 = You'd be better off with spit on a rag

**DIY DISHWASHER POWDER** $$ Free yourself from store-bought dishwasher detergent by mixing 1 cup (250 mL) of borax and 1 cup (250 mL) of washing soda (or baking soda), then tossing 2 tablespoons (25 mL) into each load. Use vinegar in the rinse compartment.

**Cleaning Cloths:** A new wave of cleaning cloths claims to be able to tackle dirt without any help from products. So how well do they stack up?

**MABU CLOTH** The best basic dishrag of the bunch, though stink-resistant claims don't hold up for more than a week. My guy keeps complaining it's the least absorbent rag in town. I argue it's a decent basic rag, though I wouldn't bother with it on surfaces like windows and mirrors. 👍👍

**ENJO**  These fleece mitts do sop up grease,  but they leave a big soggy mess behind that requires a separate drying stage with a microfibre cleaning cloth (otherwise, it's kind of like wiping up with a wet teddy bear). I prefer a one-step cloth. My mom gives it a 3 for shower-duty.

**E-CLOTH**  Love this thing. Wiped up last night's  dried greasy splatters with ease and left nothing but a shine behind. Gentle scouring power lifts caked-on crap. Works well on slimy sink too, but once cloth is wet, it's hard to shine up surfaces. As long as the cloth is semi-dry it does a perfect, streak-free job on mirrors and windows.

**BLUE WONDER**  Loved by the chemically sensitive, as  well as cleaning buffs like my mom. Its patented microfibre knit (half polyester, half nylon) is ultra-absorbent and magically enables you to shine up scummy sinks, mirrors, stoves, TVs and pretty much any surface you can think of without cleaners. Streak-free windows every time.

GREEN THUMB LEGEND    5 = A clean freak's dream    4 = Mr. Clean's green brother
3 = Decent grime fighter    2 = Ouch, my elbow hurts    1 = You'd be better off with spit on a rag

**Furniture Polish:** Just because your furniture polishing spray has a CFC-free label on it doesn't mean it won't fill your home with air pollutants. And lots of them have ingredients, like phenols, that have ties to cancer. You could buy natural wood polish from the health store, but why bother when you can make your own with a simple mix of 1 cup (250 mL) olive oil and ½ cup (125 mL) vinegar? If you find that too oily for your needs, flip it: ¼ cup (50 mL) vinegar with a few drops of olive oil makes a good wood cleaner and polish.

Some B.C. beekeepers make a great furniture polish out of beeswax, called **Clapham Beeswax Furniture Polish**, as well as an edible one called **Clapham Beeswax Salad Bowl Finish** that is great on butcher's blocks, wooden counters and more (claphams.com).

**Floor Cleaners:** We stomp all over them and track the outside world on them, but is that enough to justify washing our floors with a chemical that 12 national health and enviro organizations lobbied to have banned? Endocrine-disrupting DEGME (a.k.a. methoxydiglycol) is being ousted from cosmetics, but the feds are still weighing whether it should be banned from floor cleaners, too. In the meantime, it's found in Mop & Glo Triple Action Floor Shine and others. Hardly worth the shiny floor.

$$ Honestly, floor cleaners are one place where homemade solutions really make sense. Just add a cup (250 mL) of vinegar to a pail of water for non-wood floors. For wood floors, stick to dry mops as much as possible, or use a little castile or natural dish soap in a pail of water and make sure the mop's not too saturated. Remove scuff marks with a paste of baking soda and water. Of the health store brands, **Ecover Floor Soap** worked best on many surfaces. Though it says not to use the product on treated wood floors because the linseed oil in it might leave a film, it nourished older, worn floors well. Both **Nature Clean** and Home Depot's **Eco Mist Solutions** offer a plant-based Hardwood & Laminate cleaner suitable for cleaning wooden surfaces, though they don't really add shine, to my floors, anyway.

Juggling work, life and family obligations leaving you with zero time to clean the house? The problem with most cleaning professionals is that they use all the harsh chemical cleaners you're trying to avoid. There are, however, a few specialty green cleaning companies popping up around the country, like **Earth Concerns Cleaning Services** in Toronto (**earthconcerns.com**) or the **Green Maids Canada** chain, servicing lower mainland B.C. and Calgary (**greenmaidscanada.com**). Ask around for similar services in your hometown or just see if a conventional cleaning pro would be willing to use the natural cleaning products you provide. Many would be happy to oblige, especially when they see how effective they can be without irritating their lungs and burning their hands.

**Oven Cleaners:** Ask me why it's okay to spray our cooking surfaces with some of the most toxic cleaning chemicals around (including neurotoxic 2-Butoxyethanol). Can't tell you. But I can tell you not to waste your time on store-bought cleaners when the homemade option works like magic. FYI: don't use the self-cleaning feature on your oven—it's really energy-intensive.

$$ Just smear surfaces with a healthy helping of baking soda and hot water, let it sit overnight, then scrub with a soapy abrasive sponge. Works like a charm.

**Drain Cleaners:** Put down the skull and crossbones stuff and try these natural tips instead:

- Light jobs: Pour some baking soda and 1 cup (250 mL) vinegar into the drain, wait 15 minutes while it fizzles and pops, and then pour in a kettle of boiling water. Do this several times, until the clog clears.

- Somewhat tougher clogs: Try 1 cup (250 mL) washing soda (a stronger relative of baking soda that you can find in the laundry section of your grocery store or any health store), followed by 3 cups (750 mL) boiling water. Again, repeat until you break on through to the other side. Just don't overdo it if you have PVC pipes. You can try store-bought natural enzyme- and bacteria-based cleaners, like **Citra Drain** and **TerraCycle Natural Drain Cleaner and Maintainer**, but they won't break down drains jammed with hair, in my experience.
- Deep clogs: A good chem-free option is **Drain King**, available at hardware stores. It attaches to your garden hose and creates a hard-core water flush. Could be messy if you're not careful. For the most hard-core jobs, you'll need to snake out the drain. If you're not comfortable trying it yourself, call a plumber.

One Second Plumber is not actually as enviro-friendly as it claims to be and as we here at *Ecoholic Home* once thought; it contains acetone and tetrafluoroethane, a potent ozone-depleting chemical.

Bottom line: to avoid future sink jams, get yourself a metal strainer that fits over your drain and do monthly, even weekly, baking soda sessions.

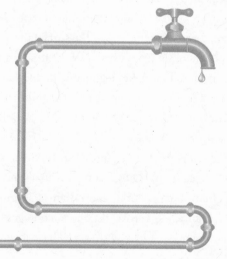

## GREEN-ISH CLEANERS

Method products are slick 'n' sexy, and their main claim to green fame is that they're "biodegradable" and "naturally derived." And although Method is far greener than conventional brands (it stays away from all the worst offenders—like triclosan, bleach, phosphates and parabens), Method comes clean about a few iffy ingredients in its extensive online FAQ section (something you always want to check on corporate sites). It fesses up to some petroleum-based ingredients and sudsy sodium lauryl sulphate, an irritant that many crunchy granolas try to avoid. Not to mention synthetic fragrances (that explains why I get a headache just sitting near an open bottle). Method's dish and hand soaps also tested positive for relatively high levels of 1,4-dioxane; the company says it has since reformulated its hand soap and dish soap to reduce 1,4-dioxane levels. Method does have a purer fragrance- and dye-free line called **Go Naked**, which will be welcomed by the scent-sensitive.

SC Johnson's new Nature's Source products don't tell you much about themselves other than alluding to ultra-vague "ingredients" (hello, "plant-based cleaning agents"!). It does admit to using synthetic fragrances, dyes, stabilizers and preservatives but says they amount to less than 1% of the product. Unfortunately, Nature's Source offers no third-party certification to back its biodegradable claims.

Clorox's Green Works website offers a pretty specific list of ingredients that, for instance, tells you the surfactant in most products is alkyl polyglucoside (you wouldn't want to squirt this in your eye, but it is considered more biodegradable than other agents). The brand passed the Organic Consumers Association's 1,4-dioxane testing and gets a thumbs-up from the U.S. Sierra Club (which, admittedly, Sierra has gotten some flak for)—although it does use sodium lauryl sulphate, dyes and a petrochemical preservative. Some say you should stay away from a cleaner made by a company that's responsible for so many caustic chems being poured down drains nationwide; others say that buying Clorox's Green Works line encourages big companies to offer cleaner products. Strictly scrubwise, I have to admit that much of this line does a really top-notch job and gives off only very mild (albeit partly synthetic) citrus scents.

Melaleuca is much more, well, mysterious. If you haven't heard of it, you're not alone. It's actually a consumer-direct marketing operation (like Avon), and a whole $780-million Melaleuca world out there pushes what it calls wellness products. But red flags pop up when I spot bioaccumulative triclosan and questionable aluminum in Melaleuca deodorants. The company claims its cleaning formulas make "EcoSense" and are free of big baddies like bleach, phosphates and ammonia. But there's no backup for biodegradability claims, and the Tub and Tile spray label, for instance, lists only "naturally derived detergents and solvents." Hmm, well, that's useful. A call to Melaleuca's product info line results in more talk of proprietary ingredients but reveals that sodium lauryl sulphate and polyethylene glycol are among them. (That last one has been linked to 1,4-dioxane.)

Some say you should stay away from a cleaner made by a company that's responsible for so many caustic chems being poured down drains nationwide; others say that buying Clorox's Green Works line encourages big companies to offer cleaner products

Shaklee is another popular consumer-direct line of products. It's not in stores, but has a more public profile thanks to many Oprah plugs. It's been around since the '50s and has funded lots of impressive eco-projects (plus, it's been certified carbon-neutral since 2000), so why can't the company share its ingredient list? Telling us the list is proprietary doesn't inspire much confidence, but the company does guarantee that its products are free of about 20 major cleaning toxins. I've also seen Shaklee trade show demo-ers swallow the stuff to show just how non-toxic it is. FYI, you need to buy a $15 membership to order the goods.

Bottom line: ask lots of questions, and if you're uncomfortable with a company's hush-hush ways, turn to brands that happily give you the real dirt on their contents. And remember, vinegar and baking soda ain't hiding a thing.

# LAUNDRY DETERGENTS

I don't know about you, but laundry is one of the last things on my list of things to get done in a day. I'll put it off till I'm down to the last pair of stinky socks. But what you shouldn't put off is getting the toxins out of your wash cycle. Who needs possible cancer causers like trisodium nitrilotriactetate (found in products like Sunlight Ultra) or asthma-linked monoethanolamine (found in Tide, Gain, Cheer, even Ivory Snow)?

Without mandatory ingredient listing, it's hard to know which products to avoid, but here are a few hints:

- If it says it contains optical brighteners, you might want to pass. These don't easily break down in nature, and many are toxic to fish. Not good, considering they get washed into the water system with every load of clothing you clean.

- You can bet that "summer meadow" or "spring rain" are synthetic scents heavy in phthalates, a hormone-disrupting family of chemicals that's best to avoid. Pick scent-free options (though just because a product is perfume-free doesn't mean it's free of other questionable chemicals; Tide Free, for instance, still contains monoethanolamine).

- The stain-fighting power of bleach might seem like a bright idea (buh-doom boom) until you realize it's pretty caustic, mistakenly poisons thousands of children a year and can end up forming deadly dioxins when it mixes with other elements in the environment (in fact, bleach-heavy detergents have been blamed for high levels of dioxins in San Francisco Bay).

- Some of the stain-digesting enzymes added to laundry powder since the '60s are essentially the same proteins you buy from the health store to help digest your food. Pretty harmless. There used to be problems with workers at detergent plants inhaling the stuff, but they say it's all been corrected and home exposure to enzyme dust would be minute. Still, many newer synthetic antibacterial pseudo enzymes are more troubling and aren't readily biodegradable. Stick to plant-based enzymes.

- "Phosphate-free" labels are fairly meaningless in the laundry aisle, considering that all major manufacturers virtually eliminated the ecology-disrupting mineral from their powdered products a decade or two ago.
- "Cold-water" brands are a soft step up because they encourage consumers to wash without energy-wasting hot water, but that doesn't mean they're made with natural ingredients in any way.

**Laundry Detergent Testing Guide:** How do you test laundry detergents evenly? Well, I took swatches of white jersey and splashed them with wine, olive oil, dirt and tomato sauce before testing them. Warning: Test stains weren't pre-treated, which, admittedly, didn't give the products much of a fighting chance. (Hell, even the control batch, tested with chemical sudser Tide Ultra, failed to remove the stains entirely.) But there were some clear winners and losers. FYI, while powder detergents come in cardboard boxes (which are lower impact than plastic jugs), I find natural powders don't do so well in cold-water washes, often leaving a grainy residue on clothes, so I tested mostly liquids.

| 🍁 NATURE CLEAN 3X CONCENTRATE LAUNDRY LIQUID | Sure, it's more powerful than my pitiful trials with the non-concentrated Nature Clean (which left tomato stains so untouched you could actually still smell the herbs and garlic a day after we washed them!), but 3X still failed to remove all evidence of ketchup and oil. Fine, as long as your clothes aren't really dirty. It is incredibly concentrated though, so you need very little. |  |

**🍁 WONDER WASH NATURAL LAUNDRY DETERGENT (POWDER)**

Oil stain looks like you can still lick it and taste the olives. Created a weird black tree-ring effect on the wine stain and did slightly better on the tomato stain than washing soda with borax.

**SOAP NUTS** a.k.a. soap berries (literally nuts you toss in a sack and into your washer).

These are good enough when it comes to washing clothes that aren't super-soiled, but they don't do so well in cold water. Bad news, since warm-water loads use much more energy.

**ECOVER LAUNDRY WASH (LIQUID)**

Love the mild, lemony scent. I've had good luck with this one in the past on run-of-the-mill sweat and dirt, and it did lift about as much tomato sauce as Tide, and almost as much wine, but the oil and dirt are still alive and well.

**🍁 ATTITUDE LAUNDRY SOAP (LIQUID)**

Not bad for basic, everyday laundry, but don't expect it to fully tackle stains. It left faint yellowy ketchup residue. The oil's gone, at least, and it definitely did better than Nature Clean. Nice mild orange scent (though you can pick others or a non-scented option).

**🍁BIO-VERT LAUNDRY DETERGENT (LIQUID)**

My original grime-fighting champ (until Seventh Gen tied for first with its 2X Ultra formula). This Quebec-made soap eliminated all traces of oil and beat Tide on tomato sauce, although, like the others, it only faded set wine stains (though it faded the wine more than the rest). N.B.: Do not overpour in high-efficiency machines! We created a suds monster of B movie proportions! Scent is pretty strong, but now comes unscented, too.

**SEVENTH GENERATION 2X ULTRA NATURAL LAUNDRY DETERGENT (LIQUID)**

Wow, way better than regular Seventh Generation, and the concentrated formula means you save cash and packaging. Erased all hints of the oil and tomato sauce. Got the grime out of a nasty white robe no problem, too. Plus, you can pick a nice mild lavender scent, if you like, or go non-scented.

GREEN THUMB LEGEND    5 = A clean freak's dream    4 = Mr. Clean's green brother
3 = Decent grime fighter    2 = Ouch, my elbow hurts    1 = You'd be better off with spit on a rag

**DIY LAUNDRY SOAP**

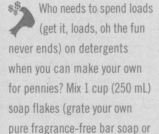

$$ Who needs to spend loads (get it, loads, oh the fun never ends) on detergents when you can make your own for pennies? Mix 1 cup (250 mL) soap flakes (grate your own pure fragrance-free bar soap or use liquid castile soap), ½ cup (125 mL) washing soda, and ½ cup (125 mL) borax. Use 1 tablespoon (15 mL) for regular loads and 2 tablespoons (25 mL) for dirtier ones.

## ARE LAUNDRY DISKS ALL SPIN?

These electrically charged or magnetized pucks are said to soften water, dramatically reducing the need for soap. Plus, they claim to work for up to 700 loads. Too good to be true? The U.S. Federal Trade Commission says the claims are totally bogus.

## WHAT'S UP WITH OXYGEN BLEACH?

Did you ever notice how one day you woke up and there was a new type of bleach being advertised everywhere? Oxygen bleaches are made with either hydrogen peroxide or sodium percarbonate (which is a mix of washing soda and hydrogen peroxide). Note that although they're considered safer for the environment than bleach and don't give off harsh fumes, both can still be corrosive in stronger concentrations, which is why you might spot a skull and crossbones on more potent brands. They can be pretty effective cleaners, though I found them to be duds on tough clothing stains.

 Hanging clothes to dry in **sunlight** is still the cheapest whitener on the market. You can also try adding **baking soda** or **lemon juice** to your wash. Warning: applying straight lemon juice to fabric will put yellow splotches on your shirt.

**Stain Removers:** Conventional stain removers are loaded with questionable chemicals, including the fish gender bender nonylphenol ethoxylates. I used to think they were worth a little spritz if it meant saving an oily tomato-stained blouse from the trashbin. That is, until I found green stain removers that actually work. Who needs Spray 'n Wash?

**ECOVER STAIN REMOVER** Love the built-in scrubber on this bottle. Really wiped out spaghetti sauce and oil. Not quite as good on wine as Nature Clean, but good effort.

| | | |
|---|---|---|
| ❁ **NATURE CLEAN LAUNDRY STAIN REMOVER** | Sloppy eaters will be pleased to see how well this one tackles garlic spaghetti sauce and wine. But while olive oil splatter is mostly gone, it's not out. At least it does a better job than the completely ineffective Nature Clean Liquid Bleach and Nature Clean Oxygen Bleach (only soda water and salt did as poorly as that one on tomato sauce). |  |
| ❁ **SIMPLY CLEAN STAIN REMOVER** | Move over, Mr. Clean—this is the real Magic Eraser. As good as chemy Spray 'n Wash anyway, but both Simply Clean and Spray 'n Wash left very faint residues of oil and wine. A steal at $1.50. Vegan alert: contains tallow. |  |
| **BI-O-KLEEN BAC-OUT STAIN & ODOR ELIMINATOR** | Loved by cloth-diapering moms for its stain-ousting power. This enzyme-based fighter wins the battle on every-thing from poop to carpets. |  |
| **PINK SOLUTION** | My top pick. This no-fail stain remover kicks ass on everything, including five-year-old carpet stains. I put the stuff on a beet stain, washed the soiled white hoodie a whole week later, and like magic it was gone. You can heat and dilute this paste (it comes in a big tub) or just use the handy-dandy stain-removing soap bar that comes with it. Only available online and at Costco. |  |

🖐 **GREEN THUMB LEGEND**   5 = A clean freak's dream   4 = Mr. Clean's green brother
3 = Decent grime fighter   2 = Ouch, my elbow hurts   1 = You'd be better off with spit on a rag

# WASHING MACHINES

In the market for a new washer? Look for a front-loading machine first and foremost. They use 40% to 60% less water and 30% to 50% less energy than top-loaders. Plus, these guys spin out more $H_2O$ than others during the spin cycle, so you can reduce your drying time.

**What to Do to Keep Your Old or New Washer Spinning Green:**

- Wash in cold. Since 90% of your machine's energy use goes to heating the water, you'll be doing your part to prevent global warming while still getting the stink out of your hockey socks.
- Fill 'er up. Washing machines are at their most energy-efficient when they're packed with a full load.
- Skip the sanitary cycle. This super-hot cycle, available on some machines gobbles up energy.
- Hit the high-speed spin button. If your washer has a high-speed or extended spin option, pick it. It means your clothes will have very little moisture left in them and won't need long to dry.

Switching to a high-efficiency front-loading washer can save you $100 a year on your water and energy bills, according to Natural Resources Canada. An Energy Star clothes washer can save you over 26,000 litres of water a year! Oh, and check with your municipality, utility provider or province to see if they already have or are coming out

## ENERGY STAR VERSUS ENERGUIDE

The blue-and-white government–Energy Star logo tells you an appliance uses 10% to 50% less energy and water than standard models.

This label doesn't tell you an appliance is energy-efficient; it just tells you how much electricity it uses, to help you make an informed decision. Federal law in Canada requires that the EnerGuide label be placed on all new electrical appliances.

## THE DARK SIDE OF NANO SILVER

Heigh-ho silver! So there's nano silver in everything from your washing machine to your cutting board—marvellous. What the hell is it, anyway? Well, nanotechnology, in case you're not up to speed, essentially creates and manipulates molecules or atoms that are 100,000 times smaller than the width of a human hair follicle. And this brave new world of science is making its way into every room in your house, folks. Manufacturers are embedding nano silver in antibacterial socks, underwear, toothbrushes, baby bottles, spatulas, plastic food containers and at least 200 other consumer products.

Take Samsung's SilverCare washing machine. According to the company's website, it releases over "100 quadrillion silver ions to sanitize clothing without the need for hot water or bleach." The claim is that, since silver kills 99.9% of bacteria on your clothes without those two eco no-no's, it's more environmentally friendly than other machines. Of course, if you don't launder with hot water or bleach anyway, it offers no ecological advantage, but that's beside the point. The problem is that silver is considered a water pollutant and has been found to cause significant reproductive damage in Californian marine life, for instance. It might have been historically useful in hospital ointments and such, but lab research on nano silver in particular has found it highly toxic to cells.

No one's really sure what impact a flood of nano silver would have on Lake Ontario or the St. Lawrence River if we all switched to silver-lined or -releasing products, and really, do you want to be part of that mass experiment? The possibilities have raised enough eyebrows to get the U.S. Environmental Protection Agency to force Samsung to register its machine as a pesticide. Though Health Canada's Pest Management Regulatory Agency argues Samsung's silver ion discharges are too minimal to worry about, eco org Friends of the Earth is calling for a full-on product recall.

with new rebates for Energy Star washing machines. A few such rebates will have expired the month this book comes out (drats!), but Toronto still offers $60 cash back on the purchase of a new high-efficiency, front-loading washer.

Does your town bar you from using a clothesline? How insane is that? Just because your prudish neighbour doesn't want to see your dirty laundry doesn't mean we should be cooking the planet with clothes dryers. For free access to a "solar dryer" in your own yard, talk to your MPP about bringing in right-to-dry regulations, like Ontario now has.

## DRYERS

Tip 1: Avoid turning it on. Seriously. You're wasting a lot of hot air in there. But if your municipality has banned clotheslines (yes, this really happens; see the Right to Dry sidebar), or you need your lucky jeans in a hurry, here are a few points to consider. For one, don't bother buying a new clothes dryer unless the one you have is really, really old. Technology hasn't improved that much. Energy Star doesn't even certify dryers, because none are all that efficient. Still, new clothes dryers generally use 15% less energy than clothes dryers built before 1990, because they have more efficient motors and controls. Read the EnerGuide logo when shopping for a new machine. It tells you how much power (in kilowatt hours) each machine uses on average per year. The most efficient average under 900 kWh per year, according to Natural Resources Canada. The least efficient: 950 kWh.

Tips for Dryer Use:
- If you've got a moisture sensor built into your dryer, be sure to use it, so you don't keep tumbling long after your shorts have been baked.
- If you don't have a moisture sensor, set your dryer on its lowest setting.
- Don't automatically turn the dial to 60 minutes. Your clothes are often dry in much less time. Start with 30 or 40 minutes (even less if you have a high-efficiency washing machine). Synthetics often dry in 10 minutes and really shouldn't go in the dryer at all.

## HANG-DRYING TIPS

- String a retractable clothesline in your basement for drying during the winter months. Moisture levels are lower in your basement in winter (though you could still try hanging lighter fabrics outside on sunny winter days).
- If you're afraid of fading dark items in the hot summer sun, hang them indoors on really sunny days or just don't leave them out there for long.
- Apartment dwellers should look into compact tub-top racks and folding clothes racks, as well as retractable clotheslines that can be installed in the bathroom or bedroom. You can get all sorts of drying racks from Canadian Tire (from cheap plastic to stainless steel) or nice wooden ones from IKEA.
- If your family hates the crunchy texture of towels that have been hung to dry, just pop them in the dryer for five minutes when they're nearly dry.
- Shake clothes out well before hanging; smoothing down jeans with your hands will make them less crinkly.
- Dry shirts upside down or hang them on hangers.

- Remove your clothes before they're bone-dry. That only leads to static.
- Clean your trap. Emptying out that lint filter could save you $35 a year in energy costs, since clogs in your dryer can increase energy use by about a third.
- Look into **natural gas dryers**. They dry your clothes in less time, and in provinces where natural gas is significantly cheaper than electricity, these babies will save you some coin (in Saskatchewan, for instance, you'll be cutting your operating costs in half).
- It costs a good $80 to $90 a year to power your clothes dryer. If you buy yourself a $20 clothing rack and/or clothesline and ditch the dryer, you'll have saved, oh, nearly $400 in the first five years alone!

**Fabric Softeners:** Love burrowing your face in warm, freshly dried clothes? You might not want to inhale, since you'll be taking in a whiff of toxins like chloroform, benzyl acetate, even neurotoxic toluene (not to mention animal tallow). Plus, dryer sheets aren't recyclable, no matter what they say on the box, and using them will void warranties on many new dryers because they clog lint traps and vents. If you're a total disposable-dryer-sheet junky and refuse to abandon your ways, then at least shift to a less harmful product, like **Seventh Generation's Natural Fabric Softener Sheets**. Not sure why **Method's Squeaky Green** or **Softener Infused** dryer cloths have to be packaged in plastic and not a basic recycled cardboard box, though at least Squeaky Green's format uses less plastic.

So is liquid fabric softener any better? Well, if you call making your terry cloth, fleece and velour clothing seven times more flammable a good thing, as *Consumer Reports* found, sure. Who needs the stink of petrochemicals and phthalates on your back anyway? Also, avoid those reusable spiky laundry balls you pop in the dryer to soften your shirts. They're made of phthalate-heavy PVC. And I know static cling is annoying, but ditch the Static Guard. It's loaded with petroleum-based ingredients, such as butane, propane and isopropanol, as well as dimethyl ditallow ammonium chloride (toxic to fish and algae) and chloromethane (which breaks down very slowly in air).

- Try all-natural health store brands of liquid fabric softener, or just add a cup of vinegar to your rinse cycle.
- To reduce static cling, get a reusable chem-free dryer sheet like the **Static Eliminator**. It combats static relatively well and lasts for up to 500 loads (just wash it periodically).
- Stave off the next static attack by hanging your clothes to dry.

## DRY CLEANING

If Martians ever flew down and saw us sending our clothes to get "cleaned" by dipping them in a chemical that officials tie to cancer, they'd probably shake their heads, then fly back home to let us stew in our own mess. Sure, Environment Canada is restricting the use of perchloroethylene (a.k.a. perc), which it considers a toxin, but we're nowhere near as smart as California and New Jersey, which are phasing the major groundwater contaminant out altogether.

California was originally pushing for a switch to a silicone-based process developed by GreenEarth Cleaning but backed off when health concerns started emerging. Then, in 2008, Health Canada declared the silicone used by such dry cleaners (known as D5) to be bioaccumulative and persistent in the environment, meaning that it can build up in the food chain and "may cause long-term adverse effects on sediment-dwelling organisms." The silicone lobby argues that the product is perfectly safe. If you're curious and want to track down GreenEarth dry cleaners, go to greenearthcleaning.com.

**Green Alternatives:** Really, your best bets are either **wet cleaning** or **carbon dioxide–based cleaners**, though they're definitely harder to find. Wet cleaners use specially formulated detergents, water and often computer-controlled machines, and can accommodate most "dry clean only" garments. Supposedly, that includes wedding gowns, wool

---

### WHAT'S THE DEAL WITH "ORGANIC" DRY CLEANING?

Honey, your clothes aren't just being washed—they're getting green-washed, and that ain't a good thing. You've probably spotted the big "organic" signs hanging in the windows of more and more dry cleaners lately. It's enough to lead anyone to believe the industry that dips your clothes in toxins and calls them "clean" suddenly went all hippy-dippy on us. Don't be fooled. That dry-cleaning compound is as organic as petroleum (in fact, it's petroleum-based hydrocarbons), meaning it's organic in the chemistry student's sense of the word, not the crunchy-granola one you were hoping for. And wouldn't you know it, the compound used by those stores flashing perc-free signs is commonly made by the grandest of eco-villains—ExxonMobil. Sure, hydrocarbon solvents are a little better than perc for your health and the planet, but they're still hazardous air pollutants.

suits, silks, leather, comforters and rayon clothing. Of course, wet cleaning is not entirely holy, since the process can release soap surfactants and bleaches into the sewers, though the solutions used are purportedly biodegradable.

Carbon dioxide–based cleaners, which use liquid carbon dioxide, have also got the green thumbs-up. Although they do add a little $CO_2$ to the air, proponents say they're still ahead of the curve because they originally removed $CO_2$ pollution from stacks to create their solvent, making them carbon-neutral. Both wet cleaners and $CO_2$ cleaners are starting to pop up in more and more towns, so keep your eyes peeled.

Bottom line:

- Avoid clothes that demand dry cleaning.
- Most clothes labelled "dry clean" or "dry clean only" can be handwashed in cool water with gentle, natural soap—especially most synthetics, blends and wool. Silk is tricky because it might shrink, and rayon can shrivel up; best to test a small swatch.

**Steam-based:** If you've got a closet full of dry-clean-only clothes, a washer that needs replacing and a wallet full of cash, marketers would love you to get a steam-based washer and dryer set. These babies are said to replace the need for dry cleaners by simply steaming the wrinkles and odours out of your clothes, as well as offering all regular wash cycles. LG's TrueSteam washer does use much less water than running your clothes through a regular wash cycle (less than a litre of water for its SteamFresh cycle), but it does use energy to heat the water into steam (and even more power if you flick on the Allergiene cycle), which you wouldn't have used if you were washing in cold water. Still, if this piques your interest, you'll be happy to know the Energy Star–certified machine does exceed Energy Star requirements by a good 110%.

## PEST CONTROL

Oh, what a wicked web we weave when first we practise to douse the shit out of living things with chemicals. I know it's tempting when a major infestation hits, but you're actually dousing your family in carcinogenic, neurotoxic ingredients that can lodge themselves in your body for years to come. Not to get all Buddhist on you, but in killing that roach, you're actually killing yourself. Very, very slowly. So take a deep breath and read on. You'll see there are plenty of effective natural solutions that won't turn your home into a karmic dead zone.

### All-Round Pest-Aversion Strategies:

- Seal up any cracks or gaps around baseboards, cupboards, vents, electric outlets and pipes (mice can squeeze through a hole the size of a dime). Perforated and sheet metal, concrete and wire-mesh hardware cloth are all rodent-resistant.
- A good caulking job should help keep ants out.
- Weatherstripping under doors is a must.
- Leaky taps and toilets are like rivers of fresh water for all sorts of pests—get them fixed!
- Food in your cupboards should be kept in airtight glass, No. 5 plastic or metal containers or sealed bags. Many containers on the market are far from airtight.
- Vacuum often, clean your kitchen daily, and be sure to sweep under, around and, yes, even behind your appliances frequently.
- Don't be a slob (says the pot calling the kettle black).

**Mice:** Got unwelcome squeaking houseguests? The old-fashioned strategy has long been to get yourself a feisty cat. While vegans might wince at the prospect of Fluffy patrolling their household parameters, it's a far more natural solution than laying out sticky traps or putting out poison powder that slowly kills the mouse over days or minutes by attacking its nervous system or triggering internal bleeding.

If you're cat-averse, use food to lure the whiskered scramblers into live traps. But you'll be defeating the point of these if you let a little mouse die of dehydration in your basement. Check the traps often, and release any captives several kilometres from your home or they'll be back. The reusable **Victor Tin Cat Mouse Trap** (available at hardware

stores or from victorpest.com) can hold up to about 30 mice, but the more traps you have going, the better.

**Creepy Crawlies:** Some mainstream bug killers list benign boric acid (borax) as their active ingredient, but they don't tell you that the (unlisted) so-called passive or inert ingredients, which make up 95% of the product, can actually be quite toxic. The group Beyond Pesticides says that more than 200 "inert" chemicals are actually hazardous air and water pollutants. Warnings have been issued in the past against buying two products, Miraculous Insecticide Chalk and Cockroach Sweeper, thanks to illegal pesticides and traces of lead.

- If roaches have taken over your kitchen, a powdery trail of **sugar and baking soda** (50:50) is said to kill them in a couple of weeks, according to Golden Harvest Organics' tip sheet on pest control (ghorganics.com).
- For all-round creepy-crawly control, try sprinkling straight **natural borax** (which you can buy for a few bucks in the laundry section of your grocery store) on cracks, in garbage cans and under appliances to kill roaches, water bugs, silverfish, fleas, ants, millipedes— pretty much anything that crawls. Note that borax shouldn't be swallowed by anything or anyone you don't want to make ill.
- If borax didn't work, or if you're worried about toddlers or pets swallowing that borax, track down harder-to-find **diatomaceous earth**. It's made of crushed fossilized algae that won't harm pets if swallowed (though it can be irritating on the lungs). It kills off all sorts of wigglers, such as earwigs, roaches, ants and fleas. Sprinkle it around cracks, in crevices, along baseboards, under appliances and above kitchen cabinets, and roaches, for instance, should be dead within a few days.
- Vacuuming is a great non-toxic way to suck up roaches, wasps and ants. Most will suffocate in the bag, but sprinkling diatomaceous earth in the bag should kill the others.
- Spritz a spray bottle full of **soapy water** on ants, roaches and other bugs. This surprisingly lethal cocktail also works on garden pests.

**Moths:** So you've pulled out your favourite sweater and discovered that it's been somebody's breakfast. Mothballs seem like the right thing to do, but don't go there. They're loaded with coal tar–derived naphthalene, a possible human carcinogen. Inhaling a lot of this stuff is linked to liver damage and neurological damage, according to government sources. In fact, the U.S. Environmental Protection Agency says infants born to mothers who sniffed this chemical during pregnancy had higher chances of hemolytic anemia. Even moth-repellent blocks labelled "cedar" or "lavender" could contain the same toxin.

- Try all-natural **herbal moth bars**, made with essential oils and plant-based wax, available at some health stores or from Wise Ways Herbals (wiseways.com). Or make your own moth-repelling sachet with a mix of dried lavender, thyme, cloves and, ideally, cedar shavings.

- Lay your woollens out in the sun every summer to kill any sun-loathing larvae. If you don't have outdoor access, you can also run them through a hot dryer for a bit (just don't toss them in wet, or you might shrink them).

**PANTRY MOTHS**

Got moths flying out of your pantry? You're not hallucinating! Indian meal moths love a good bag of rice/flour/cereal/nuts/dried fruit. You'll spot a telltale white webbing inside food containers before you see their young (wriggling larvae). Ditch any sack of dried food mentioned above, wash everything down well with a little borax water, and then be sure to keep any new supplies in well-sealed containers. If your pantry gets really infested, you'll have to toss everything out. And they still might come back. Sorry. They're particularly persistent. Next outbreak, try trapping the adults by sticking a pheromone-based moth trap in your pantry to prevent more breeding (see page 48).

- Store sweaters in airtight containers during the warmer months.
- If you suspect moths, shove that sweater in the freezer in a plastic bag for a few days.
- Stick a natural **pheromone-based moth trap** in your closet. Order one from the Urban Nature Store (urbannaturestore.ca) or Grassroots Environmental Products (grassrootsstore.com), or search for them at Home Depot.

**Ants:** It's hard to look at an ant the same way after you've heard Woody Allen's voice coming out of one of them. Yet despite the Hollywoodization of colony life in the late '90s, most of us have no problem crushing the little buggers. Still, you've gotta admit, they're pretty damn fascinating. Some of these mini Navy SEALs emit propaganda pheromones to confuse enemy ants. Others are odd little farmers that actually "milk" aphids by stroking their bellies until they release a sugary juice. Killing them should definitely be a last-resort option. But if your yard or home has become the New York City of ant colonies, here are some greener ways to make your move.

- One popular route involves pouring a large pot of **boiling water** into the anthill. It kills most but not all of them instantly, but it'll also kill your grass and won't necessarily put an end to your problem. You need to get to the queen. This requires stealthy assassination plans along the lines of the CIA plot to poison Castro. Another method involves sprinkling lots of **cornmeal** around their home. They'll all chow down, including the queen, and the next time they drink water, they swell up and, well, explode. No joke. This should even work on fire ants.
- Put some **citrus peels** or **cucumber parings** out. They hate the stuff so much, they should vacate. You can even sprinkle **orange peels** in your garden if you get ants eating your sweet peppers, like I used to.
- For carpenter ants, you'll want to **prune nearby trees, patch up entry holes** to your home and start praying they don't find a way inside. If that happens, you'll need a pro.

**Raccoons:** Have I told you about the night a raccoon snuck into my house and stole a granola bar from my gym bag? By the looks of my mangled windowsill, he wanted out more than he wanted to spend his evening locked inside with my hulky cat, so he wedged himself out through a 5-centimetre gap in my window and never looked back. Well, other than plotting against my compost bin whenever the sun goes down. So what do you do with masked bandits that just won't go away? It depends on what kind of headache they're causing. Without a good latch system on your trash bins, you might as well put out a menu and some tablecloths. If you've got the space and deep pockets, get yourself a fancy **cedar garbage shed** from a site like Bin Solutions (binsolutions.ca). DIYers can build one themselves. Here are some other strategies if they're tearing up your veggie garden/shed/deck.

- Mist the area with a **jalapeño-water solution** (boil several chopped fresh hot peppers for 20 minutes, then steep for a day) every three to five days. (Warning: open windows when boiling!)
- Release **beneficial nematodes** into grassy spaces to naturally eliminate the tasty grub population that can lure hungry raccoons (garden centres should carry them).
- Experiment with ambient deterrents like **motion-sensing floodlights and sprinklers**. Hell, some people even leave a **radio out overnight**, with an all-talk station on low, to keep them away. The efficacy of these methods depends on how people-sensitive your creatures are—and in urban centres, good luck.
- If they treat your patio like a giant latrine, try laying down **plastic painter's sheeting** everywhere (raccoons don't like the slippery surface).
- You might be tempted to call in a pro who promises humane wildlife removal. But unless you catch the whole fam-damily, this is pretty cruel. And in some jurisdictions, services are allowed to release the crafty critters only a kilometre away, so

they could easily make their way back. Any further and their chances of survival are sadly slim.

- For those of you hosting guests in your attic like a Motel 6, get a responsible wildlife control company to install a one-way door wherever the creatures are getting in. Once you're sure they're gone, block all entry points with galvanized metal or rust-proof mesh, cap your chimney, fix your shingles, trim overhanging tree branches and pray to the raccoon gods that they don't excavate an entrance somewhere else.

### "PREDATOR URINE"

Stay away from deterrent sprays made with "predator urine." Raccoons may not like the scent of coyote pee, but coyotes enjoy being locked into wire pens to have their urine harvested even less.

**Bedbugs:** Whether you live in the lap of luxury or a crusty roach motel, no one is immune to love bites after dark. If you're finding tiny dots of blood on your sheets and itchy ringed bites on your skin, you've got vampires, baby—lentil-sized ones. And let me warn you right now: expect a prolonged military engagement. The last several years have seen a serious resurgence of bedbugs, according to exterminators and public health officials. Not that they're anywhere near as common as, say, roaches, and some say the media are stirring up a panic. But if you find these buggers on your turf, you have good reason to freak. Now that DDT is a big no-no (thankfully), our chemical defences against the nibblers are, well, limited. Word is, bedbugs have built up resistance to the pyrethroid family of pesticides we've been using on them, and many exterminators won't guarantee their work, often having to spray two to three times. Trouble is, these land-based piranhas are way too good at hiding. Besides making themselves at home in box springs and mattresses, they lurk behind electrical plates and loose wallpaper, in the tiniest of cracks or crevices. So getting them all is tough. But there are ways to tackle them without resorting to toxins.

- First things first: **steam-clean** your mattress (heat kills these creeps), then body-bag it in a tightly woven **barrier sheet**. You can find polyester microfibre ones online for cheap if your budget's tight, or invest in organic cotton barrier sheets (which also keep dust mites out) from green home stores like Grassroots or Organic Lifestyle (see Resources: Good Green Home Websites).
- Fire up that washing machine. All drapes, bedding and removable upholstery need to get sudsed up in hot water (one of the few times this energy-hogging practice is justified), and do this often.
- Vacuum vigorously (and ditch the bag right after).
- Remove clutter.
- Caulk all cracks, even the tiniest ones.
- Sprinkle diatomaceous earth everywhere.
- Short of calling in a pro saddled with synthetic chemicals, the brightest hope for health- and planet-conscious residents is a product that doesn't yet have approval to make bedbug claims (though it's waiting on it). It's an all-natural enzyme-based liquid spray called **Kleen Green Naturally**, carried by licesquad.com, or **Kleen-Free**, carried by Ecoginesis Inc. at ecoginesis.com. Testimonials from Brooklyn to New Brunswick attest to its ability to kill bedbugs dead when sprayed everywhere. Just don't expect Kleen Green's label to say so until it gets clearance to make such claims. South of the border, Kleen-Free is very clear about its bedbug-fighting properties. If you're rigorous about spraying every last surface, maybe, just maybe, enzymes will be the pesticide-free solution.
- From now on, carefully inspect curb finds and antiques before taking them home.

So your sweet little Fluffy/Fido brought friends home and they're not the adoptable kind. What do you do next? First, bathe your pet in mild soapy water to drown any existing fleas. Try dipping your pet's comb in **Natural Ginesis's Kleen Green** enzyme-based solution as you brush your pet. You can even use the diluted product to clean your home and bathe your pet. Otherwise, get your hands on some diatomaceous earth (it's a fine white fossilized algae powder that grinds away at the fleas' exoskeleton). You can sprinkle this on your pet and your home (spread over couches, carpets, pet bedding, then vacuum) every few days, though it can be quite drying on their skin and irritating for you to inhale.

Vacuum often, even daily, to remove eggs, larvae and adults—making sure to vacuum furniture (both under and over), baseboards, cracks and crevices. Throw some **diatomaceous earth** or **borax** in the vacuum bag to kill any eggs and sprinkle some around your house as well, under rugs and furniture. Make sure to get them at the source, too, by sprinkling diatomaceous earth in your backyard and/or releasing microscopic nematodes, which prey on flea larvae and pupae (you can pick up nematodes at garden supply stores).

**Mould:** Don't even get me started about life with mould. I found water dripping into a basement closet one day—that was moments before I found an old pair of boots growing blue and white fuzz. The horror! While fungi are quite multi-talented, with powers to clean up chemical spills and heal ailments, they're very rarely welcome inside your home (other than in a risotto). In fact, people sharing spaces with mould are, according to Health Canada, "more likely to suffer from health problems, especially symptoms such as coughing, wheezing, and headaches." In all honesty, most types of mould shouldn't hurt you if you're healthy, but if there are young kids, someone with allergies or anyone with a weakened immune system around, I'd take extra precautions.

If your mould patch is larger than a square metre, it's time to call in a pro. Especially if you keep trying to clean it and it keeps growing back like creepy B-movie slime, if it has a strong odour or, worse still, if it is blackish-green in hue. In my case, mould remediators came in and found, surprise, spores climbing behind closet walls. I came home to find that my bedroom had been cordoned off *X-Files* style. For that kind of work, call your local Canada Mortgage and Housing Corporation office for a list of individuals who've completed the CMHC Residential Indoor Air Quality Investigator Program. However, if you think you can manage the mould yourself, here are a few tips:

- Invest in a good dehumidifier (see page 135 for more on dehumidifiers). They aren't problem solvers and won't get rid of the source of your moisture, but they will control the amount of moisture in the air.
- Check the foundation for leaks. Patch cracks with hydraulic cement. If walls are just damp rather than leaky, try putting a low- or no-VOC waterproof coating over exposed foundation. AFM Safecoat's **Penetrating WaterStop** is a good choice.
- Check plumbing for leaks and take corrective action.
- Make sure downspouts are disconnected from eavestroughs, especially if you live in a concrete-heavy city (heavy rainfalls can flood the sewers with millions of litres of water, some of which can spit up into your basement). And make sure your downspouts are directed at least 1 metre from your house onto a grassy patch.
- Check for crappy drainage happening outside your home (my backyard, for instance, slopes, rather ridiculously, towards my apartment, and all the concrete walkways around the house were broken, allowing water to seep downwards way too easily. But hosing down the outside of the house revealed the ultimate source of basement leaks and, in turn, mould—water coming in through cracks in the mortar between the bricks).
- If bathroom mould is a problem, install an Energy Star–certified ventilation fan.
- Stay away from harsh chemicals like bleach whenever possible. Try an alternative and all-natural enzyme-based cleaner like

**AllerAir's Mold Away** spray—this is the same company that brings you top-notch air purifiers, so they wouldn't think of contaminating your air quality with chemicals (the only Canadian retailer to sell Mold Away is Grassroots [grassrootsstore.com]; you could also ask your local green home store to special order some for you).

- Tackle existing mould with straight-up vinegar or put 1 tablespoon (15 mL) of tea tree oil or 1 cup (250 mL) of borax in 4 cups (1 L) of hot water. Spray it on, but don't rinse. Try washing it off a few days later.

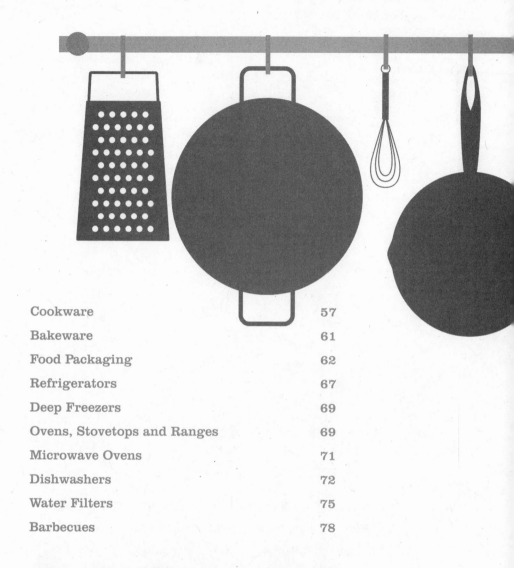

# COOKING

Eat, drink and be wary
(of your kitchen tools, that is)

**Ever fantasize about having your own**
Food Network show? Mine would be called **The Explosive Chef
and Company**. Ads would beckon viewers to "Tune in as Adria's
organic kitchen descends into chaos nightly." (Trust me, you
don't want to follow me on cleanup duty.) Whether you're part
Jamie Oliver, part Nigella or part Chef Boyardee, we all rely on
our kitchens to fill our bellies. How you stock this room, however, determines whether you're serving up a healthy, green
meal or an energy- and chemical-heavy one that leaves you and
your family, well, bloated.

# COOKWARE

I have good news and bad news—which do you want first? Okay, the good news: you know that chemical used to make non-stick pans, found in over 95% of our bloodstreams (and 100% of umbilical cords, according to the Johns Hopkins University)? The über-persistent one that sticks to our tissues indefinitely and is considered a likely human carcinogen? It's called PFOA (perfluorooctanoic acid), and the eight largest manufacturers of that chemical, including DuPont, have agreed to a request from the U.S. Environmental Protection Agency to phase out its use by 95% by 2010. Since none of it is actually made in Canada, that agreement should seriously reduce and eventually elimi-nate the amount of PFOA used to make the pans, colanders and whisks we cook with. Since we can thank the manufacturing of Teflon-everything for the mass bioaccumulation of PFOA in everyone from polar bears to babies, this change should help lower the concentrations of PFOA in our bodies (which were already down 25% in 2004 from 1999). It should also put an end to the worrisome habit of using the slippery grease-proofer on burger wrappers, popcorn bags, french fry cartons and candy packaging, which has been an especially easy route for PFOA to get into our systems. Luckily, many companies—including Burger King, Frito-Lay, Kellogg's, Kraft and most recently McDon-ald's—have told Ohio Citizen Action that they don't use or have phased out the use of PFOA-coated packaging.

**We can thank the manufacturing of Teflon-everything** for the mass bioaccumulation of PFOA in everyone from polar bears to babies

The bad news is that an investigation by the Environmental Working Group found zero evidence that the PFOA's replacement chemicals being rushed to market are much safer. It's hard to say, when consumers are being left in the dark as to their make-up. Also, while health officials still insist that your PFOA exposures through cookware are minimal, Health Canada does admit that "non-stick coatings are a risk if they are heated to temperatures greater than 350° Celsius or 650° Fahrenheit." In fact, a non-stick pan heated to a very high temperature begins to emit a variety of toxins (including possible carcinogens such as TFE, or tetrafluoroethylene) and has, in the past, killed pet birds innocently tweetering away in kitchens.

So what to do with your old, chipped pan now that you're completely turned off? Well, I wouldn't, in good conscience, donate it to Goodwill. And since the government doesn't consider it to be hazardous waste, you have no choice but to send it to the dump (though I'd hate to see what happens when non-stick pans end up in old municipal incinerators). Unless, of course, you want to send it to DuPont, with a sweet thank-you note for poisoning our environment for decades.

As for alternatives, there is no number-one choice here, but you do have a few pots to cook in comfortably.

**Stainless Steel:** The most popular alternative for non-stick–weary cooks. Forget the surgical-grade stuff with zero recycled content— unless you want to empty your bank account. Still, you'd be wise to invest in a good pan instead of cursing the uneven hot spots on your cheap one. Stainless steel can be a little sticky, so Starfrit has recently come out with a Quicklean pan with microscopic peaks and valleys that allow food to "float" without sticking (though, in my experience, unless you maintain that surface carefully, you'll lose the non-stick factor fast). I prefer a good old stainless steel pan you can take a steel scrub brush to if things get extra sticky. Quick tip: If you're allergic to nickel, look for the nickel-free variety, since most stainless is cut with the stuff.

**Cast Iron:** If treated properly, these can last for decades (generations, even). And if you season cast iron pans and woks regularly with an oil high in saturated fat, like coconut oil, you can create a fairly non-stick finish. Make sure to dry the surface well after washing (and many say you should wash only with water and a scrub brush, avoiding soap). Most are made with scrap iron filtered of contaminants, though cheap versions may not be properly filtered. U.K.-based **Biome Lifestyle** makes a pricy "eco-luxury" frying pan with 75% recycled content.

"Green" Cookware: If you're longing for truly non-stick surfaces, you should check out ceramic-coated pans, often marketed as green cookware. They're non-leaching, chemical-free and as slippery as any Teflon pan without the worry. Even Cuisinart is dishing out a ceramic-coated line called **GreenGourmet** (cuisinart.ca). The base is made of either anodized aluminum or stainless steel.

$$ A few quite affordable Starfrit lines (including **Eco Chef**, **Alternatives** and **Heritage**) coat 99% recycled aluminum bases with non-leaching ceramic linings (starfrit.com). Eco Chef is available from Canadian Tire, and the more durable Alternatives cookware can be found at Wal-Mart. These come with a three-year warranty, so if the coating starts to chip and reveals the non-anodized aluminum beneath, Starfrit will give you a new one.

I've had a good experience with BergHOFF's **Earthchef** series (though as with all non-stick coatings, even these pans can lose a little of their slipperiness with time) (earthchef.ca). Beyond ceramic-coated pans, which can withstand metallic cooking utensils, Earthchef also has griddles, woks, muffin trays and more with the same solid coating,

## SAVE WITH SECOND-HAND COOKWARE

$$ Okay, so I might not recommend getting a used non-stick pan, but you can score some seriously good deals buying stainless steel, glass and cast iron cookware second-hand. I got my whole five-piece stainless steel Cuisinart set from a friend's moving sale for, like, $30. But you don't need to wait for your pals to move across the continent—just trawl garage sales and Goodwill stores or hop online. I just jumped onto a couple of virtual second-hand sites (like **Kijiji.ca** and **Craigslist.org**) and spotted an eight-piece stoneware set for $30, a seven-piece stainless steel cookware set for $15 and an old Danish cast iron enamel pan for $5! You can even score old blenders, coffee makers, bread makers and kitchen knives for killer prices. Now you'll have no excuse not to have a well-stocked kitchen.

all at really good prices. Plus, with every 11-inch (28 cm) pan sold, they'll sponsor a tree planting with Tree Canada (earthchef.ca).

My least favourite is probably pricier GreenPan. It's got a silicone-based Thermalon ceramic coating they call a nano-composite. Honestly, though, the whole realm of nanotech is way too unregulated and controversial for me to want to cook on the stuff. (See The Dark Side of Nano Silver sidebar, page 39.)

**Titanium:** Touted at health shows as a healthy, lightweight choice for people with fat wallets. You'll find some woks and thin camping cookware that are solid titanium but solid titanium isn't the best heat conductor, so most are titanium-coated aluminum with non-stick titanium dioxide surfaces; these are considered non-toxic. Many surfaces are made of safe, non-leaching titanium-ceramic blends. Just beware of PFOA-based (a.k.a. Teflon) coatings on titanium cookware.

**Anodized Aluminum:** Hard anodized aluminum cookware is said to seal in the aluminum and create a non-stick surface that can handle acids like tomato sauces with minimal leaching (but it is not leach-free). Worrywarts take note: pots and pans give us 1 or 2 milligrams of aluminum daily (versus the 50 milligrams that you get from swallowing

## CRYSTAL CLEAR: THE PROBLEM WITH STEMWARE AND OLD CHINA

You know that fancy crystal stemware you never use? And that antique china? Yeah, well, let them sit there gathering dust if they're heavily scratched or chipped. They're heavy in lead. Oh, and Health Canada says you shouldn't serve up any food on lead-containing tableware to pregnant women or children. Chances are pretty slim, but lead poisonings have occurred from old crystal, and I doubt your guests fancy a real-life version of Clue where the plates are the culprit.

one antacid). The anodizing process is pretty chemical- and energy-intensive though, involving an acid bath and electrical currents.

**Copper:** This fancy-schmancy cookware will always be coated with stainless steel (a little copper isn't bad for you, but too much of it can be poisonous, and safe daily-exposure doses haven't really been determined). Great heat conductor, so chefs love it.

**Glass:** A top pick. Glass is the ultimate renewable resource. Totally inert. One hundred percent non-leaching. Be careful your rice doesn't burn in one of these, because it'll stick like hell and will need some serious soaking.

## BAKEWARE

Put down those non-stick muffin tins and reach for something that doesn't stick to your bloodstream long after your cupcakes go stale.

**Ceramic:** A good choice as long as the glaze is lead-free. In Canada, glazed ceramics and glassware are regulated, and cookware made of these materials cannot be sold, advertised or imported if it releases more than trace amounts of lead and cadmium.

Big budget? Get some **Le Creuset** ceramic enamel-coated cast iron bakeware.

 **Earthchef** makes affordable ceramic-coated muffin tins and bakeware (earthchef.ca).

**Stoneware:** This stuff is oh so earthy and somehow seems to make your food taste better. Digging for clay isn't always welcomed by the planet, so make sure your brand is using sustainably sourced clay. **Pampered Chef**'s stuff is made with American clay and comes with a three-year unconditional guarantee, so even if you drop and crack it, they'll give you a new one (pamperedchef.com). After having a few greasy dishes baked in it, it forms a non-stick layer. FYI, always get the unglazed kind, the same colour as terra cotta.

## IS SILICONE BAKEWARE SAFE?

You don't have to fit in with the Hugh Hefner crowd to get yourself a pair of these. (I meant silicone oven mitts, you perv.) This manmade fusion of silicon (basically sand) and oxygen is moulded into colourful and bendy heat- and cold-resistant muffin trays, baking sheets, bread pans, ice trays and, yes, mitts. No real dirt on this can be found, other than that sand mining can be pretty damaging to an ecosystem—but so can digging for steel, iron and clay. Silicone is touted as the safest bet for everything from baby bottle nipples to sex toys, so you should be fine. At the same time, research on the effects of baking with this stuff is scanty at best, which means not everyone's convinced they should test them out in their kitchens. You're not going to have silicone gel leaking into your food like a bad implant job from the '80s, but with every Tom, Dick and Mary making cheap versions of this bakeware, it's hard to say what you're getting. Health Canada says you have nothing to worry about, you just don't want to bake the stuff at temperatures higher than 425°F (220°C), since it could melt.

## FOOD PACKAGING

**Tips to Avoid Packaging:** A whopping 35% of municipal solid waste is packaging, according to Waste Reduction Week Canada. Want to minimize the amount of trash that comes clinging to everything you buy? Here are a few tips:

- Pass on produce bags. Trust me, you don't need a plastic bag for every apple and chili pepper you buy. They'll weigh them loose. But if you're really hooked, get mesh produce bags by Montreal-based **CredoBags** (check credobags.com for stores near you). Kootenay-based **Kootsac** makes cotton and nylon-based produce bags that are perfect for filling up on bulk flour, grains and more (punch in "kootsac" at etsy.com for orders).
- Get your meat and cheese from the deli counter and ask for butcher paper only, please. Who needs the polystyrene foam and

plastic wrap that comes from the ready-packaged kind? Butcher paper isn't necessarily from recycled sources and often comes with a petroleum wax to make it more water-resistant, but at least you can compost it in municipal composting systems.

- Cart your own containers to the bulk store. Most will be happy to preweigh your vessel (be it a sack, reusable food container, empty peanut butter jar, you name it) before you fill it with flour, cereal, nuts or whatnot. You might even have a shop in your home town that sells shampoo and soap in bulk (see Resources: Green Home Storefronts).

## THE GREAT PURGE: GARBAGE-FREE CHALLENGE

It's garbage night and you're elbow-deep in trash, trying to make sense of the landfill-bound packaging in your bin. With all the diligent recycling you do, you're still left with an ever-morphing pile of plastic. And don't think that pile is heading for plastic heaven, where it'll be infinitely reborn into new plastic. Nuh-uh, it gets downcycled—a.k.a. downgraded into dead-end products like plant trays or shoelaces that, after one kick at the can, end up in a landfill. Throw in all the stuff that goes straight to the dump, and in total Canadians churn out on average 1,000 kilograms or nearly one whole ton of garbage, per person per year. You can't get rid of it all, but surely we can shave off a few kilos. What if you tried just one week without producing any garbage at all? You might just get hooked.

**Ground Rules:**

- Packaging is to be avoided at all costs.
- Nothing disposable can be purchased (that means no gum, no Swiffers, no straws, not even a bag of organic chips).
- If for some reason an unpackaged substitute can't be found, the container the product is sold in must be recyclable. Otherwise, said item must be forfeited. Sorry.

- Size matters. If you can't buy your peanut butter or cereal in bulk in refillable containers, better to get one large container of PB or bran flakes than two smaller ones. Larger volumes will also keep you from having to travel to the grocery store often (and one large box should contain less packaging than two smaller boxes). But read the weight labels (e.g., 450 grams) to be sure the large box of cereal isn't actually stuffed with the same quantity as a smaller box.
- Give a hoot and dilute. Buying soap or soup concentrate means you can add the water yourself at home instead of having it watered down for you.
- Stash reusable shopping bags everywhere: your coat, your gym bag, your briefcase, your trunk.
- We all know we should BYOM (that's bring your own mug) to the coffee shop, but try bringing your own reusable food containers to your favourite takeout spots too. I've brought mine everywhere from Chinese restaurants to fast-food courts and no one flinches. They might even smile, since you're saving them a dime's worth of packaging! (Oh, and be sure to forgo the plastic bag, plastic utensils and wad of napkins that come with your takeout, too.)
- Make a statement: leave that bulky unrecyclable packaging that comes with your razors, headphones or toys with the cashier. This action passes on a message to management that you'd like to see packaging-reduction programs in place. You can even mail some to your provincial representative with the same message!

Plastic Wrap vs. Aluminum Foil: Okay, so which is worse for the planet, a wrap made of destructive petroleum or one made of destructive aluminum? Well, you can now buy plastic wrap that's PVC-free (Glad and Saran make some), so it doesn't leach hormone-disrupting phthalates into your food (which cheaper generic brands could). But you can bet there's no recycled content in this petroleum-based product, and good luck reusing the sticky wad of plastic left

## NO SUCH THING AS "MICROWAVE-SAFE" PLASTIC!

So we've finally woken up to the fact that microwaving plastic baby bottles is plain tantrum-worthy. Not only does estrogen-mimicking bisphenol A (BPA) leach from polycarbonate plastic during regular use, but studies have found that one zap in the microwave can cause as much leaching as 60 to 100 rounds in the dishwasher. Kind of erodes your confidence in the whole "microwave-safe" label, doesn't it? Especially when you find out that no one regulates the term. Maybe we shouldn't be surprised that when the *Milwaukee Journal Sentinel*, in the fall of 2008, lab-tested 10 plastic food containers for microwave leaching, they found even plastics Nos. 1, 2 and 5 had BPA leaching. These included frozen food trays, microwaveable soup containers and plastic baby food packaging. What? Isn't BPA only in No. 7 polycarbonate plastic? Guess not. Stay safe and follow these tips:

- Never microwave food or drinks in any plastic. Period.
- Never microwave or heat plastic wrap.
- Don't put plastics in the dishwasher. Heat (including hot water from dishwashers) boosts leaching from purportedly dishwasher-safe polycarbonate, so who's to say your dishwasher-safe plastic won't leach when someone decides to test that too.

behind after wrapping half a watermelon in the stuff. Yes, aluminum is incredibly resource-intensive to mine and refine. Yet foil is technically recyclable (check with your municipality) and reusable (I wash mine and save it for next time), and you can buy aluminum foil made with recycled content (**If You Care** makes some that's 100% recycled content, requiring 95% less energy to make than non-recycled foil; available at health food stores or see ifyoucare.com). I wouldn't store food, especially acidic food, in aluminum but I wouldn't store food in any disposable vessel, including plastic wrap. Better to reach for something that can be washed and used again, like a reusable food container. Tupperware, Gladware and Ziploc containers are phthalate- and PVC-free plastic. But you'd be much wiser to get glass storage containers. There are tons of brands on shelves today. Oh, and there's always my quickie plate trick: instead of wrapping up half-eaten produce, like a grapefruit, just put it face down on a dish. In a pinch, plates can also be used to cover bowls full of leftovers.

**Cans:** If the popular tool in your kitchen is a can opener, listen up. Those butt-kickers at the Washington-based Environmental Working Group tested the contents of 97 cans of soup, soda, veggies and fruit, and over half registered positive for the same controversial estrogen-mimicking chemical that's been banned from baby bottles in Canada, namely bisphenol A (BPA). The chemical has been linked to growth in cancer cells, as well as developmental and reproductive damage in infants. One in 10 canned items showed disturbingly high levels of the chemical, the worst being canned veggies and pasta (not good for those kids growing up on canned ravioli and peas).

That's because steel and tin cans are lined with an epoxy resin heavy in bisphenol A to keep the metal from leaching into your food (go figure). Government officials will tell you they're more worried about the bisphenol A lining in baby food than adult food, but plenty of young children eat canned soups, pastas and veggies on a regular basis. Not to mention the fact that newer research is linking high levels of bisphenol A in adults to heart disease and type 2 diabetes.

Canada has yet to set limits on how much bisphenol A in cans is too much. In the meantime, you'll have to regulate your own habits. If you eat canned foods once in a while, I wouldn't worry too much. If you eat canned food every day, including canned vegetables, pastas and soups, you might want to reconsider your shopping habits:

- Cook from scratch with fresh ingredients.
- Buy dried beans and soak them yourself. (I know, I know, this will be tough for last-minute cooks, but the texture is a million times better.)
- Go for glass. Look for soups, sauces and random items like artichoke hearts or anchovies in glass jars.

# REFRIGERATORS

Picture it. Canada. Pre-1950s. If you wanted to keep your perishables cooler than your root cellar, you stocked your icebox with, you guessed it, hunks of ice delivered on a horse-drawn wagon. Today, electric refrigerators zap 15% of our energy bills. The older it is, the more energy it uses. A 20-year-old refrigerator uses 60% more power than modern models, and really old models have often lost their insulation completely (the fibreglass inside basically disintegrates), so they're outrageously inefficient.

If you want your fridge to really save on power, stick to models that come with the Energy Star logo. What makes Energy Star so great? Well, it's not without its flaws (see the Is the Energy Star Label All It's Cracked Up to Be? sidebar, page 74), but in the case of refrigeration, these models should have more energy-efficient compressors and better insulation. A brand-new Energy Star model uses half the energy of a 10-year-old fridge (saving you enough power in one year to light your house for three months, say government stats). FYI, I was told by fridge salesmen that some cheaper imports pushing ultra-high efficiency (e.g., Samsung and Haier) have had some reliability issues. LG models (LG also makes GE-branded stuff) are also considered troubled new kids on the block.

**Sun Frosts** are in a league all of their own. These babies are made in California and are some of the most energy-efficient in the world. They're super-insulated, extremely quiet and even come in DC versions

## UNPLUG THAT BEER FRIDGE!

A third of Canadian households have a second fridge in the basement or garage, which tend to be serious clunkers. Unplug that ancient beer fridge and you'll save yourself $150 in utility bills a year. Just getting rid of all the secondary fridges that are 10 years old or more would save us enough energy to power 100,000 suburban homes!

## IS YOUR REFRIGERATOR RUNNING . . . EFFICIENTLY?

Hold on, I'm getting flashbacks to my early crank-calling years. Let me take this moment to apologize to anyone I might have irritated. I offer up these energy-saving tips as an olive branch. Clean the condenser coils with a long-handled brush. The thick blanket of dust building up back there (or under there) is making the condenser work harder. Clean the seals around the doors so they're nice and tight. If your fridge is right next to your stove, you should consider moving it, since you're making it work harder to keep cool. And my dad would also add that you should make up your mind about what you want to eat before opening the door. I kind of sucked at this one as a kid.

for those who live off the grid. They're also made to last 20 to 50 years. Pretty impressive. Though they'll cost you roughly $3,000, you'll save on power bills, as they use 80% less energy than conventional fridges. Check sunfrost.com for more info. Other ultra-low-energy refrigerators for homes powered by renewable energy include **ConServ** (equatorappliance.com) and **SunDanzer** (sundanzer.com).

### Fridge Features to Consider:

- Side-by-side models swallow up to 7% more energy than freezer on the top or bottom.
- Fancy types with ice and water dispensers on the outside use even more power (15% more, to be exact).
- Fridges with anti-sweat (a.k.a. anti-condensation) features use 5% to 10% more energy.
- Stay away from fridges that push antibacterial features, like Kenmore's Microban-infused crisper bins. Microban is made with triclosan, which is a big eco no-no (see page 8 for more on triclosan).
- Oversized fridges sitting half-empty only suck up more power.

Full fridges and freezers use less energy to keep items cool but, duh, the answer isn't to buy more food that'll only go to waste, the answer is to buy a smaller fridge.

- Do look for a temperature dial that allows you to determine just how cool your fridge needs to be to keep your beer crisp.

 • Got an old fridge to offload? In British Columbia, BC Hydro will pick up an old fridge, recycle it and give you 30 bucks. Anyone living in the Northwest Territories can get up to $200 in rebates towards a new Energy Star fridge. Check with your utility provider, home province and municipality for similar deals. Truth is, there's some valuable scrap metal in those appliances, and most municipalities are happy to make a little cash off it.

## DEEP FREEZERS

If your deep freezer is sitting in your basement empty but for two meat pies, it might be time to unplug. But if you're making use of it (by, say, storing a summer's worth of fresh local veggies), note that freezers made after 2004 use less than half the electricity gobbled up by those made 15 years earlier. And the Energy Star kind will be 10% more efficient than its competitors (compact Energy Star freezers, with less than 7.75 cubic feet, will be 20% more efficient than those without the blue-and-white logo).

- Chest freezers are generally more energy-efficient than upright models with the door at the front.
- Manual defrosters that force you to unplug your freezer now and then suck back less power than the automatic kind.
- Set your freezer temperature at –18°C for maximum efficiency.

## OVENS, STOVETOPS AND RANGES

As much as we tout the idea of a gas stove, the fact that they burn cleaner than coal-fired electric ovens isn't what draws most chefs to them. Still, 97% of Canadians are stuck with the electric variety, according to the Alberta government's Utilities Consumer Advocate. What's more, stoves tend to live a good 18 years, so it's important to

## MOVE OVER, EASY-BAKE: HIGH-TECH OVENS

- **Induction cooktops:** These babies are the fastest cooks in the west. They magically keep the stovetop element cool, while your pan sizzles away. These nifty magnetic inventions don't heat cookware made of non-conductive cooking materials like ceramic or glass (even aluminum cookware can be iffy here). Plus, they don't do so well with rounded cooking surfaces like woks, since they require surface-to-surface contact to work. You can get single induction burners for, like, $150 or four-burner induction cooktops at Sears from $2,000.
- **Fancy electronic steam ovens** (**Viking** and **Miele** make some): These are said to use water and energy pretty efficiently, in large part because they cook food quickly. Manufacturers say you can also cook pasta and soups or sterilize baby bottles in there. Still, in my mind, these are up there with warming drawers as totally unnecessary (read wasteful) appliances for those with cash to burn.
- **Speed ovens:** If you're cool with microwaves and are in the market for one of these as well as an oven, consider a speed oven, which fuses energy-efficient convection oven powers with even more efficient microwave powers.

purchase yours right the first time. FYI, the Energy Star logo isn't available for cooking devices, because all ovens are fairly comparable in energy consumption. That being said, some have features that will help you save more energy than others.

### Stove Features to Consider:

- Check the EnerGuide sticker. The lower the kWh/yr number, the more energy-efficient the appliance.
- Natural gas stoves are three times more efficient than electric. If you have natural gas heating your home already, it might be worth making the switch.
- Self-cleaning ovens rule, not because you actually use the self-cleaning feature (which is quite energy-hogging when turned

on), but because the extra insulation in them makes them more efficient (especially if you don't use the self-cleaning feature more than two or three times a year).

- Convection ovens not only save you time, they save you cash, since they use a third less power than a regular oven.
- Smooth-top electric stovetops are generally more efficient than the old-fashioned coiled type, but they can take longer to heat up (and can be impossible to clean if messes aren't wiped up right away). Radiant versions are cheaper than halogen (note: there's some kvetching that halogen cooktops aren't all that good at their job).

## MICROWAVE OVENS

In all honesty, this is probably the most energy-efficient way of cooking food. But do you want to nuke all your meals? I'd keep veggies and any

### TEA TIME: ELECTRIC VS. STOVETOP KETTLES

Don't you just love the sound of a whistling kettle? You never know when a conductor might pop his head in and yell, "All aboard." Yet as much as I fancy a spot of tea made the old-fashioned way and instinctively scoff at the notion of plugging in an electric kettle, it looks like instincts aren't always right. At least when it comes down to energy efficiency. It seems that stovetop kettles waste all that energy heating the whole vessel before even starting on the water, while an electric kettle targets the $H_2O$ directly with a heating plate on the inside. Doesn't mean all electric kettles are built equally. Despite assurances that plug-in kettles made of solid plastic won't leach into your tea leaves, it's best to avoid the whole mess and get one lined with stainless steel. Invest in an electric kettle with automatic shutoff and even one that has a "warm" setting for when you want to heat, but not boil, water for hot cocoa or whatnot.

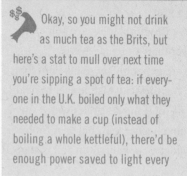

## DRINK NOT, BOIL NOT

Okay, so you might not drink as much tea as the Brits, but here's a stat to mull over next time you're sipping a spot of tea: if everyone in the U.K. boiled only what they needed to make a cup (instead of boiling a whole kettleful), there'd be enough power saved to light every U.K. streetlight for nearly seven months, according to the U.K.'s Energy Saving Trust.

nutrient-rich foods (including breast milk) out, since studies have found that microwaving can drain things like flavonoids and some B vitamins. Officials assure us the tiny amounts of non-ionizing radiation emitted within close proximity to the ovens aren't the cancer-causing kind. To avoid leaks, make sure the door's seal and hinges aren't damaged or dirty.

You definitely don't want to nuke polycarbonate plastic or polystyrene foam. These bad boys leach. Better to go with glass or ceramics. If your microwave harkens back to the days when Dire Straits was singing about them, consider keeping anyone with a really old-generation pacemaker away from it (microwave radiation used to interfere with pacemaker signals).

## DISHWASHERS

After the first *Ecoholic* book declared dishwashers more efficient than handwashing, I had a couple of exasperated skeptics write in. "You'd better double-check your stats," they said. "There's no way dishwashers could win." So double-check my stats I did. The University of Bonn study is probably the most thorough out there, having tested 113 handwashers in seven European countries (to account for variations in technique) and pitted them against two top-rated energy-efficient machines. To clean 12 place settings, the average hand-washer used 103 litres of water, 2.5 kWh of energy and 79 minutes' time. The machines: 15 litres of water, just over 1 kWh of energy for a full load and no time at all.

That's not to say your "No. 1 dishwasher" apron isn't well deserved or that you couldn't beat some of the Euros surveyed, especially if you're going up against an old dishwasher cranked on energy-heavy settings, but you get the point. I will, however, give you points for having one less bulky appliance that'll eventually end up in a landfill and bonus points for using *Ecoholic Home*'s Water-saving Hand Dishwashing Tips (see page 23).

---

### WASH 'N' SAVE

 Replacing a pre-1994 dish-washer with an Energy Star one can save you more than $30 a year in utility costs.

---

**Dishwasher Features to Consider:** If you are in the market for a new dishwasher, here are a few points to keep in mind.

- Make sure your dishwasher has an air dry button (and that you use it religiously so no added heat is created to dry your dishes). Or just open the door after the rinse cycle.
- Look for models with energy-saving and light-wash modes and use them.
- Stick with Energy Star. The logo tells you your dishwasher uses at least 41% less energy than federal standards require and sucks up much less water than conventional models.
- Read the EnerGuide sticker for an inside line on how much power the dishwasher gobbles up. The most efficient dishwashers use about 300 kWh per year. The least efficient? Closer to 700. Bosch's Evolution 800 series **SHE98M** line is the most energy-efficient of all, using only 190 kWh per year (73% above the Energy Star requirement).
- Research your features. Whirlpool's new PowerScour option seems wasteful, since it has 36 targeted jet sprays, but the company insists it doesn't suck up one additional drop of water. Its Sani Rinse option, however, is said to eliminate bacteria by shooting the water temperature up to 68°C, which isn't exactly energy-saving.

- Sensors that pick up on how dirty your dishes are and use more or less water/soap/heat accordingly (like Bosch's **EcoSense** system) could potentially cut your energy use by 20%; that is, if your dishes aren't heavily soiled (which they could be if you're not pre-rinsing, see below).
- Once you've picked your dishwasher out and taken it home, make sure you run only full loads and try to avoid pre-rinsing dishes.
- If you have to pre-rinse a bunch of dirty dishes, try setting up a mini basin of warm water so you don't have to leave the tap running.

## IS THE ENERGY STAR LABEL ALL IT'S CRACKED UP TO BE?

All that glitters is never really gold, is it? Energy Star may be the brightest twinkle in the sky when it comes to highlighting energy-efficient products (it's the most popular green label on shelves), but that doesn't mean it couldn't use a little polish. In the fall of 2008, *Consumer Reports* came out with a major dig against the government-led program started in the U.S. but adopted globally, including by Canada, Japan and Australia (see "Energy Star has lost some luster" at **consumerreports.org**). It seems the 17-year-old program has been too lax about what gets the star of approval, which is supposed to alert consumers to products that are anywhere from 10% to 75% more efficient than their competition. Until recently, 92% of all dishwashers qualified for the label. Part of the problem was that lab coats were gauging their energy use by running clean dishes through them. The standards have recently been tightened up, so about 50% of dishwashers should now get the star.

Critics also say Energy Star's judgment criteria are just plain behind the times, or rather, behind the tech. Samsung claimed that one of its 2008 Energy Star–labelled fridges used 540 kWh of energy a year. But in tougher testing that *Consumer Reports* says "better resembles how you use a refrigerator," the fancy ice-dispensing French-door fridge actually used 890 kWh per year. That's 60% more power-sucking than advertised. A similar LG model used a good 50% more. Why the gap? Turns out that Energy Star's outdated standards call for icemakers to be turned off during testing, but with these new models, doing so would actually melt all the ice inside.

Which leads us to the next major question: who's policing this henhouse anyway? Why, that would be the fox, of course. Manufacturers are currently doing their own compliance testing, and there's very little verification from Energy Star going on. Consumers Union, the org behind *Consumer Reports*, says it's time for more random spot checks and independent testing to make sure products are living up to the label. A Euro-style ranking of product energy efficiency from 1 to 5 would be nice. The U.S. Congress has mandated that Energy Star start updating its test standards more frequently, so that should help us at least keep up with the times. U.S. president Barack Obama has also promised to amp up energy-efficiency standards for appliances. Why does that matter to Canadians? Well, even Natural Resources Canada's Office of Energy Efficiency's website admits that most products that qualify in the U.S. automatically get the little blue-and-white star here (**oee.nrcan.gc.ca**).

Bottom line is, don't throw the baby out with the bathwater. Overall, Energy Star is a good program that needs some tweaking. Even if Energy Star appliances save half of the 40 million tons of greenhouse gas emissions they claim to prevent, they're still helping us all breathe a little easier and spend a little less on hydro bills. Oh, and just to give you a little update, in the fall of 2008, LG ended up agreeing to suspend its use of the Energy Star logo on its French-door fridges with icemakers and is offering consumers a free in-home modification of these fridges to make them more efficient.

## WATER FILTERS

Okay, so the water coming out of your tap isn't as crystal clean as you'd hope and you're pining for a water filter. The market is flooded with options on how to purify your agua, but not all are created equal, even within the same type. Look for certification by the Canadian Standards Association (CSA), the Underwriters Laboratories or the National Sanitation Foundation (NSF). NSF-certified filters have to meet particularly stringent standards (in fact, you should look up your product on the NSF site—nsf.org—before you buy). You'll be able to see exactly what each filter is certified to remove. As for how to make your choice, well, it depends on what you're hoping to filter out. If you just want to remove chlorine taste, a simple granulated carbon pitcher will do. If you want to go one notch up, get a solid block carbon filter you attach to your faucet or under your sink (it does a better job of removing lead, chlorine, pesticides and asbestos). If you have bigger worries (like heavy metals or fluoride), you might consider forking out for reverse osmosis in tandem with a carbon filter or a distiller, but both are costly. Distillers are the godfathers of purity when it comes to

## Water Filter Features to Consider

| FILTER TYPE | CARBON | REVERSE OSMOSIS | DISTILLER |
|---|---|---|---|
| USED IN | Pitchers like Brita, faucet-mounted, under-the-sink | Under-the-sink or larger whole-house system | Countertop or whole-house system |
| HOW IT WORKS | Positive charge attracts and traps particles | Pushes water through a fine membrane | Boils water, condenses purified steam; repeats |
| WHAT IT REMOVES | Bad tastes, smells, chlorine, can reduce heavy metals like lead, pesticides, asbestos | Fluoride, minerals, heavy metals, parasites, pollutants like arsenic, but doesn't remove chlorine or chemicals like pesticides | Bacteria, viruses, minerals, fluoride, arsenic, heavy metalslike lead and even VOCs; doesn't remove chlorine |
| DOWNER | Filters not generally recycled | Wastes four to nine gallons of water for every gallon filtered $$$ | Uses a lot of electricity, and boils about five times more water than you end up with; slow process $$$ |
| BONUS | Doesn't need to be plugged in | Softens hard water | Filters out more than any other system |
| TIPS | Pitcher types with loose carbon don't work as well as solid carbon block | Best when combined with carbon block | Don't put these under a counter or in a closet; they need ventilation |

getting rid of the largest number of chemicals, as well as bacteria, viruses, fluoride, heavy metals and VOCs. You'd probably be wise to find out what's lurking in your water before you decide what system you need. Ask your water provider for a copy of its annual water quality report and get your water tested for lead. FYI, most in-home systems won't really do much for major bacteria problems like *E. coli*—you'll have to boil your water if you have serious concerns.

Many quality filter systems combine multiple filter types, but you should expect to pay more for purity. Some go beyond the usual routes

| UV | CERAMIC | IONIZER |
|---|---|---|
| Under-the-sink | Under-the-sink or countertop | Under-the-sink |
| Ultraviolet light kills bacteria, sterilizing water | Traps impurities in small ceramic pores | Claims to alkalanize water by running electric current through it |
| Bacteria, parasites, some viruses | Asbestos fibres, some bacteria and parasites | Doesn't filter contaminants unless teamed with other filters (it's often paired with a carbon filter) |
| Class A types disinfect water; class B's, not so much, more for non-disease–causing bacteria | Not recognized by certification bodies like NSF | Debatable health claims like anti-aging; not much cred in scientific community |
|  | All natural |  |
| Best when combined with carbon block | Best when combined with carbon block | Take this with a grain of salt; still, if you're keen, be sure it's combined with a carbon block |

and try to put beneficial minerals back into the water they filter. For a couple of hundred bucks, you can buy the B.C.-based **Santevia** gravity water system, which has several stages of filtration, including ceramic, activated carbon, silica sand and zeolite granules. In addition, the water is run through mineral stones to add vital minerals back to the otherwise stripped water (santevia.com). For a few hundred more and lots of sex appeal, Montreal-based **Aquaovo**'s slick porcelain, glass and metal egg, a.k.a. OVOPUR, uses a combo of a recyclable activated charcoal filter, microporous bioceramics and quartz crystal to remove impurities from the water (aquaovo.com). Note that smaller companies like Santevia may pay for one level of certification on, say, their carbon filter, but they argue that prohibitive costs keep them from getting additional certification.

### BRITA STARTS RECYCLING FILTERS AGAIN

Open up many a Canadian fridge and you're likely to spot a Brita purifying device. They're not fancy, but they do remove chlorine flavour and a little lead. Their big downside is that once Clorox bought out Brita, it cancelled its filter recycling program. Well, good news. Clorox is bringing back Brita's filter recycling program! Just mail in your used pitcher filters and they'll be recycled into toothbrushes, cups and more (**filterforgood.ca**). FYI, although many worry that the Brita pitcher is made of polycarbonate, it's actually made of styrene acrylonitrile, which is so far free of controversy. If you're still worried, get a faucet-mounted system instead and avoid the whole plastic problem altogether.

## BARBECUES

So they tell us grilling foods at high temperatures gives us cancer. Now show me a steak lover who cares. After all, you can take the charcoal out of the barbecue, but you can't take the barbecue out of the yard — at least, not without pissing off your home's grill man (or woman). By the way, you should really get rid of that charcoal hibachi. Charcoal and wood send soot and smog-inducing carbon monoxide into the air. That applies to both lump charcoal (which is basically unprocessed charred wood) and the pillow-shaped briquettes (made of scrap wood). Though briquettes are worse, because they could contain hidden chems left over from the scrap wood. Then again, lump charcoal chops down trees (especially bad when you're talking tropical woods,

## SAVE ENERGY, ORDER TAKEOUT (JUST JOSHING): 8 FRESH POWER-SAVING COOKING TIPS

**#1** What the bleep, don't preheat (unless you're baking).

**#2** Slow down, you cook too fast: Slow cookers will slow your energy flow, since they're so damn energy efficient.

**#3** Slip sliding away: If a piece of paper can be shoved inside the oven door when it's closed, it's time to redo the seals.

**#4** Put it in neutral: Turn your burner or oven off a few minutes before it's done and coast on free heat.

**#5** Get toasted: Ovens will burn you come bill time. Use a toaster oven for smaller jobs.

**#6** Eat it raw: Try delicious raw food recipes. They're not only ultra-healthy, they use less energy, since you're not cranking the oven and stovetop (although raw foodies have been known to rely on electric food processors to grind up seeds and nuts, etc).

**#7** You have the power: Who needs a fossil-fuel-fired dinner when human power works just as well. Look into manual hand beaters, foodmills and mortar and pestles. Heck, the Amish have even developed cool hand-cranked blenders and food processors (**lehmans.com**).

**#8** Say no to mush: Don't overcook your food.

even if they're certified by the Forest Stewardship Council). If you're looking for a grill-on-the-go, **Lokkii** makes one that runs on recycled charcoal (lokkiicharcoal.com).

**Grill:** Stay away from aluminum grills and go for sturdy, non-leaching **cast iron** or **stainless steel** instead. The **porcelain-coated** kind, which is quite common, is also good and provides a non-stick surface. If you're buying non-stick grill-top or grill-side trays, rib racks, baskets and roasting pans, make sure they're coated with ceramic or porcelain. You wouldn't want any Teflon-coated stuff cooking at high temps.

**Fuel:** The sun's rays are definitely the cleanest fuel around, so you might want to check out solar cookers. They don't give you that flame-roasted effect, and they work only when the sun's up, but they're still pretty damn cool (solarcooking.ca). Electric grills are your second greenest option, but again, no flame. Fire-lovers should go for natural gas, electric or liquid propane (which is extracted from natural gas) over charcoal any day. And here's a kernel of good news: outdoor grilling on your BBQ is more energy-efficient than baking in your hot oven. Now make me a veggie burger, will ya?

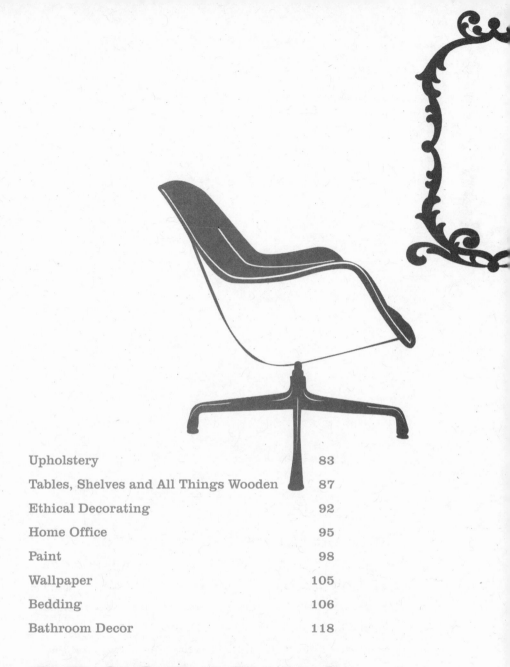

# DECORATING
## Not just a pretty house

## Come on, do you really need to

tear down walls and rip out kitchens to refresh your home?
It's not only wasteful, it's damn pricy (and technically impossible
if you're a renter)! Try working with what you've got first and
just, you know, shift things around a little. This is where green
home decor philosophy comes into play. You know, paint the
wall, instead of gutting it. Get a new tablecloth instead of a
new table. But hey, if you do need a new dining set, sheet set or
wall finish, you want to make sure it's as one with the planet as
possible—while still looking drop-dead fabulous.

# UPHOLSTERY

Whoever invented the overstuffed couch is a genius. Melting into a comfy sofa at the end of a long day is one of the best rewards a home can offer. Why, oh why, did they have to go and spoil things by filling our furniture with polyurethane foam that's manufactured with carcinogenic toxins (like toluene diisocyanates), off-gasses air-polluting chemicals (like volatile organic compounds) and sheds harmful flame retardant (like PBDE—see Flame Retardants, page 85) dust into your home?

Here are a few things to keep an eye out for when browsing for a new place to park your derriere. Warning: truly eco-friendly furniture can cost you from 30% to 40% more than the mass-produced kind, partly because the materials themselves are inherently more expensive and partly because they're often handcrafted and sweatshop-free (so they actually pay humans a living wage—imagine that!).

Soy-Stuffed: A couple of companies make PBDE-free furniture foam that mixes conventional polyurethane with 20% soy (**Preserve** is made with American soy and **BioPlush** is Canadian-made). Depending on your perspective, you might applaud it as a solid move away from conventional petroleum-based stuffing; others say it's only a half-assed step. Maybe it's both, but it's certainly better than the status quo and more affordable than going totally organic, so it's a popular choice with greener designers. **Natural Lee** stuffs its sectionals, pull-outs, chaises and ottomans with Preserve, plus the throw pillows are made with 100% recycled bottles, the coils are 80% recycled, the wood frames are certified by the Forest Stewardship Council (FSC), and they offer organic fabric choices (check naturallee.com for retail vendors in Alberta, B.C., Nova Scotia, Ontario and Quebec). The furniture chain The Brick also uses Preserve stuffing in its **ECO** line of upholstered couches and chairs (thebrick.com). Winnipeg-made **Pulse Furniture** offers soy stuffing, as well as recycled fabrics and FSC-certified wood options for an extra fee (pulsefurnituredesign.com). **Whitewash & Co.** is an Ontario-based source for sofas, upholstered accent chairs and ottomans padded with soy foam on FSC maple frames (shop.whitewashco.ca).

**Latex-Stuffed:** Back in the day, couches were stuffed with natural latex, and green furniture makers are now turning to the tree-tapped substance once again to fill their sofas. **Upholstery Arts** in Vancouver is one such furniture maker. It uses natural latex, wrapped in fire-resistant wool padding, as well as FSC- and Rainforest Alliance–certified wood, recyclable and biodegradable textiles and non-toxic glues and sealants (upholsteryarts.ca). The sassiest latex-stuffed designer is definitely **Pure** by **Ami McKay** (purebyamimckay.com). DeBoer's **everGreen** line is also latex-filled and is encased in wool, organic cotton, hemp, flax, linen, silk, bamboo or recycled textiles. Montreal's **Zia & Tia** (ziaandtia.com) use water-based glues, natural latex foam, hemp, and wool batting, as well as FSC-certified and reclaimed wood to make their custom organic sofas, chaises, daybeds, ottomans and upholstered bed frames. Toronto indy **608 Design** makes funky modular couches with built-in storage using either natural latex or more affordable soy foam, FSC-certified wood frames and coverings of recycled polyester, wool and other options (sixoeight.com). A few green home stores also carry eco upholstered furniture (see Resources: Green Home Storefronts).

**Buying Used:** Given the pocket-straining costs of getting a healthy, happy, sweatshop-free organic couch, going the second-hand route is definitely less intimidating. Yes, second-hand always seems like the greenest (and cheapest) way to go, but you have to be cautious with stuffed furniture. If that couch was made anywhere between the late '80s and, say, 2006, I'd veto the idea of having all those crumbling cushions in my house. It'll only kick up toxic PBDE dust into your household (I've got enough crumbly Goodwill cushion dust in me to last a lifetime). If you're buying a vintage 1960s couch, it was probably stuffed with latex. If you're considering getting it reupholstered, find out what kind of foam they're planning to use first. If you can't track down an all-organic upholstery shop near you (like **reCraft Custom Sustainable Furniture** in Etobicoke, Ontario: recraftfurniture.com), try to find one open to experimenting with vintage or other earth-friendly materials (see sidebar, opposite).

## GREEN FABRICS FOR DIY AND CUSTOM PROJECTS

Planning on making your own curtains or reupholstering an old chair? Keep in mind that conventional cotton sucks up 25% of the world's chemical insecticides, and the stuff you buy from fabric stores or suppliers could be treated with dodgy finishes like formaldehyde or Teflon-based stain-proofers. Stay away from tainted bolts and look for truly natural, planet-friendly options. You can order all kinds of gorgeous green fabrics, from boldly patterned organic cotton and hemp herringbone to wild silk (produced by moths that weren't boiled alive in their cocoons, as with conventional silk). Scan these sites for ideas: **modgreenpod.com**, **rubiegreen.com**, **greensage.com**, **nearseanaturals.com**, **aurorasilk.com**. You can also find eco fabrics at some green home stores like **thezeropoint.ca** (see Resources: Green Home Storefronts). Snoop around on **eBay.ca** and you might just score yourself some ultra-eco vintage fabrics.

**Flame Retardants:** For decades now, manufacturers have been adding chemicals to furnishings to keep them from bursting into flames when an idiotic smoker ashes on them. Sounds logical, but many of those chems are incredibly toxic—especially a whole family of flame retardants called PBDE (polybrominated fire retardant) that have been in common use since the late '80s. They stick to your fatty tissues and mess with thyroid and liver functions; even low levels have been shown to affect fertility. Not good, considering they're everywhere: in furniture foam (couches and pillows), fabrics (upholstery, drapes) and plastic casings (think electronics, wiring). They've also been found in wildlife, breast milk, umbilical cords . . . you name it. Yes, a lot of that comes from factory emissions, but the stuff also breaks down into contaminated dust that's been found to coat every surface in our homes. One U.S. Environmental Protection Agency researcher, Matthew Lorber, published a report fingering household dust and household products for 80% of our PBDE exposure.

## CAN I MAKE MY OLD COUCH STAIN-RESISTANT?

Remember when we'd grab a can of Scotchgard and mist every piece of furniture in our homes like we were in one of those crazy Febreze commercials? In 2002, after 50 years in commercial use, Scotchgard phased out the nastiest, most persistent chemical in its formula, the one that lodges itself in our fatty tissue and stays there indefinitely: PFOS. But that doesn't mean I'd recommend going nuts with its reformulated products. Manufacturer 3M says its new recipe has a "low risk" of building up in the food chain, but there's a big difference between "low" and "no." And you should know that lots of other brands use PFOS's sister chem, PFOA. That's the one used in Teflon. You know, the likely carcinogen that's in 95% of our bloodstreams. It'll be largely phased out by 2010, but it's still on shelves. So what's a life-loving, earth-hugging citizen to do about all that furniture that's bound to see some spaghetti splotches or wine drops?

- Don't buy a white couch. I nearly did a few years ago, then flashbacks to all the times I'd spilled food and booze in my life made me ixnay the idea.
- Jump on stains as soon as they occur. If the old salt and soda water options fail, try blotting a mix of laundry detergent and cold water on there (unless it's an oil-based stain; then use hot water) using a damp but not dripping-wet cloth or sponge, or lightly scrub with a brush. Or keep a bucket of seaweed-based **Pink Solution** on hand (you can order some at **pinksolution.ca**). It gets everything out and can be used in a rented steam cleaner for heavy-duty jobs.
- As for pretreating, there is no readily available all-natural stain repellent on the market for furniture fabric. You could theoretically wash your slipcovers in **Nikwax Cotton Proof**, a non-toxic, water-based, fluorocarbon-free water repellent used on outdoor gear and clothing. This stuff does, however, contain mineral oil, which is petrol-based (**nikwax.com**).

- Try sticking to your mom's rule of not eating on the couch, but stop short of your grandma's strategy of covering furniture with plastic.

The whole PBDE family is considered toxic by Environment Canada. Trouble is, Canada only phased out two of the three PBDEs of concern (back in 2006). The feds have done diddly squat about decaBDE—which means this bioaccummulative flame retardant could still be in textiles, mattresses and furniture. Enviro orgs are freaking out, wishing Canada had the nerve to take on a deca ban like a growing number of U.S. states. Although we should definitely thank our lucky stars we don't live in California, where the world's toughest flame-retardant laws mean furniture sold in that state has some of the highest concentrations of flame-resistant chemicals in the world. According to a 2008 report by Friends of the Earth, which tested 350 pieces of California furniture, 52% of all furniture tested in domestic residences contained high levels of toxic flame retardants. Yowsers.

There's no way to sugarcoat this stuff, but there are measures you can take to minimize your exposure.

- Dust often! Sounds trite, but it's important. But don't pull out chemical cleaners. Just dust with a damp cloth, and vacuum regularly.
- Ditch crumbling couch cushions. Especially if you have an old beater with foam peeking out.
- Shop for furniture that's PBDE-free. If you can't afford eco-furnishings made of latex or organic materials, IKEA opted to phase out brominated flame retardants and antimony compounds in 1998 and totally phased them out by 2002, so all textiles, mattresses and upholstered furniture sold by IKEA are in the clear.
- Look for furniture that's treated with natural flame retardants such as borax (a.k.a. sodium borate/boric acid, which has been used on furniture for two centuries) or made with naturally flame-retardant materials such as wool or latex.

## TABLES, SHELVES AND ALL THINGS WOODEN

If a tree falls in Indonesia to get you a dining room set, does anybody care? Sure, wood is natural and "renewable," but axing down the world's dwindling old-growth forests and replacing them with mono-culture plantations is hardly sustainable. Stay away from tropical woods entirely, including woods like teak, nyatoh, ipê (a.k.a. Brazilian walnut,) jatoba (a.k.a. Brazilian cherry) and African or South American mahogany. Even so-called plantation-grown teak isn't often wise. Only Central and South American plantation teak from land cleared in the past for, say, cattle ranching, gets the green light. Indonesian plantation teak, on the other hand, is often 200-year-old, rich, second-growth forest that really shouldn't face the axe. And an astounding amount of logging in places like Indonesia and Brazil

**Stay away from tropical woods entirely, including woods like teak, nyatoh, ipê (a.k.a. Brazilian walnut,) jatoba (a.k.a. Brazilian cherry) and African or South American mahogany**

happens illegally. Even if the wood is labelled as coming from one country, it could be coming from another. According to Rainforest Relief, one study found that much of the wood being exported from Vietnam was actually swiped from Cambodia, and Indonesian-labelled wood is being pinched from highly deforested Burma. Greenpeace International and Greenpeace China put out a report in 2006 warning that a startling amount of illegally logged Indonesian, Burmese and Papua New Guinean wood is laundered in China.

Even woods from developed countries aren't always well protected. Cypress trees are in trouble in the southern United States. Jarrah is being axed from old-growth forests in Australia. Western red cedar is being knocked down in old-growth Canadian and American forests. Yellow cedar, western hemlock and Alaskan cedar should also be avoided.

Here's a breakdown of your greener choices. (Whichever option you choose, ask about low- and no-VOC finishes and stains.)

**Salvaged:** Salvaged, a.k.a. reclaimed, or antique wood is your number one choice. Getting solid wood furniture second-hand from antique markets, garage sales or Craigslist-type sites is ideal, but there are also plenty of amazing furniture designers working with gorgeous old timber salvaged from construction sites, dilapidated barns and more. Check out leveldesign.ca and ethosmillwork.com on the west coast; heritageartisanfurniture.ca in Alberta; cityandnorth.com, foreverinteriors.blogspot.com and kimberleyjackson.com in Ontario; and villagewoodworks.com in Quebec. And what about you east-coasters? Chad Everett does beautiful stuff with wood that has washed up into the Bay of Fundy, as well as old windows and barn wood (personal.nbnet.nb.ca/chadever). You'll also find great pieces at renovators-resource.com. Check green home stores nearest you for reclaimed furnishings too (see Resources: Green Home Storefronts).

**FSC-Certified:** Homegrown Canadian FSC-certified wood is your second-best choice (tropical wood with FSC certification can still

---

**THE FAKERS: PARTICLEBOARD/MDF/PLYWOOD**

You'd assume that if you're going to make a plank of wood out of little bits of wood, you'd be using leftovers of the mill industry and saving a few trees, but nope. Very little of it comes from recycled sources. Sure, it's cheap, but what the hell is holding all those wood chips together? Why, that would be carcinogenic and allergy-inflaming urea formaldehyde, which can off-gas from your furniture as a lung-irritating VOC for years. Although the industry has reduced emissions by 80% over the last couple of decades, VOCs such as formaldehyde are still out there causing headaches, allergic reactions and nausea in unsuspecting home dwellers. Phenol formaldehyde isn't considered as bad.

Now, veneers need not be a bad thing, as long as they come from FSC-certified North American sources and the MDF behind them is formaldehyde-free and made from non-virgin wood sources (still easier to find south of the border, from online sources like abundantearth.com). Note that the FSC label on these kinds of products doesn't guarantee that 100% of the wood is FSC-certified. If it's labelled "FSC Mixed Source," only 70% of the wood is FSC-certified. Best to double-check with the company for details.

FSC has long been one of the most trusted acronyms in the world of forestry. In fact, this not-for-profit was the first and remains the only logging certification program supported not only by industry but also by big-name environmental organizations around the world like WWF and Greenpeace. However, in the last few years, its reputation has taken a bit of a beating. There were already rumblings that the FSC label was too lax (it was letting paper makers use the mixed-source label even if only 50% of their pulp came from FSC forests). Tension really started to mount when it came out that wood from one of the largest Asian forestry companies (responsible for devastating a Delaware-size tract of rain forest on the island of Sumatra) was going to be sold under the FSC mixed-source label (not as the FSC-approved 50%, but the other half). After the *Wall Street Journal* covered the controversy in 2007, the FSC recanted the company's approval. Since then, FSC rules have been tightened (as of 2009, anything with the mixed-source label has to be 70% FSC-certified). But critics still remain. In early 2008, for instance, the Swedish Society for Nature Conservation pulled its support for the forestry org, saying FSC "functions badly in Sweden" and that there's not enough monitoring going on.

Nonetheless, after a review of forestry labelling programs in late 2008, WWF came out publicly stating "FSC is still the best," maintaining that the program "still drives significant improvements in forest management on the ground." And, in all honesty, all the other labelling systems for wood are considered way weaker. Bottom line is, we shouldn't turn our back on FSC products. FSC is the best we've got. An FSC-labelled coffee table is generally made with far more responsibly managed wood than one that isn't. We just need to keep pressuring our green labels for better monitoring and tougher rules. In the meantime, support FSC wood you can keep an eye on, namely the stuff that's sourced right here in Canada.

come from old-growth forests, according to Rainforest Relief, though it says a limited number of FSC-certified plantation-grown imports, like eucalyptus, get the green thumbs up). FSC is certainly not without its critics (see sidebar, page 90), but it's really the best certification system we have for wood furniture. Furniture makers working with Canadian-made sources include wiggersfurniture.com, franksmith.ca and durantefurniture.com. Even Crate and Barrel carries a bedroom set made with FSC-certified wood, using Vermont-harvested maple, birch veneer and engineered wood (crateandbarrel.ca). About 7% of IKEA's wood products are FSC-certified, but, irritatingly, the company does not say so on labels (Rainforest Relief does, however, say that IKEA has pretty responsible forestry practices overall). Note: If you spot the industry-run Sustainable Forestry Initiative (SFI) label, keep in mind that it doesn't get much respect from environmental organizations.

**Bamboo and Rubber:** Furniture made of super-fast-growing bamboo shoots is sprouting up absolutely everywhere. You didn't kill a tree to get it, but were natural forests cleared to plant it? Hard to say. (For a full discussion on the dark side of bamboo, see page 201 under Flooring.) I'd steer clear of most conventional bamboo furnishings unless they have sturdy credentials. Luckily, the FSC has started certifying

## SECOND-HAND STEALS: ONLINE ANTIQUE HUNTING

Shopping for pre-loved furniture? Avoid the sticker shock of investing in new eco-furniture and prowl sites like **Craigslist (craigslist.org)**, **Kijiji (kijiji.ca)** and **Freecycle (freecycle.org)** for second-hand furnishings at amazing prices. Some of it is pretty junky, but you'll find some serious steals—both retro and modern—if you keep your eyes peeled.

bamboo plywood, so hopefully you'll start seeing more bamboo furniture with this logo. You also want to make sure the stuff is free of formaldehyde. Montreal-stationed **Greene Bamboo** is one very reputable (and stylish) source of bamboo furnishings. Its bamboo is sustainably harvested from its own groves in Thailand, then finished in Canada with zero-VOC, zero-formaldehyde coatings and adhesives. It's backed by Quebec-grown FSC-certified plywood.

One imported wood that scores well comes from **unproductive rubber trees**. Once rubber trees no longer produce latex sap, they face the chop. Might as well make a bedroom set with them, as the national furniture chain **The Brick** does.

## ETHICAL DECORATING

Truth: you usually pick stuff out for your home because it looks pretty/sleek/cool or whatever adjective you're going for (that, and it's got an attractive price tag). I don't blame you. But guess what, honey, the same ethical quagmire that applies to the world of cheap clothes shopping applies to the design realm. So put the vase down and read up on some ways to bring a little soul back into your housewares shopping.

100-Mile Decorating: You might be trying to eat more local produce in season, but let's face it, the stuff we buy to deck out our kitchens, bedrooms and bathrooms tends to be about as local as a hunk of pineapple in Yellowknife. Finding a couch made completely of materials grown near you is near impossible (you try finding native latex and cotton sprouting on Canuck soil—even most of the hemp fabric out there comes from eastern Europe or China), but you can make choices that bring your house's style closer to home, literally. Ask for furnishings and decor items made in Canada or, better yet, in your home province or town. No, they won't be as cheap as that oh so inexpensive stuff imported from China or India, but they should be more affordable than those European designs that get fawned over in design circles.

Though, of course, just because it's made in Canada doesn't mean it's made with sustainable material. The greenest pieces are both local

## FLORAL DERANGEMENT: CENTREPIECES GONE WRONG

Nothing brightens up a room like a bouquet of fresh-cut flowers. But is a rose really just a rose when the world's 100 million blooms suck up more neurotoxic and carcinogenic pesticides than any other crop? Enough toxins, in fact, to curse up to two-thirds of flower workers in countries like Ecuador with headaches, nausea, blurred vision, rashes and dizziness, as well as distressing rates of birth defects and miscarriages. Definitely not worth the 58 cents a day they get paid to pick 'em. Or the $20 or $50 you paid for them.

Okay, so organic and fair-trade flowers aren't a dime a dozen. You won't find them at every corner shop and they'll cost you more when you do, but they're definitely worth it. Depending on where you live, you can just jump online or get on the horn, order a gorgeous organic and fairly grown bouquet and have it delivered straight to your mom's door. If you live in Nova Scotia, New Brunswick, Ontario or especially Quebec, you'll probably find it easiest to track down flowers certified by **Sierra Eco (sierraeco.com)**. Farms that carry the Sierra Eco label not only offer fair wages, they fund housing, education, daycare and medical care for their workers. And while they may not be totally organic, they use way less pesticides, relying instead on sustainable, integrated pest management techniques.

If you've got your heart set on organic *and* ethical petals, Montrealers should try **Karisma (floristkarisma.com)**. Torontonians can call **Ecoflora (ecoflora.ca)** or **Hatcher Florist (hatcherflorist.com)**. Some, like **My Luscious Backyard (mylusciousbackyard.ca)** and **EcolStems (ecostems.ca)**, even grow their own blossoms. Vancouver and the entire lower mainland are serviced by **Amoda Flowers (amodaflowers.com)**, which provides sustainable floral decor (including organic, local, fair-trade buds, as well as flowers certified by **VeriFlora**, the European equivalent of Sierra Eco). By the way, Whole Foods sells some organic, fair-trade and local blooms—but it also sells a lot of conventionally grown plants (with set limits on pesticide residues). Best to ask. Can't find an eco-florist near you? Voice your interest in fair-trade/organic blooms and ask for local flowers in season.

*and* made with earth-conscious components. And the greenest of the green designers form their furnishings with recycled or reclaimed objects. That means candle holders made from old wine barrels (grassrootsstore.com), a lounge chair made with the conveyor belts from a felt machine (brothersdressler.com) or a coffee table made of driftwood (wildwooddesigns.ca). For more Canadian-made designs, ask around at storefronts like Vancouver's **m-smart design** (m-smartdesign.com), Toronto's **Made** (madedesign.ca) and **Koma** (komadesigns.com) or **Galerie CO** in Montreal's Mile End (galerie-co.com).

**Fair-Trade Decorating:** The complete opposite of 100-mile decorating in many ways, fair-trade shops are rammed with items that come from all corners of the globe, just like most of the household items you buy in conventional stores. The big difference here is that the workers were actually paid fairly to make wonderfully unique tablecloths, vases, teapots, sculpture, chairs, you name it. Certified fair-trade goods tend to be made by independent worker cooperatives with an emphasis on fair working conditions, gender equity and respect for the environment. Bringing fair-trade projects to a group of artisans with weaving or pottery skills, for instance, creates amazing economic opportunities for those who might otherwise be peddling their wares for pennies. And more and more fair traders are folding green materials into their product lines. One of the easiest places to access feel-good furnishings and housewares is at one of the dozens of **Ten Thousand Villages** storefronts across Canada. They sell all sorts of ethical and eco-conscious items, including recycled glassware, vegetable-dyed tablecloths, coconut shell salad servers, salvaged wood bowls and furniture, and a slew of super-cool decor items made with recycled phone books and magazines (tenthousandvillages.ca).

Bringing fair-trade projects to a group of artisans with weaving or pottery skills **creates amazing economic opportunities** for those who might otherwise be peddling their wares for pennies

# HOME OFFICE

Yes, working from home means you get to avoid the morning commute and bad office coffee. But we home workers face different struggles, like cats walking across our keyboards and kids screaming during a phone-in with the boss. With all those distractions, you might as well make your home office set-up as green as possible.

- If you're in the market for a new desk, keep your eye out for ones made of rich reclaimed wood or gorgeous antiques (like those at johnsonsantiques.com). Or look for more modern options made with recycled content and FSC-certified wood by companies such as **Krug** (krug.ca) and **Wiggers Custom Furniture** (wiggersfurniture.com).

- Scan second-hand office supply stores near you (check the Yellow Pages for listings) for solid wood desks (not that cheap off-gassing MDF stuff). You'll find great vintage discoveries at bargain-basement prices through online sites like Craigslist.

- Make sure your office supplies aren't overworking the planet. Get your hands on 100% recycled, chlorine-free paper, planners, folders and calendars. And don't stop there: look for pens, desktop organizers, mouse pads and filing systems made with recycled plastic. Or just get a complete Office Starter Kit from B.C.'s own green office supply shop, **Frogfile Office Essentials** (frogfile.com).

- Stock your office with Energy Star equipment (e.g., computer, cordless phone, scanners, printers). If every home office product purchased in North America this year were Energy Star–qualified, we'd save $200 million in annual energy costs and prevent greenhouse gas pollution equivalent to taking 250,000 cars off the road!

**Office Chairs:** It's amazing what people working from home put up with when it comes to seating arrangements. A friend of mine was a teleworking marketing exec in England, and the poor girl used her coffee table as a desk, with the drafty wooden

## THE IKEA FACTOR

Let's get real here—when you were dreaming of a greener home, you weren't picturing a house full of IKEA furniture. It can be hard to imagine how a company with a catalogue rammed with 12,000 incredibly affordable products manufactured largely in developing countries can be mentioned in a book like *Ecoholic Home*. But way back in 1992, IKEA (the world's largest furniture manufacturer) came out with a forward-thinking environmental action plan that kick-started a long list of eco-measures like ousting the grand villain of plastics, PVC, heavily restricting the use of formaldehyde, phasing out controversial brominated flame retardants long before our government did, and using wood from responsibly managed forests. More recently, IKEA has been redesigning its furniture to reduce trucking needs (so, say, twice the number of Klippan couches can fit on one truck, cutting transport emissions in half), as well as funding research into affordable renewable energy technology (think solar panels for the masses), water and energy-saving devices and eco-friendly materials, in the hopes of getting new offerings to the market in three or four years. It already has a solar-powered desk lamp in stores, which is pretty cool (see page 161). IKEA's even working with the WWF (World Wildlife Fund) to have its cotton growers in India and Pakistan retrained to use less water and fewer pesticides.

Not that IKEA gets a free pass. It's still using conventional, pesticide-laden cotton, petroleum-based plastics and plenty of synthetics. Its stores are still crammed with goods shipped in from halfway around the world, and anyone who's bought a cheapy IKEA shelf or desk knows IKEA products aren't always that durable (quite the opposite, in fact). They're also not without labour concerns. A 2006 report commissioned by Oxfam found that while IKEA supply factories in Vietnam had decent conditions, several Bangladesh supply factories had major problems with excessive overtime and abusive management, both clearly against IKEA's code of conduct. IKEA has since terminated relations with the worst offenders and reps say it has worked to improve compliance with its 10 existing suppliers in the region (IKEA says fulfillment of the IKEA code of conduct in Bangladesh has risen from 45% in 2006 to 80%

in 2008). IKEA's own reports admit it's "not at journey's end, even if huge efforts are being made to meet [labour and environmental] goals."

If you ask organizations like International Save the Children Alliance, Rainforest Alliance or WWF for their thoughts on IKEA, they'll agree IKEA isn't problem-free but it's certainly more open to improvement on these issues than most other imported furniture stores with zero human rights or green issues on the agenda. And since it's safe to say that most Canadians simply can't afford to buy a $3,000 organic couch or reclaimed wood cabinets, at least you can get a couch free of persistent flame retardants and cabinets ultra-low in formaldehyde from these guys. And that's a start.

floor acting as her bench. As for me, the first *Ecoholic* book was written from a crappy office chair I purchased in university for, oh, $100. It was probably loaded with off-gassing PVC and toxic flame retardants. Plus, it had bolts poking through the seating and it left my bones in agony. This time around, I was going to get it right. Ergonomically advanced, ecologically superior, ultra-durable — the works. I gotta say, I'm a much happier writer now (or, at least, I curse a lot less).

Here are some of my top picks on where to park your working butt hour after hour. All are GREENGUARD Indoor Air Quality Certified, and though they'll cost you a mint at full retail price, you can look for used chairs on sites like eBay or Craigslist or from second-hand office stores. FYI: all these chairs note their recyclability, which is cool, but in all honesty, where are you going to recycle them? They win more points for durability (you're more likely to be using it for decades or reselling it on Craigslist for a good price than blue-boxing it). **Think chair by Steelcase:** An eco office standby that is 99% recyclable and made with up to 41% recycled content. **Teknion Contessa** is the first and only office furniture manufacturer to have all major products and manufacturing facilities in Canada certified to Environment Canada's **EcoLogo**

**Program**. And they're 85% recyclable. **Herman Miller Aeron** is an ergonomic classic but a little firm for my taste. It's made of 62% recycled materials and is 94% recyclable. **Haworth Zody** was the first task chair certified as Cradle to Cradle gold and the first one endorsed by the American Physical Therapy Association. It contains up to 50% recycled content, and the energy that goes into making this chair is offset with wind energy certificates. My personal fave, comfort-wise, is the **Human-scale Liberty**. This form-sensing mesh technology is great for anyone who likes lots of lower lumbar support, plus it's 54% recycled and 95% recyclable, so your conscience can feel as good as your back.

Note: Sit before you buy. Every back is different and craves different support.

## PAINT

Humans have been freshening up their homesteads with a splash of paint for, oh, 35,000 years now. Debbie Travis's *Painted House* is proof enough that our techniques have evolved from the old cave-painting days. Too bad it took us so long to realize that slapping lead on our walls was a bad idea or that adding mercury—yes, neurotoxic mercury—to latex paint as a mould inhibitor was just plain dumb. We finally got rid of both entirely by the early '90s, but that doesn't mean today's paints are free of hazards.

**Low VOC and No VOC:** Low-VOC paints are all the rage, but most of us have no clue what VOCs actually are. Volatile organic compounds help make paints spreadable and dry the way we like them to, but these chemicals can continue to off-gas from your walls for weeks or months. Not good, considering the VOCs in paint include known carcinogens and neurotoxins like benzene, formaldehyde, kerosene, ammonia and toluene. No wonder laying down a coat of paint can make the air quality in your home 1,000 times worse than that of outdoor air. As you can imagine from the smell, oil paints are much worse than water-based latex paints when it comes to air-polluting,

## THE NEW DESIGN PARADIGM: CRADLE TO CRADLE

You know that whole Industrial Revolution–style way we just take, take, take from nature then express our thanks with a heaping mass of garbage? Well, instead of designing cradle-to-grave products primed for the dump, William McDonough and Michael Braungart are hoping to power the Next Industrial Revolution in a more nature-friendly way. Through their groundbreaking 2002 book, *Cradle to Cradle: Remaking the Way We Make Things*, as well as their design firm **MBDC (McDonough Braungart Design Chemistry)**, they're transforming industry by creating products for cradle-to-cradle cycles, where materials are "perpetually circulated in closed loops." Under their system, all materials, including the fabric of that chair you're parked on, would either cleanly return to the earth as organic nutrients or be harm-free "technical nutrients" that can be recycled in perpetuity or "upcycled." Meaning those manufactured goods would have to be endlessly reusable, not the one- or two-use wonders of today's plastics. And they've put their vision into practice with nearly 200 products (including office chairs by Herman Miller, Steelcase and others, wall coverings by Milliken and carpet tiles by Shaw) that they've fostered through their Cradle to Cradle certification system. The end products aren't necessarily perfect (no item has received platinum certification, for instance, and not all have upcycling infrastructure in place), but McDonough and Braungart are trying to keep the trajectory moving ahead to a brighter, greener future (**mbdc.com**).

headache-inducing VOCs. Still, acrylic-based latex paints contain up to 10% VOCs. It's no wonder, then, that the trendiest paints hitting stores these days are the low-VOC kind.

Canada's just developing its own standards in 2009, and it looks like low-VOC flat paint will be capped at 100 grams of VOCs per litre, with high-gloss paint capped at 250. The Green Seal logo from the U.S. and Canada's own EcoLogo are a lot stricter. Green Seal– and EcoLogo–certified paints have to have less than 50 grams of VOCs per litre for flat paints and less than 150 grams per litre for non-flat paints with colourants added. Plus, they have to be free of "carcinogens, mutagens, reproductive toxins, hazardous air pollutants or ozone-depleting compounds."

Many certified paints go beyond low-VOC into no-VOC territory. **YOLO Colorhouse** (yolocolorhouse.com), **Sico's Design** line

## WALL OF SHAME: LEAD PAINT

Pop quiz time. Do you **a)** plan to reno a home built between 1960 and 1980? **b)** live in a home built before 1960 with preschool-age children crawling around? or **c)** plan on sanding down exterior paint on a home built before 1992?

**a)** If you answered yes to this one, then you might want to get your paint tested. Get a lead-testing kit from your local hardware store or online (**leadinspector.com**) before you start sanding and grinding things down—or demolishing entire walls. Paint companies started phasing out lead in the '60s (back when paint was up to 50% lead!), but small amounts were still used through the '70s. You wouldn't want to kick up lead dust now, would you? If your lead test comes back positive, you'll need to take extra safety precautions. Call in a lead remediator.

**b)** If you've got young kids putting random objects in their mouths, then you need to move into high gear. Especially since pediatricians say your kids are at higher risk of lead poisoning from paint dust and flakes than from lead in toys. You have a few options here: if the surface is in good condition and not peeling, just paint over it; if the surface is cracked and peeling, cover it with drywall or vinyl-free wallpaper. Also, replace all the old base-boards, doors and window frames, then vacuum very well. If you're worried about your family's lead levels, ask your doctor for a blood test.

**c)** If you answered yes to this one and plan on sanding down exterior items such as window panes, you'll want to be extra careful, since lead could have been used in exterior paint until, oh, 1992. Wear protective masks and goggles, and wash shoe soles and clothing when you're done.

(sico.ca), **Olympic's Flat Enamel** line (olympic.com) and **General Paint's Z-Coat** (generalpaint.com) are all good zero-VOC, Green Seal–certified paints. **AFM Safecoat** also makes great zero-VOC wall paint. For green retail paint stores in Canada, consult Resources: Green Home Storefronts at the back of the book. Many of the regular green home storefronts listed there also carry eco paint.

No- and low-VOC acrylic paints have generally been limited to dull, muted shades in eggshell and flat finishes. Truth is, big bright colours in high gloss still generally require more VOC-releasing petrochemicals, but few paint companies will come right out and tell you this. So to this day most of your greener acrylic options will start with a low- or no-VOC base then add whatever hue your heart desires, which in turn spikes your VOC content. **Benjamin Moore**, though, says it's developed a **Color Lock** waterborne colourant system in its **Aura** and new zero-VOC **Natura** lines that doesn't add VOCs to its paints and is so effective it often gets the job done in one, max two, coats, saving you paint and money.

Keep in mind, throughout all this paint shopping, that VOC-free doesn't mean it's all natural, chemical-free or necessarily non-toxic. It just means it's free of a particular family of air-polluting chemicals, namely VOCs. Your paintbrush might still be dipping into some pretty harsh fungicides and biocides. Best to ask.

FYI, low-odour oil paints aren't greener, they just don't smell as bad. And low-VOC oil paints don't have to meet the same VOC standards as latex.

Natural Paint: Want to really paint your walls green? (Well, not literally, though sage is a lovely colour.) **BioShield** paints, stains, thinners and waxes are made from mostly naturally derived raw materials like tree resins, citrus peel extracts, essential oils, mineral fillers, beeswax and natural pigments (bioshieldpaint.com). **Green Planet Paints** offers plant-based paints with mineral colours (greenplanetpaints.com; available through green Canadian home stores listed at sipdistribution.ca under "where to buy").

If you love the southwestern look of plaster walls, you can't get much greener than **American Clay**'s products. It uses clays, recycled and reclaimed aggregates, and rich natural pigments, all from the southern U.S. (americanclay.com; available through green stores listed at sipdistribution.ca). **BioShield** also makes clay paint, using different types of clay to achieve different hues. A little closer to home, **silicate mineral paint**, manufactured by New Brunswick–based Eco-House, is ideal for concrete, stucco, brick, stone and new drywall, though it doesn't work quite as well on repainted surfaces (eco-house.com). This 19th-century German invention uses a liquid mineral (potassium silicate) as the binder and is guaranteed to never peel or blister, plus it's naturally antibacterial and solvent-free. It comes in 10 rich, earthen colours that can be diluted, creating 50 shades to pick from. There are interior and exterior versions, as well as semi-transparent stains.

Your most benign choice has got to be **milk paint**. This ancient decorative finish has been around since Cleopatra was bathing in milk herself. It's more commonly used to get that antique finish on wood furniture, but this milk powder, lime protein and mineral mix can also be applied on drywall, plaster and stucco. Parents are turning to milk paint as a worry-free nursery wall finish, and people with chemical sensitivities trust it in their homes. Just steer clear of fakers who sneak in plastics or formaldehyde. Trusted sources include **Homestead House Paint Company** (homesteadhouse.ca) and **Old-Fashioned Milk Paint Company** (milkpaint.com) or inquire at any green home store. Wanna try making your own? Check out realmilkpaint.com/recipe.html and add colour with saffron threads, turmeric or clay-based hues.

To source natural paint products, see Resources: Green Home Storefronts.

**Sealants, Waxes and Paint Strippers:** Looking for non-toxic, environmentally preferred sealants, adhesives, caulking compounds and paints? **AFM Safecoat** is the go-to company. Plus, it makes a natural line of oils, waxes and thinners (afmsafecoat.com). B.C.'s **Broda Coatings** makes great low- and no-VOC wood finishes that stand up to rainy and snowy west coast conditions. **CBR Products**, the same company that distributes Broda, also sells greener graffiti removal, paint strippers, concrete coatings and more (cbrproducts.com). New Brunswick's **Eco-House** makes a wonderful beeswax wood finish, tree-resin wood and cork finish, carnauba floor wax and more (eco-house.com). **Osmo** is another greener source for wood stains and finishes, though it has to travel from Germany (raincoastalternatives.com).

Peeling paint off furniture or walls can bring some seriously hazardous chemicals, like methylene chloride, into your home, unless you smarten up. There are methylene chloride–free paint removers at cbrproducts.com, like **ABR Citrus Gel Paint Remover,** which should strip layers of latex, oil, stains and varnishes. **Soy Gel** strips urethanes and all paints, including lead-based paint (franmar.com or greenbuildingsupply.com). Though remember, you don't want to be stripping lead paint without advice from a pro.

**Cleanup:** Even though your municipality says you can wash your latex paintbrushes in the sink, that doesn't mean you should get cocky and pour a half-empty quart down there. And don't be a jerk and pour paint down a storm drain. If you do, the next time it rains and those storm sewers overflow into local water bodies, those toxic chems from your last paint job will be killing fish.

- Wipe off your brushes with a newspaper. If you're putting a job on pause for a day or two, just wrap your brushes and paint tray in a plastic bag.
- Oil paint should never be rinsed into your sink (just good old common sense, really). Once your brushes have been wiped in newspaper, soak your brushes in some eco-friendly paint thinner (**Bioshield Citrus Thinner** and **AFM Safecoat Naturals Diluent/Reducer** are two good alternatives; bioshieldpaint.com, afmsafecoat.com or from green building supply stores—see Resources: Green Home Storefronts) and wipe them with a rag.

To soften them up for the next paint job, just soak them in some diluted shampoo, rinse and dry.

• Used paint thinner shouldn't be trashed! If you let the paint settle to the bottom and pour the clear liquid off the top into a labelled jar, you can reuse a large portion of that thinner. Just take the leftover sludge to a local household hazardous-waste depot.

Disposal: Nearly 40% of Canadian households have old paint cans kicking around gathering dust, and we have no clue what to do with them. So what *should* you do with those rusty, half-full cans? Why, you call your municipality and ask them the same question. It might recycle paint cans and even the paint itself. In fact, paint stewardship programs have sprouted up in many provinces, including Quebec's **Paint Recovery Program** (eco-peinture.ca), Saskatchewan's **Post-Consumer Paint Stewardship Program** (saskwastereduction.ca), Nova Scotia's **Paint Recycling Program** (rrfb.com) and, most recently, Ontario's **Do What You Can** initiative (dowhatyoucan.ca) and Alberta's **Too Good To Waste** program (albertarecycling.ca). The programs are largely

---

### WHAT GOES AROUND COMES AROUND: BOOMERANG PAINT

What goes around really should come around. If you're a true believer in 3Rs. Quebec-based **Boomerang Recycled Paint** manages to reduce the amount of new paint Canadians use, reuse old paint and recycle metallic paint cans, all in all processing 5 million kilograms of paint a year from all over Quebec, Ontario, the Maritimes and B.C. into sixteen lovely new colours of latex, four shades of oil paints and six hues of wood stains, for only, like, $12 a gallon. Bonus: Boomerang paints are even low-VOC! Really, you can't get paint any greener or cheaper, unless you smear blades of grass clippings on your walls (**boomerang-paint.com**).

funded through fees paid on new paint, though old paint cans are dropped off for recycling or swapping at no charge. Even if your town or province isn't doing the right thing and recycling old paint into new paint, your local hazardous-waste depot should be happy to take your old paint cans for recycling. (See Resources: Household Hazardous Waste Disposal Guide.)

## WALLPAPER

Were you as shocked as I was when wallpaper made a design come-back a few years ago? All of a sudden, bold prints and crazy patterns weren't just a thing of the '70s. At interior design shows and in maga-zines, wallpaper was once again chic, new, reborn. Problem is, it's still largely made with PVC/vinyl. You know, that nasty plastic you don't want to get rolled up in. Especially since it's softened with hormone-disrupting phthalates now banned from kids' toys on both sides of the border. Not only can those phthalates keep off-gassing from your walls, they can erode and become part of your household dust over time. Then there are the smoggy VOCs (including significant quantities of formaldehyde) given off by wallpaper glues (even low-VOC kinds can contain eye- and lung-irritating chemicals such as methyl formate). Meanwhile, we slap cuddly vinyl wallpaper stickers up in kids' rooms without even thinking about it. Plus, if you tack them onto bathroom walls, you're just laying out a mould trap.

Eco Options: Why smother your walls when you can go wild with funky green options made of recycled paper, bamboo, cloth, sisal, gorgeous dried grasses (a.k.a. grasscloth)—even cork—in all kinds of beautiful and interesting designs? Just ask around at local high-end paint stores or inquire with interior designers. Warning: this won't be cheap. Vancouver's **m-smart design** has a collection of vinyl-free, flame retardant–free, hand-screened wallpapers by special order (m-smartdesign.com). Toronto's **Schoolyard** crafts small batches of charming fibre-based wallpapers to order (schoolyardstudio.com). **Green Design Studio** carries recycled leather wall tiles, as well as bamboo ones (greendesignstudio.ca). **The Zero Point** carries **Mod Green Pod**'s super bold vinyl-free cellulose wallpaper (thezeropoint.ca). U.S.-based **Phillip Jeffries** makes a massive range of sophisticated hemp, raffia, cork, grasscloth, rattan, woven bamboo and much more (phillipjeffries.com). For bold designs that would make any hipster (with cash) go weak in the knees, check out **Woodson & Rummerfield**'s recycled-paper wallpaper dyed with vegetable inks, as well as its printed grasscloth (wandrdesign.com).

## BEDDING

The moment you touch your head to the pillow, the most you want to be counting is sheep, not formaldehyde and pesticide levels. Alas, in the harsh light of day, that's the reality you have to consider whenever you're buying a fresh set. Do I recommend pulling the ol' tablecloth trick and ripping the bedding out from under your family, mid-sleep? Let's not be rash; the cotton's already been picked and the formaldehyde's long dissipated. But next time you're in the market for new bedding, it's best to put an end to your synthetic affair.

Pillows: What's that you're drooling on every night? Probably a toss-up between petroleum-based polyester fillers and fluffy feathers/down plucked from geese/chicken/ducks either before or after their death. Feathers, might I add, that were sterilized with formaldehyde, bleached and sprayed with chemical anti-allergens. IKEA makes a point of not using down and feathers from living birds; instead, its pillows and comforters are made with by-products from the poultry biz. It also steers clear of formaldehyde. But there are greener options for you to bury your face into. You'll find several types of natural pillows at eco bedding stores like Nelson's willownaturalhome.com or Calgary's myorganicbedding.com, as well as at green home stores like organiclifestyle.ca (see Resources: Green Home Storefronts for more stores).

• Like a heavier, firmer pillow? One hundred percent **organic cotton fill pillows** are ideal for you.

- Looking for something fluffier and more breathable? **Organic wool fill** is great for those who get night sweats and anyone with allergies (it's naturally resistant to dust mites and mildew). **Alpaca wool** is naturally lanolin- and oil-free (hankettes.com and naturalbeautycanada.com carry organic alpaca bedding). Creative accent pillows (and hand-knitted throws) made of organic wool and ramie blends are available from looolo.ca.

- Sears is selling 100% organically grown, Canadian-made hypo-allergenic wool fill pillows by **Natura** from $59.99 (about $30 cheaper than most places). But your most affordable options are all-wool pillows for $52 from **Shepherd's Dream** (woolbed.ca) or Kapok pillows from **Dream Designs** (dreamdesigns.ca) at around $45 each.

- **Natural rubber** (either fluffy or firm) is another excellent option for those with asthma or non-latex allergies, since it's naturally dust-resistant and hypoallergenic. But if you've got a latex allergy, stay away. **Green Sleep** carries some that come in an organic velour casing (greensleep.ca). You can now also score all-natural latex memory foam pillows from **Essentia** (myessentia.com).

- Ergo-heads that like it hard love **buckwheat husk** pillows, since they form to your head. Still, they're far from cushiony and I can't say the one I got helped relieve the pinched nerve in my neck. **Many Moons Alternatives** has a huge selection of options if you want to give it a shot (manymoonsalternatives.com).

- If you're looking for the feel of down without the animal cruelty and allergens, you might want to check out pillows stuffed with **kapok pod fibres**. The seeds on this majestic tropical tree produce silky threads and are hand-harvested without the tree itself being axed. **Dream Designs** (dreamdesigns.ca) sells Canadian-made, fair-trade kapok pillows. **Loop** (looporganic.com) makes kapok-filled accent pillows with a hemp casing.

- Putting disposable plastic bottles to rest with pillows stuffed with **old water bottles** seems like a great idea, especially

Latex pillows and mattresses are starting to pop up in more and more stores as Canadians begin to shy away from the idea of synthetics. The thing is, not all latex comes from the sap of rubber trees. In fact, a good chunk of latex products are fakes (made of petroleum-based rubber and plastics) and many are blends. You might see pillows and beds marketed as Talalay or denser Dunlop latex. Neither is a type of latex; rather, they are ways of processing the latex. The product could be all synthetic, a blend of synthetic and natural latex (like Natura's Aloe Dream Mate Pillow) or, in rarer cases, all natural (like Natura's Organic Dream Mate). Natura is one manufacturer that's fairly open about the fact that it offers different grades of purity throughout its bedding line, from green lite to all organic, to cater to varying budgets. You'll never know unless you press for details, so call the manufacturer and ask.

when they're encased in 100% unbleached organic cotton (bedbathandbeyond.ca). The only reservation I have is that water bottle plastic leaches the heavy metal antimony. Might not be an issue (hell, fleece jackets made with old pop bottles are a good thing), but I'm not totally convinced I'd want to plant my face in it every night. Bed Bath & Beyond also carries pillows with certified organic cotton dust-mite-proof exteriors, but they're oddly stuffed with conventional polyester.

- **Hemp** enthusiasts will want to bed down with rawganique.com's 100% hemp pillows to complete their hemp bedding sets. It's one of the few sources for pure hemp in this category.

**Duvets and Comforters:** Wouldn't it be great if we could spend all winter nestled under giant duvets? And I don't just mean when we go to bed. I'm talking duvet housecoats, duvets for offices — the works. We'd definitely save on heating bills. In the meantime, you might want to avoid down for the same reasons listed under Pillows.

- The most popular eco combo for beds is toasty and breathable **wool in an organic cotton casing**. **Euphoria**'s organic wool comforters or duvets, available from allergybuyersclub.com, are handmade in Canada with organic cotton outer shells and lightweight certified organic lamb's wool on the inside. **Hankettes** (hankettes.com) and **Natural Beauty** (naturalbeautycanada.com) offer some made of **alpaca wool**.
- Vegans might prefer comforters stuffed entirely with **organic cotton** or **hemp** (see rawganique.com), or even naturally antibacterial bamboo (dreamdesigns.ca). True vegans will definitely want to steer clear of silk-filled duvets (most silk is made by boiling silk moth cocoons before the moths have emerged).

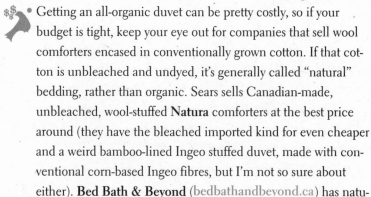

- Getting an all-organic duvet can be pretty costly, so if your budget is tight, keep your eye out for companies that sell wool comforters encased in conventionally grown cotton. If that cotton is unbleached and undyed, it's generally called "natural" bedding, rather than organic. Sears sells Canadian-made, unbleached, wool-stuffed **Natura** comforters at the best price around (they have the bleached imported kind for even cheaper and a weird bamboo-lined Ingeo stuffed duvet, made with conventional corn-based Ingeo fibres, but I'm not so sure about either). **Bed Bath & Beyond** (bedbathandbeyond.ca) has natural wool duvets made with low-impact dyes at a good price (they also sell **Eco Luxe** conventional down-filled duvets with

## PURE GROW WOOL

Keep an eye out for wool labelled "Pure Grow." It comes from farmers in Sonoma County, California, who follow sustainable, humane sheep-ranching practices. Manitoba's all-wool bedding store **Shepherd's Dream** uses Pure Grow Wool (**woolbed.ca**).

unbleached organic cotton casings). **IKEA's Mysa Ljung** duvets have a silky **lyocell** casing (lyocell's made with FSC-certified eucalyptus) stuffed with 50% modal (a European beech wood fibre) and 50% polyester.

Sheets: Slip between silky sheets with a moan-worthy thread count and you might as well have died and laid down in heaven. Too bad great swaths of the world's ecosystem had to suffer thanks to water- and pesticide-heavy genetically modified cotton sucking up 25% of the world's chemical insecticides. Then there are the 1 million children working Egyptian cotton fields, 11 hours a day, 7 days a week, in 38°C heat, all to get you luxury Egyptian cotton sheets. And you know that lovely sheen that comes with new sheets? Well, that's carcinogenic formaldehyde, baby, and even if you wash your sheets before bedding down on them, about 40% of that formaldehyde will still linger. Dodgy chemicals and human rights not something you want to get twisted up in each night? I don't blame you.

**One million children work in Egyptian cotton fields, 11 hours a day, 7 days a week, in 38°C heat, all to get you luxury Egyptian cotton sheets**

- One hundred percent **organic cotton bed linens**, free of bleaches and dyes, are a conscientious classic. **Coyuchi**'s bedding gets its hues in part from naturally coloured cotton strains from Latin America (coyuchi.com). Loop makes lovely autumn- and thistle-hued sweatshop-free organic bedding with low impact dyes (looporganic.com). Montreal-based online shop **Zia & Tia** (ziaandtia.com) has a whole collection of fair-trade, organic, naturally dyed pillow cases, duvets and even matching curtain panels.
- You can't get any softer than **bamboo linens**. It can, of course, take a lot of chemical processing to turn bamboo shoots into creamy sheets, so make sure they're processed ecologically by asking about Oeko-Tex certification (Oeko-Tex Standard 100 basically screens for harmful chemicals like formaldehyde on

the finished fabric, while Oeko-Tex Standard 1000 involves auditing and certifying that a product is manufactured from start to finish in environmentally conscious facilities free of child labour). Stay away from suspiciously cheap bamboo sheet sets without green certification. (See Resources: Decoding Eco Labels for more.)

- **Organic hemp sheets** (said to be surprisingly soft) and **organic flax linen** aren't as common, but you can score some from rawganique.com for a pretty penny. **Dream Designs** has sheets that blend hemp and ramie, a member of the nettle family (dreamdesigns.ca).

- You can now buy organic bedsheets at really low prices through mainstream stores like Home Outfitters, Sears and Bed Bath & Beyond (BB&B actually uses natural vegetable dyes for the Simply Organic sets, which can't necessarily be said for the others). Bed Bath & Beyond also sells ridiculously silky sheets made of **modal** (which is a great pesticide-free, totally chlorine-free, Oeko Tex–certified fibre made of European beech wood pulp) or lyocell, a.k.a. Tencel (a fibre made from mostly FSC-certified eucalyptus pulp by the same people who make modal), for only $110 for a queen set. If you score eco-sheet sets for under $100, just make sure they're not blended with conventional cotton or polyester. And remember, there's no guarantee, at these prices, that they're sweatshop-free.

**Mattresses:** Mattress shopping is a funny activity. It's the only time you walk into a store and lie down, trying to simulate a night's rest in five minutes of tossing and turning. But while salespeople hover, trying to convince you that the pricier mattress will keep your back from aching, they never talk about the VOCs off-gassing from your polyurethane foam. Luckily, the most bioaccumulative flame retardants have been phased out (see Flame Retardants on page 85 for more on PBDEs), but troublesome fire retardants (including harmful chlorinated tris) might still be used.

## FUHGETABOUTIT: MEMORY FOAM

Wow, a mattress that forms to your body! The prospect used to seem so totally space-aged, especially since every mattress pusher talks up how memory foam was invented for the aches and pains of astronauts (truth is, NASA never did use them in space). And how could it be toxic if all the Swedes of the world seemed to be sleeping on Tempur-Pedics (at least, that's what marketers tried to imply)? While dealers might tell you this stuff is special thanks to a visco-elastic foam, we now know that it's plain old petroleum-based polyurethane with mysterious density-boosting chemicals added to the mix. And all that polyurethane means that smoggy lung- and skin-irritating volatile organic compounds (including the neurotoxin toluene) are off-gassing as the mattress hugs your body. Supposedly, the VOCs dissipate over time, and North American–made brands also insist they're free of the super-persistent family of flame retardants, PBDEs, that can accompany cheap imports. Some brands like SleepLevel tell you their particular breed of memory foam (in their case, something called Biogreen) is VOC-free, but they remain suspiciously hush-hush about what exactly it's made of. Come on, you're spending a third of your life sleeping on the thing; you want to know what you're lying on.

And don't be duped by memory foam mattresses that tell you they're made of soy. Dig a little deeper and you'll see that they're maybe 5% to 20% soy-based and the rest is the usual polyurethane fill! That's basically the story for the so-called natural Aerus memory foam mattress available at Wal-Mart and other stores. Sure, it comes with a nice bamboo cover, but its maker, Foamex, won't tell you how much of the fill is actually from "renewable sources." It does, however, claim to have "the most environmentally friendly process for the manufacture of polyurethane foams worldwide," exceeding Clean Air requirements.

Keetsa sells memory foam mattresses made with BioFoam that replaces 20% of the usual petroleum oil with castor bean oil. And the "calming" green tea component of that foam? That's just added as a deodorizer. Talk about greenwash! It also comes with "natural antibacterial protection" made with nano silver particles. Considering how, in the spring of 2008, a coalition of consumer, health and environmental groups petitioned the U.S. EPA to block the sale of products containing nano silver, I'd reconsider (for more on nano silver, see The Dark Side of Nano Silver sidebar on page 39). Still, they do use recycled steel coils and natural wool padding, and offer organic cotton as a cover option.

Canadian-made Foamite has better numbers: its Koosh Hybrid beds are made with soy foam that's purportedly 60% soy (and the company's hoping its Koosh foam will be fossil-fuel-free within two years). But don't get those confused with many of Foamite's mattresses that are plain old regular memory foam. Foamite does offer all-natural latex beds, but they're not memory-foam-type products.

There is one Canadian memory foam bed that's totally natural. Hand-made in Montreal, **Essentia** beds are made of natural latex whipped into a froth, then set in a mould. There are no VOCs and no toxic glues, and they deliver for free anywhere in North America (**myessentia.com**).

Be leery of stain-resistant finishes. Ask questions to find out exactly what chemicals were used to make it so. There are even some mattresses embedded with highly unregulated and experimental stain-repelling nanotechnology. If your mattress was treated with Scotchgard or Stainmaster before 2002, back when 3M was still using dangerously persistent PFOS, I'd consider upgrading to a newer model. Today's stain repellents are often based on Teflon (or PTFE), and due to persistent chemicals created in the manufacturing process, manufacturers have till 2015 to phase that out too. In the meantime, you might as well stay away. Think about the box spring too: less expensive frames made of plywood or particleboard are generally bound together with carcinogenic urea formaldehyde, which continues to off-gas while you sleep.

I gotta be honest with you, though, eco-friendly mattresses are a huge investment. They just can't compete, price-wise, with cheap petroleum-based stuffing found in conventional mattresses.

But they cream the competition when it comes to helping you sleep with a clear conscience, plus they're super-comfy and they're also guaranteed for up to 25 years (see if the big boys can match all that). Here's a breakdown of options that should leave you dreaming in green.

- **Inner spring-based mattresses with organic cotton and wool batting** are a solid pick. Especially when paired with sustainable wood slats, which **Obasan** does (obasan.ca). Wool, by the way, is naturally fire-retardant, so you don't need weird chems to pass fire safety tests. Plus, wool is a great humidity regulator, which should help minimize night sweats. Most natural mattresses will have wool batting below the surface.

- For an all-wool mattress, visit Manitoba's **Shepherd's Dream** (woolbed.ca).

- Break the mould and try a **natural rubber bed**. Latex is naturally fire-safe and impervious to mould and mites. It's a nice, springy, supportive base for organic cotton and wool toppers, and you can choose the level of firmness you prefer. Obasan beds are crafted with 100% organic cotton and/or organic wool blends and natural rubber. You can pick between a traditional box-spring base or a wood slat base made of sustainably harvested Quebec timber. European-made **Green Sleep** beds come with organic velour casing, natural rubber from its own tree farms and wooden dowel-based frames free of synthetic glues, dyes or finishing sprays. They're available at dozens of retail stores across Canada (listed at greensleep.ca). **Soma** (somasleep.ca) carries a broad selection of alternative mattresses, though not all are eco.

- Wanna sleep like Swedish royalty? Bed down on **horse hair**. **Hästens Naturally** beds are literally stuffed with genuine horse-hair, as well as a cotton wool blend, on a traditional spring frame. They even make adjustable versions (great for the eld-erly). These guys actually supply beds to King Carl XVI Gustaf of Sweden. As you'd expect, these don't come cheap, but if

If your mattress is too grungy to donate to charity, ask your municipality about mattress recycling in your area. The springs can get melted down and born into new springs, the stuffing can go into furniture padding, the wood can get mulched for use on gardens. Way better than sending it to landfill, where hundreds of thousands of these babies end up every year, hogging more space than any other curbside item. Some municipalities, like Moose Jaw and Toronto, are recycling mattresses as we speak (Toronto's are collected with regular garbage pick-up and few residents are aware they're actually being recycled). Montreal's **MattCanada** actually does the dirty work for Toronto and has drop-off centres in Calgary and Montreal, plus they're hoping to bring mattress recycling to Vancouver and Halifax soon. Call MattCanada for details on your area (**mattcanada.com/english.html**).

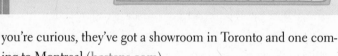

you're curious, they've got a showroom in Toronto and one coming to Montreal (hastens.com).

- For green memory foam, see the sidebar on page 112.
 • Green penny pinchers take note: IKEA has a new green mattress, the **Sultan Heidal** bed. It's made with latex that's 85% natural, organic cotton, a wool topper and some corn-based fabric (for only $999 for a queen). It does, however, contain old-school springs, which many greenies like to avoid, preferring to go all natural with solid latex cores. All IKEA beds have been free of brominated fire retardant since at least 2002 (they use salt-based fire retardants instead), and IKEA has pretty decent forestry policies.
- **Sealy** says it stays away from chemical flame retardants and uses new fibre-based flame-retardant barriers instead. And though its

mattresses are still polyurethane foam–based, they're free of Teflon-based stain-resistant treatments. Sealy also makes an all-natural latex spring-free mattress, but it's almost impossible to find now that Sears stopped carrying it. You're more likely to come across Sealy's SpringFree latex-core mattress made with synthetic latex.

**Cribs:** There's nothing cuter than a babe sleeping snugly in a crib. The question is, what's the crib made of? Composite woods are bound together with carcinogenic urea formaldehyde, which off-gasses smog- and asthma-inducing VOCs long after we assemble the furniture. Same goes for all the other pressed-wood furniture we buy. In fact, a 2008 report by Environment California found that 12 of 21 composite cribs and changing tables (including products from Child Craft,

StorkCraft, Delta Enterprises, Jardine and Quebec's South Shore Industries) emitted formaldehyde at levels known to encourage allergies and respiratory problems in kids. Even a solid oak crib with one composite-wood drawer was enough to spoil air quality in a nursery. In fact, in the fall of 2008,

California's attorney general sued the companies cited in the report for failing to warn consumers about the emissions.

Get **solid wood** that you can finish yourself with natural hemp oil, a beeswax polish or some sort of VOC-free wood finish. Look for low-emission furniture. **Nurseryworks** uses low-VOC finishes and formaldehyde-free glues, and all their baby furniture is air chamber–tested to confirm low emissions (nurseryworks.net). At the big-brand level, IKEA makes brominated fire retardant–free cribs, cabinets, changing tables and high chairs from farmed trees, rather than pillaging from natural forests. And all of IKEA's pressed woods are ultra-low in formaldehyde. FSC-certified kids' furniture is a little tougher to come by in Canada, but Montreal's Zia & Tia carries whimsically handpainted VOC-free FSC-certified cribs and kids' furniture by Lilipad (ziaandtia.com). Or head online to specialty shops like **Argington Modern Children's Furniture,** which uses only FSC-certified woods and non-toxic finishes for their adjustable cribs, high chairs, changing tables and beds (argington.com).

Crib Mattresses: First off, you might want to read up on big people's mattresses (starting on page 111) to inform yourself about your natural mini-sized options. If you're ready to buy, green home stores like willownaturalhome.com or organiclifestyle.ca often carry crib mattresses (see Resources: Green Home Storefronts) as do eco-conscious baby stores like **Baby on the Hip** (babyonthehip.ca) in Toronto, **Mom Knows Best** (momknowsbest.ca) in Calgary and Vancouver's **Little Treehouse** (littletreehouse.ca). **Obasan** has a good selection of ultra-pure spring-based and latex options for wee ones (obasan.ca). **Natura** makes mattresses with breathable natural latex innards instead of springs, in both organic and non-organic versions, depending on your budget (naturaworld.com). All of the above stores should also carry organic cotton sheets, crib skirts, bumper pads and organic cotton/wool comforters.

Pass on vinyl mattress covers. Vinyl off-gasses potentially hormone-disrupting phthalates, now banned in American baby toys and mattresses (as of February 2009) and found in babies' urine. If you can't find a vinyl-free crib cover, just buy clear plastic polypropylene sheeting used for house painting and wrap that like a flat sheet around the mattress. Better yet, buy a wool puddle pad for under $50 from a green baby store.

## BATHROOM DECOR

Unless you're doing major gut 'n' purge renos, there's really only one way to give life to a new bathroom on a budget, and that's with the accents. But why should colour be the only criterion by which we judge our towels? You're wiping your privates and your face with this stuff, people! Whatever you do, get rid of those weird puffy cushioned toilet seats. They're made soft and squishy with hormone-disrupting plasticizers.

Towels: Yes, organic towels are gorgeous (and oh so soft), but, honestly, don't run out and buy new ones if you don't need them. If yours are wearing thin, though, you want to make sure you avoid the conventional pesticide-heavy kind tied to child labour abuses in Egypt. Luckily, green towels are popping up almost everywhere these days, and at better and better prices.

- Your top pick, sustainability-wise, would be **100% certified organic cotton fair-trade towels**, like those made by **Coyuchi** (see coyuchi.com for store listings).
- Keep an eye out for **low-impact dyes** or, even better, **colour-grown cotton** (cotton that grows naturally in subtle earth tones). **Native Organic Cotton** makes some (nativeorganic.com).
- **Bamboo** is ultra-soft but much more chemical-intensive to manufacture than cotton. You can find cheaper bamboo/conventional cotton blends in more mainstream stores, but **Organic Lifestyle** (organiclifestyle.ca) carries some made in Japan with low-impact dyes, certified by Oeko-Tex (see Bamboo, page 201). **Shoo-foo** bamboo towels are made in Canada and are Oeko-Tex-certified, and Shoo-foo is working on getting Forest Stewardship Council certification (shoo-foo.com).

- Ridiculously silky luxury Italian **Legna** towels are made of sustainably harvested beechwood trees (they're also from the Lyocell family of products, which are mostly made from FSC-certified wood pulp cellulose processed with non-toxic dissolving agents—sort of like rayon, but greener). Manufacturers recycle 99.6% of the bleach-free solvent in a closed loop system, but the fibre is blended with conventional cotton.

- You'll find the cheapest 100% organic cotton towels at Sears and Bed Bath & Beyond. But if they're not fair trade, there's no guarantee they're sweatshop-free.

**Shower Curtains:** Those plastic curtains do a lot more than keep your bathroom from getting wet. A 2008 report by the Centre for Health, Environment and Justice found some serious chemicals off-gassing from vinyl shower curtains. One of the curtains they tested released as many as 108 VOCs into the air (including the neurotoxin toluene), some of which persisted in the air for nearly a month. Best to stay away from the vinyl kind and be wary of conventional fabric curtains; they could be treated with dodgy chemical fungicides and water repellents. Instead, go for one of these:

- **Hemp** is a great naturally fungus-resistant choice. But that doesn't mean you won't find things growing on your shower curtain if you don't wash it once a month. Expect to pay $90 or so. **Dream Designs** (dreamdesigns.ca) carries Canadian-made ones in four hues.
- It'll cost you more upfront, but a **glass shower door** or sliding enclosure will last you decades and works best at keeping water off your floor.

- You can find the safer chlorine- and phthalate-free sister of vinyl, PEVA (polyethylene vinyl acetate), at **IKEA** and south of the border at **Target**. Bed Bath & Beyond has some cheap shower curtains made with recycled fabrics, but they need a liner.

**Bath Mats:** What do you stand on when you get out of the shower dripping wet? Hope you didn't get one of those antibacterial bath mats. And fingers crossed you didn't invest in one of those trendy teak bath mats taken from an old-growth tropical rain forest (see page 88 for more on tropical wood) or a PVC mat embedded with pebbles. Instead, wipe your feet on organic cotton bath mats from organiclifestyle.ca or rawganique.com. Keep your eyes peeled for cushy bath mats made of sustainable cork. One Swiss designer came up with an awesome "moss matt" literally made from living moss fed by humidity in your bathroom. If only you could buy one at your local garden centre or green store, I'd be the first to line up for one.

Also keep in mind that those anti-slip mats and decals people add to the bottom of their tubs are often made with PVC, which causes the same problems as vinyl shower curtains. Instead, look for some made of natural rubber or polypropylene.

**Toilet Paper:** I know having toilet paper that's as thick as a face towel is all the rage, but come on, people: we're clear-cutting the boreal forest just to wipe our backsides. While any and all brands without recycled content get vetoed by Greenpeace, the org has spent extra-special time targeting Kimberly-Clark (maker of Kleenex, Scott and Cottonelle). In 2008, Greenpeace came out with a new report charging, "Since Kimberly-Clark started logging the [Kenogami forest] in 1937, 71% of the forest has been fragmented. Woodland caribou have been driven out of 67% of the forest, and wolverines have completely disappeared from within its boundaries." Between 2001 and

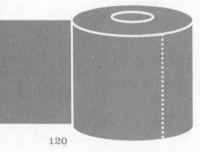

2006 alone, an area more than twice the size of Dallas was "fragmented" for the sake of disposable tissue products.

Of course, Kimberly-Clark stood by its earth-loving ways. But funnily enough, in its 2007 sustainability report, it confided, "We believe there is no environmental preference between using recycled or virgin fibre in the manufacture of our products."

## KLEENEX SAYS "EXCUSE ME"

The nose-blowing market is saturated with products that claim to keep your schnozz happy, but 99 times out of 100 that means zero recycled content. Well, hold on to your tissue because in mid-2009, after a 5-year Greenpeace campaign, Kimberly-Clark (maker of Kleenex) told the world it's boosting its recycled content and will be free of endangered forest by 2011. Until then, blow on 100% recycled brands or reach for washable hankies (**hankettes.com** has organic ones).

Um, okay. To appease customers, however, Kimberly-Clark came out with Scott Naturals paper towels and Kleenex Naturals facial tissues, which contained some recycled content. But that didn't wipe their record clean (see sidebar for update).

If everyone stopped wiping their asses with virgin pulp from the boreal forest, we could make arboreal history. In fact, if every household in Canada switched the roughly 100 rolls of TP they buy a year over to the recycled kind, we'd save 4,800,000 trees! Here are a few more tips:

- Look for 100% recycled toilet paper labelled "totally chlorine-free" or "processed chlorine-free" (to avoid the carcinogenic dioxin pollution created by the bleaching process).
- Don't use any. Some very serious back-to-earthers (can't say I'm one of them) have said no to disposable TP culture and are using cloth instead. While that's great for the forests, they'll lose points for washing the cloths in energy-intensive hot water. More points lost if they use bleach. Better that the curious try this for, ahem, "No. 1" only.
- No matter what you've heard about bidets saving trees, stay away from electronic bidet seats! These monstrosities attach to your

toilet and use energy to warm the seat, warm the water that sprays you and warm the fan air that dries you. The Brondell brand claims its bidet seat costs only pennies a day in electricity, but any toilet you have to plug in is too much for me. And don't tell me an antimicrobial "finish" should be part of anything branded an EcoSeat, as Brondell's is.

# BREATHING
## Waiting to inhale

## Think you're safe when you

close your front door, walk into your home and don't find a burglar? Well, your lungs ain't. Anyone with chemical sensitivities knows how harmful our houses can be, but this isn't just a health issue, kids—the planet's also choking. What's behind all this bad air? Well, besides basics like cigarette smoke, dust and mould, there are plenty of serious air crimes being committed by air fresheners, candles, incense sticks and pretty much every aerosol in your home. The good news is there are a few tools at your disposal to help regulate indoor air (from purifiers to houseplants), but the only way to truly remove pollutants from your home is simple: stop using them.

## VOCs

You might have heard me kvetch about them in paint or in carpets, but VOCs (or volatile organic compounds) are a whole-home problem. They're basically chemicals that contain some carbon and may not only give you headaches, make you dizzy and irritate your lungs to varying degrees, but also help form ground-level ozone, a.k.a. smog. Oh, but how much harm can your hairspraying and deck refinishing do? Well, the Ohio Environmental Protection Agency just reported that source emissions of VOCs (including lawn mowers, beauty care products and paints) are responsible for nearly a third of all ground-level ozone woes! It's forcing companies to reformulate their products so they contain fewer VOCs, to conform with voluntary federal EPA standards. Still, the new standards allow air fresheners to be up to 40% VOCs; hairspray 55%; nail polish remover a whopping 75%.

Other home sources of VOCs? Here's a little list to give you a taste (try and say them all in one breath): glues, cooking sprays, windshield washer fluids, carpet cleaners, fabric refreshers, aerosol degreasers, aerosol deodorants, insect repellents, shaving gels, tile cleaners, wood cleaners, waterproofing footwear sprays and more. VOCs can also off-gas from new carpets and pressed wood furniture. No doubt some are minor offenders, like hair gel or metal polish. And some types of VOCs are more potent than others. Nonetheless, thanks to these compounds, the air in your home is on an average day two to five times worse than outdoor air, VOC-wise. That can rise to 100 times worse fairly regularly, and up to 1,000 times worse if you've been stripping paint or sealing floors. The rate of emission may decrease over time as the VOCs off-gas, but formaldehyde, for instance, has been found to off-gas from old desks years after they were purchased. And while you might think you're hurting no one but yourself, 5,900 people die from smog pollutants in Canadian cities every year.

The air in your home is on an average day **two to five times worse than outdoor air**

How do you shift your home from VOC villain to VOC-free haven?

- Ask for ultra-low- and no-VOC options whenever you go looking for paints, sealants, glues, cabinets and pressed wood furniture and engineered floors.
- Avoid cabinets, furniture and any pressed wood bound with urea formaldehyde (a heavy off-gassing VOC).
- Always choose the non-aerosol option if you're buying antiperspirants, air fresheners, cleaners, degreasers, etc.
- Get rid of partially full containers of old, unneeded chemicals. Why? Turns out gases can leak even from closed containers! The U.S. EPA says, "This single step could help lower concentrations of organic chemicals in your home." Just be sure you dispose of them safely (see Resources: Household Hazardous Waste Disposal Guide).
- Air out curtains and other permanent press fabrics for several days before you bring them into enclosed spaces (they're often treated with formaldehyde).
- If you are bringing VOCs into your house, you can help your indoor air quality by opening the windows.

## AIR FRESHENERS

Have you noticed how the word "fresh" is in nearly every commercial these days? I don't care what they say, spraying an old gym bag with chemicals does nothing to remove the stink. Yet no one admits to pushing "odour maskers." No, no, they're odour *eliminators*. Magical, really. Truth is, there's an epidemic of air "freshening" going on, so much so that sales have doubled since 2003. It's a nearly $2-billion industry in the U.S. alone, and a whopping 75% of households use the stuff. They might smell like gentle summer rain, but those fancy plug-ins, weird gels and fan-propelled perfumes are filled with carcinogenic formaldehyde, benzene and other chems linked to asthma and developmental problems in young 'uns. And really, any consumer product with the word "fragrance" in the ingredient list almost always contain phthalates, that freaky family of hormone-disrupting plasticizers.

The Natural Resources Defense Council tested a dozen air fresheners in 2007 to see how many phthalates they contain. Most of the heavy hitters aren't common in Canada (I'd never seen the industrial deodorizer Ozium before a pest controller tried to pawn it off on me after a skunk sprayed my bedroom window one summer). But you'll recognize some of the brands found to have "moderate" levels of several phthalates: Air Wick Scented Oil, Oust Air Sanitizer, Glade PlugIns Scented Oil, Febreze Noticeables and Glade Air Infusions. Even a spray marketed as "100% natural," Citrus Magic, had trace levels of a particular phthalate associated with low sperm count and infertility. At least SC Johnson, the maker of Glade, recently announced that its air fresheners will be free of phthalates by 2012.

Air fresheners are also to blame for high levels of smoggy VOCs in the home. In fact, the U.S. EPA found that plug-in air fresheners containing pinene and d-Limonene can combine with ozone in the air to create harmful smog. No joke. Mixing ozone with air-freshening chemicals actually creates nasty formaldehyde-related compounds like those found in a freshly painted room! What can a few VOCs really do? A large Bristol University study following the health and development of 14,000 children since before they were born found that babies living in homes where air fresheners (including sticks, sprays and aerosols) were used daily suffered diarrhea 30% more frequently than those whose homes were spritzed once a week or less. The bambinos also had way more earaches. Moms suffered, too. Mothers in freshener-obsessed homes averaged nearly 10% more frequent headaches and had a 25% higher risk of depression. Do air fresheners cause depression? Might be a bit of a leap, but air fresheners are definitely worth making a stink about.

Natural Air Fresheners: So how do you usher odours away with genuinely natural scents?

- Unplug those plug-ins pronto and dab a few drops of real essential oils (the stuff from the health store, not the fake kind from places like The Body Shop) in a clay diffuser instead.
- Make your own spray by filling an empty spray bottle with warm

water, ¼ cup (50 mL) of baking soda and a few drops of either natural vanilla extract, lavender essential oil or any essential oil. Just shake and spritz.

- Stash an old nylon full of odour- and moisture-absorbing zeolite (a volcanic mineral) near your kitty litter or in a gym bag.
- If you'd still prefer the pre-made kind, **Nature Clean** and **Citra-Solv** both make lovely natural air fresheners (though the Nature Clean scent doesn't hang around very long compared to Citra-Solv's Air Scense). Quebec's **Attitude Natural Air Purifier** is an odour-trapper made with activated carbon that seems to be wrangling mildew smells in my basement guest room.
- Sprinkle old-fashioned baking powder on carpets and couches and vacuum (stay away from the scented Arm & Hammer versions).
- Open the windows!

## CANDLES

Light up one or two of these and all of sudden you've got romance, intrigue or just a really cozy dinner party. But while you're taking in all that atmosphere, you're also inhaling a lungful of benzene, toluene, formaldehyde and soot that goes up in smoke when you melt petroleum-based waxes. Sort of like what happens when you burn petroleum in your car. No wonder the EPA found that burning one candle with multiple wicks or burning nine candles in a single room led to pollution levels higher than the legal limit for outdoor air. And all those deliciously scented candles on the market? They give off way more lung-penetrating soot that can also create dark oily deposits, a.k.a.

### PASS ON PALM OIL CANDLES

Clearing forests for palm-oil plantations is a major cause of deforestation in Asia and Central America, so it's generally best to steer clear of palm wax candles. Although, Botani does make certified organic, fair-trade palm wax candles with certified organic essential oils and veggie dyes (**alohabay.com**).

ghosting, on your walls, blinds and belongings. Don't buy the aroma-therapy BS. If it's actually made with natural essential oils, you won't smell it for more than a few minutes, max.

And talk about foot-dragging—while the U.S. brought in a ban on lead wicks in 2003, Canada is still drafting our regulatory ban. Jeez. Ousting the neurotoxin lead in wicks should be a no-brainer, especially when Health Canada says one lead-wick candle-burning session a week can put a child at risk of lead poisoning. And yet Health Canada estimates 10% of candles on the Canadian marketplace contain lead-core wicks. Test your wick by peeling apart any fibre in the wick and seeing if it has a metallic core. If it does, rub it on white paper—if you see a grey smudge, it's probably lead. If it tests positive, toss it. Or just stay away from wicks with metallic cores altogether.

- **Beeswax candles** will cost you more, but they're worth it. These long-lasting sticks don't just smell heavenly, burning them emits calming negative ions and helps purify the air in your home, rather than polluting it like paraffin does. Be sure to get 100% unbleached beeswax candles—there are lots of watered-down versions on the market that are mixed with paraffin. Also, beware of artificially dyed beeswax. If it's blue or lemon yellow, it's a fake.
- Slow-burning **soy-based wax candles** are great because they're virtually soot-free. Manufacturers say that, dollar per hour, they're actually cheaper than paraffin and definitely more afford-able than beeswax. The only thing is that a good chunk of soy is genetically modified. And some companies are getting their 100% soy wax in bulk through the multinational agro-giant Cargill. **Lumia** is the first company to put out certified organic soy candles (lumia.us). **Scents Alive**'s candles aren't organic, but it makes the first candle certified by Environment Canada's EcoLogo program—though its mix of vegetable-based waxes remains hush-hush (vegewax.com). FYI, just because it's soy doesn't mean its scent isn't totally fake.
- Reduce soot by keeping wicks trimmed and away from drafts.

# INCENSE

Lighting an incense stick still seems so crunchy granola, how could it possibly pollute dear ol' Gaia? Unfortunately, many are loaded with chemical binders, petroleum distillates and synthetic perfumes. (How the hell else can you get incense to smell like green apple?)

 Here's a tip: if you can smell it from a foot away before you even burn it, you know it's a chem-laced poser. Price is another indicator—cheapie dollar store brands tend to be super-synthetic.

Not that an all-natural ingredient list should put your mind at ease. Overexploitation and unsustainable harvesting have led to the decimation of popular ingredients for both incense and essential oils. The popularity of agarwood (or aloeswood) in incense and perfumes is pushing it towards the point of no return. Same goes for the tamarind tree in Burma and the rosewood tree in Brazil. And, sorry folks, but that super-popular hippie staple sandalwood faces similar threats. The situation has grown so bad in India that the government has banned the export of sandalwood timber, though sandalwood still gets exported in the form of incense. Red sandalwood is particularly endangered.

It's virtually impossible to find any incense makers that use organic ingredients, but there are a few things to keep in mind when you're meditating on which incense to buy:

- Incense labelled "natural" means no synthetic fragrances and petrochemicals should have been used. It doesn't mean it was sustainably harvested.
- Avoid agarwood incense like the plague or look for companies with sustainable harvesting practices. **Scented Mountain's** agarwood comes from Vietnamese plantations instead of wild sources. **Shoyeido** says all its agarwood incense is compliant with the Convention on International Trade and Endangered Species.
- Stay a cut above potentially overharvested tropical trees altogether by getting your incense from trusted North American sources. **Juniper Ridge** incense is made entirely from leaves, wood and resins that have been wild-harvested from the Pacific

While that incense stick might send you into a meditative trance, Taiwanese temples were found to have carcinogenic polycyclic aromatic hydrocarbon levels 40 times higher than those found in cigarette smokers' homes. And a 2008 study of over 60,000 Singaporeans found the more incense they burned, the higher their chances of lung disease.

mountains and deserts. Plus, 10% of all profits are donated to wilderness defence groups (juniperridge.com).

- Look for **fair-trade incense**. The workers are better paid and the manufacturers can't use endangered ingredients. **Ten Thousand Villages** stores carry a variety, including **Silence** incense cones, made by deaf workers in Calcutta.

## AIR PURIFIERS

If you're reading this section, twenty bucks says you've got one of two A's: allergies or asthma (hell, roughly 25% of Canadians suffer from some form of allergy or chemical sensitivity). Although, if pet dander, dust mites and mould don't drive you to madness, shopping for air purifiers could. There are a lot of crappy contraptions making big, bold claims. If you can't afford a decent air purifier, fear not. Most people don't really need one. You can get rid of a good chunk of allergens by dusting your home with a damp cloth and vacuuming regularly (even daily if you have serious allergies). But cracking the windows may be the simplest and cheapest way of all to clear the air—that is, of course, if outdoor air isn't the culprit. And when cigarette smoke is the problem, you're better off asking all smokers to simply step outside. You can put up with their moaning more than you can your wheezing.

Air Purifier Features to Consider: If you still need cleaner air, here are some things to mull over:

- Heard the hoopla about HEPA purifiers? They're used in hospital operating rooms and can indeed be excellent air filters,

If you have serious allergies and/or multiple chemical sensitivities, you have to pull out the big guns. According to the *Allergy Consumer Review*, AllerAir MSC is considered the best air purifier for heavy smokers and those with multiple chemical sensitivities. It has five, count 'em, five, stages of filters, including a medical-grade HEPA filter, activated carbon filter and two antimicrobial filters. The all-around winner, endorsed by the American Lung Association and used by hospitals around the globe, is Swiss-made IQAir's HyperHEPA system.

but cheaper models, like the kinds we often reach for in home and hardware stores, are often more hype than help. Still, if you invest in a decent one, it'll rid the air of allergens like mould, dust, pet dander and pollen and some larger-particle bacteria and fumes. They are noisier, though. Some models combine HEPA filters with ultraviolet light, purportedly to sterilize bacteria, but the verdict is still out on whether cheapy ultraviolet filters actually do this successfully. For product reviews, browse allergyconsumerreview.com.

• Carbon filters are said to rid your home of funny odours and gases, but not all are created equal. According to the Allergy Consumer Review, activated carbon filters are best at removing some heavier lung-irritating VOCs from the air. However, they don't get the lighter ones, like formaldehyde off-gassing from cabinets and flooring, and they don't work so well in humid conditions. (Hello! Half of Canada is dripping with humidity in summer!) Bother with carbon only if it's combined with a good-quality HEPA filter. Look for one with a pre-filter to keep large particles like pet hair from clogging things up.

• Negative ionizers are not worth your time. The American Lung Association says the harmful particulates that have been ionized by these electronic air filters have a better chance of sticking to your lungs. Sharper Image, the maker of the popular Ionic Breeze purifier, tried to sue *Consumer Reports* for slamming its product, even though the poor rating was confirmed by the Air Purifiers of America. The case was thrown out of court.

- Ozone machines are perhaps the dodgiest of electronic air purifiers. Hotels sometimes use them to rid the air of smoke smells after guests leave. They also kill bacteria and mould. But airing out is required, since too much ozone is definitely harmful for both your body and the environment, and it may react with chemicals in the air to create other harmful pollutants.

- Forced air? *Consumer Reports* says a cheapy furnace filter like 3M Filtrete Allergen filter to control airborne dust, pet hair and dander should do just fine (available from Canadian Tire). Make sure to change these every few months, at minimum.

## HUMIDIFIERS

If you're one of the many people whose lips chap and sinuses crack at the mere mention of electric heating, winter can be pretty painful. Cold air holds less moisture than the warm winds of summer, and baseboard, central and, hell, really most forms of heating can make matters worse. The result? A spike in humidifier sales come winter. Okay, maybe that's obvious, but betcha didn't know that a humidifier can help you cut back on energy consumption. Moisture from a humidifier can actually boost what the U.S. Department of Energy calls the "heat index," making a room that's kept at 20°C feel like 24°C.

### Humidifier Features to Consider:

- Get one with a **programmable humidistat**: While moisture levels above 50% are great if you're into tropical vibes, you may as well put out a welcome mat for mould, bacteria and dust mites. A programmable humidistat can turn the machine off whenever moisture levels go above, say, 40%. It's also a good tool to help you cut back on energy wastage, especially useful if your living companion is the type who forgets to turn the machine off. Ahem.
- Popular **evaporative models** actually use a fan to blow water

133

## SOMETHING'S SPREADING IN YOUR HUMIDIFIER

Not to start fear-mongering or anything, but improperly maintaining your humidifier won't just lead to visually unappealing bacteria growth, it can also potentially trigger Legionnaire's disease (especially dangerous for children or the elderly).

- The EPA says tanks should be emptied, wiped dry and refilled every day. That's right, *every day*. Then every third day you're supposed to scrub the tank with a brush and clean all surfaces with hydrogen peroxide. Damn, that sounds like way more work than I've ever done on any humidifier. Am I alone here? Clearly you should do as I say, not as I do in this case.

- Change your filter regularly (yes, more regularly than you do now). Damp filters can really attract bacteria. If you see mould, run, do not walk, to the garbage bin.

across a wick filter that traps bacteria, minerals and pollutants. These tend to be among the most energy-efficient.

- Impeller types are basically the same thing but without the filter. The U.S. Environmental Protection Agency says these could lead to white dust problems associated with ultrasonic types (see below) unless you're using distilled or demineralized water. Who has distilled water to waste on this? Higher maintenance, for sure.

- Vaporizers put warm vapour into the air the same way kettles do, by boiling water. While boiling kills off any nasty bacteria that may build up, eliminating the need for a filter, it also requires way more energy than the cold-mist process. Some people swear that the steamy moisture makes the room feel warmer (as opposed to cool mists, which can make you feel clammy), so you can set your thermostat down a notch. Still, these energy suckers can cost two to ten times the amount it takes to run a cool mister.

- Avoid ultrasonic types. These old-school high-frequency vibrating humidifiers are super-cheap at bargain stores, but the weird white "dust" they emit (mostly minerals from hard water and microorganisms) started freaking people out, including the EPA.

Distilled water will minimize the problem, but, again, who has distilled water to waste?

- Avoid antibacterial filters made of Microban, which is just another name for the ever-present chemical triclosan, which is turning up in rivers, lakes and breast milk everywhere. Do we really need this stuff in the environment?

$$ • For super-tight wallets, there's always the old pan-of-water technique. Just hope your pet doesn't lap it up before the air does.

## DEHUMIDIFIERS

If you've got a dank basement, you should probably invest in one of these. They suck the water from the air at a remarkable rate (mine pulls out a few gallons a day!). They also act like little furnaces, creating some serious heat, so it can be tempting to leave it off in the warmer months, when you might need it most. Cool and true, keeping humidity levels down, especially in warmer months, can help reduce the levels of VOCs off-gassing from pressed wood products, says California's Air Resources Board.

- Look for an Energy Star label: all qualified standard- and high-capacity humidifiers have to exceed the minimum Canadian energy-efficiency standard by 20% and 50%, respectively.
- Get a model with a removable plastic bucket and warning lights that tell you when the bucket is full. There should also be a

### LIVING, BREATHING WALLS

Magnify the air-purifying power of plants by building a whole wall of greenery in your home! Living walls are basically vertical gardens that can be installed inside or out. So far, most have been put into corporate headquarters, universities and condo lobbies, but Ontario-based ELT sells some perfect ones for the homeowner. Its indoor/outdoor living wall display kits, framed with solid unfinished cedar, go for about $200 to $400, depending on the size (eltlivingwalls.com). Verticiel also offers living walls (verticiel.ca).

fitting that allows you to hook a hose up to it that you can then place directly in your floor drain if you so choose. Though I prefer to use the water on my houseplants.

- Buy one with a **built-in humidistat** so that the dehumidifier turns itself off when your desired level of dryness is reached, instead of staying on day and night.

## HOUSEPLANTS

Forget calling in a design crew; windows full of greenery can transform a drab, lifeless living room into a lush, vibrant forest in seconds. Plus, thanks to their seratonin-boosting properties, greenery seems to speed up recovery in hospital rooms, reduce stress and boost worker productivity in office spaces. (Maybe that's why computers come with all those soothing forest screen savers.) Plants may also do a lot to boost indoor air quality, which is particularly handy in sealed office environments or come winter, when we batten down the hatches to keep the cold out. About when Cyndi Lauper was first hitting it big, NASA tested a dozen common houseplants and concluded that they're really good at absorbing and destroying certain VOCs like formaldehyde and benzene. Having 15 leafy creatures in a 2,000-square-foot home should do the trick.

### PLANT POWER: LEAFY AIR PURIFIERS

| | |
|---|---|
| Chinese evergreen | Cornplant |
| Peace lily | Devil's ivy |
| Snake plant | Bamboo palm |
| Spider plants | Weeping fig |
| English ivy | Philodendron (including heartleaf, elephant ear and more) |

Some houseplants may be poisonous if ingested by children or pets and/or may cause skin rash upon contact, so do your research or just keep them out of the way.

# GADGETING

Turn on, tune in, green out

## Slimmer, faster, sleeker, stronger.

Our lust for new electronics creates some serious fidelity issues in our culture. Let's just say, if Moses were to write a slab of green commandments, coveting thy neighbour's gadgets would have to be up there on the list of earthly sins. Especially when you consider all the toxic waste they reap.

# ELECTRONIC WASTE

Canadian homes and businesses will be spitting out 400,000 tons of toxin-laced electronic waste by 2010. What's wrong with having electronics at the dump? Leaching, that's the problem. Not good, when you consider that millions of old lead-filled TVs became obsolete in July 2009, thanks to a mandatory switch to digital signals south of the border (Canadian signals will go digital by August 2011). That means 23 million *American Idol* and *CSI* viewers who received "over the air" TV signals (as opposed to cable or satellite subscribers) found their TV stations going dark. They had to buy a brand-new set with a built-in digital receiver or get a digital converter box—and guess which option most people chose? Scary when you consider the two to three kilograms of lead in every cathode ray boob tube. Add old, unwanted cellphones, DVD players and computers to the mix, and you've got a heap of trouble. Bottom line: it's time to think twice about how you purge your used gear and just what tech you're replacing it with.

Disposal: Even with take-back programs in place at major corporations like Sony, Hewlett-Packard and Dell, and recycling drop-boxes at every cellphone store in the country, Canadians still blow at electronics recycling. Only a tiny fraction (some estimate 11%) gets recycled. The rest sits gathering dust in our basements or oozing hazards into landfills (PCs alone carry 4.5 tons of cadmium and 1.1 tons of mercury into landfill every year in this country). So how do we get rid of this stuff once we've had our way with it?

First things first: call whoever made that gizmo you're looking to toss and find out if they'll take it back. They put it into this world, they should cover the bill for recycling it. If they won't take it back, call your provincial government and find out what recycling programs it has in place. Several provinces have started to pull up their bootstraps and take on some e-waste recycling initiatives of their own.

> Call whoever made that gizmo you're looking to toss and find out if they'll take it back. **They put it into this world, they should cover the bill for recycling it**

Wouldn't you know it, Alberta was the first to take the reins and get the recycling horse a-movin'. Since 2004 it's collected around 30,000 tons of TVs, computers, printers and computer accessories (mice, keyboards, speakers). You won't have to pay to drop off a dusty old desktop monitor at one of the 250 depots, but Albertans fund the program when they fork over an extra $45 to buy a jumbo-screen TV and $5 when they purchase a laptop (albertarecycling.ca). That consumer fee structure has since been replicated across the country, and now Saskatchewan (sweepit.ca), Nova Scotia (acestewardship.ca) and British Columbia (env.gov.bc.ca/epd/recycling/electronics) have similar programs. Ontario finally kick-started the most extensive e-waste take-back program in the nation in the spring of 2009—they'll eventually be recycling everything with a cord and plug. Just punch in your postal code at dowhatyoucan.ca for drop-off points near you. By the end of 2009, Torontonians will be luckiest of all, with curbside e-waste recycling

## DUMPING E-WASTE ON THE DEVELOPING WORLD

So you've dropped off your old computer for recycling. Who's to say it doesn't end up getting dumped on developing nations (where extractables are dangerously dismantled by hand, and toxic fumes, acid spills and contaminated groundwater are common)? Sure, Canada signed the Basel Convention, which says it's illegal for wealthy countries to ship their e-waste to poorer countries, but too few recyclers are listening. Canada's intelligence agency, CSIS, says the shifty practice is so lucrative, organized crime is already in on the action. The only way to avoid the whole dodgy dismantling scene is to ask for guarantees that electronics are being recycled in Canada. That means turning only to local recyclers that have been audited and certified by industry-led Electronics Product Stewardship Canada (epsc.ca/recycle). Good news is, this standard is used by the provincial e-waste programs in Nova Scotia, Saskatchewan, B.C. and Alberta, as well as Ontario's incoming program.

## WHEN YOUR IPOD'S ALL PLAYED OUT

First things first: downloading music (legally, of course) is generally lighter on the planet than buying case after plastic-wrapped case of largely unrecyclable CDs trucked from halfway across the continent. But what if that MP3 player of yours keeps breaking down? The U.K.'s *Guardian* did a big exposé on iPods in 2006, citing reports that over a quarter of 40GM Click Wheel iPods (now discontinued) failed after the first two years and, what's more, iPod owners were twice as likely to have had repairs done than owners of other brands (12% of iPod owners compared to 6% of non-iPod owners). Apple denies that its products were or are unreliable. Either way, Apple has made it a pain in the ass to fix your own iPod when it dies, since even changing your own battery voids the warranty. And sending your iPod into Apple for battery replacement outside of warranty will cost you up to $90. Even if your iPod breaks down after six months (while still under warranty), the company has the nerve to charge you a $29.95 shipping and handling fee to fix it. Customers were so pissed off that they sued Apple, and in the summer of 2008 Apple agreed to give a $45 store credit to all those who bought their iPod on or before June 24, 2004, and have experienced battery problems.

Whatever your MP3 player of choice, be persistent about getting it fixed before nixing dying tech (see **irepair.ca** or **iShopRepair.ca**). Ask for the extended warranty and make sure the company has a good take-back program in place. Even Apple is now taking back and recycling all iPods at the end of their

life, free of charge (**apple.com/environment/ recycling/ipodrecycling**). For info on a cool new wind-up media player, see the Solar and Crank Battery Chargers sidebar, page 153.

coming to single-family households; apartments and condos will be serviced by an ElectroVan.

If your province hasn't yet signed up for an e-waste recycling program, call your municipality about local options and look into e-waste collection events in your home town.

## ELECTRONICS BUYING GUIDE

Here's a handy three-step guide to buying your next electronic device in a green way.

### ☐ 1: Keep Your Wallet in Your Pants

The first rule to green electronics purchasing is not to get lured into buying stuff you don't really need. Easier said than done with all the sexy new products continually streaming into stores. But take a deep breath, smack yourself upside the head and ask yourself, can I make do with what I already own? If it's broken, is it still under warranty? Can I repair it instead?

### ☐ 2: Do Your Research

If you've answered no to all three questions, you can proceed to the research phase, which consists of finding out which electronics makers are eco-fying their products and which are full-on eco-slackers. Every few months (since 2006), Greenpeace ranks companies on their green cred. It's a great barometer of how electronics manufacturers are doing on eco-commitments. For instance, Hewlett-Packard was one of the first to score well on green rankings, but HP slipped in the rankings when it was discovered that an HP laptop contained a type of fire retardant (deca) that it claimed to have stopped using years before. Dell's score has also plummeted dramatically over the years, since it has backtracked on eliminating PVC and brominated flame retardants (BFRs) by the end of 2009. (Dell did at least gain points for committing to reduce its greenhouse gas emissions by 40% by 2015.)

A quick scan of the Greenpeace charts will tell you that Nokia and Samsung came in first and second, respectively, in the first two quarters

of 2009 and that Microsoft and Lenovo are almost as bad as Nintendo
(which always comes in dead last). It'll also tell you specifics, like only
1% of Lenova's plastics came from recycled sources in '08. Or that,
after years of lollygagging, all of Apple's computers now meet the latest
Energy Star standards and are, as of 2009, free of PVC and BFRs, but
that it still scores only a 4.7 out of 10, thanks to "unreasonably high
threshold limits for BFRs and PVC in products that are allegedly
PVC/BFR-free."

To check out the Greenpeace Guide to Greener Electronics yourself, go to greenpeace.org/international/campaigns/toxics/electronics.

### ☐ 3: Consider Earth-Friendly Criteria

Once you've identified a brand you can live with, make sure the specific
product you're looking at meets all the latest earth-friendly criteria.

- **Look for the Energy Star logo.** All Energy Star–qualified
  TVs, DVD players, audio products, etc. consume up to 75% less
  electricity than conventional products when they are turned off
  (see sidebar on phantom power, page 144), saving you a good
  $100 a year. And now that the U.S. government has mandated
  that Energy Star update its standards more regularly as technology advances (see the Is the Energy Star Label All It's Cracked
  Up to Be? sidebar, page 74), the label will be even stronger, on
  both sides of the border. Historically, the Energy Star logo failed
  to regulate how much phantom power electronics like TV sets use
  when they're "on" (totally ludicrous when you think about it), but
  Energy Star sets made after November 2008 will be up to 30%
  more efficient than conventional models and will actually save
  energy while they're on and off. Starting in 2009, you'll also find
  Energy Star set-top cable, satellite and Internet boxes that are at
  least 30% more efficient than the major energy hog you have now.
- **Ask if it's RoHS-compliant.** Those suave Europeans are
  always so ahead of the curve, so see if your product meets
  Europe's Restriction of Hazardous Substances directive, which
  largely prohibits use of six hazardous materials found in electronics

## STOP PHANTOM POWER FROM HAUNTING YOUR BILLS

Who's that sucking power from all your electronics when you're not home? Why, that would be your in-house e-ghost, quietly draining electricity from the wall to power clocks, lights, timers and other bells and whistles on the 20 to 27 electronics sitting in standby mode in the typical North American home. All that phantom power—sucking adds up to a startling 10% of your home's energy bill. You're actually spending more money to power your DVD player when it's off than when you're watching the latest Will Smith flick! New regs should curb phantom power to 1 or 2 watts by 2013, but what to do until then? Buying Energy Star—approved products is one way to minimize the problem, but running out to buy all new electronics before you need them isn't wise for your wallet or your local dump.

• Figure out who's the biggest user: With an energy monitoring device you can see which gizmo or appliance is using the most power when on and off. All you have to do is plug the portable meter into a wall socket then plug the TV, microwave, fridge or portable phone you're monitoring into the device to figure out watts going on (yuk yuk). Your local public library branch might have loaners, or head online to sites like **store.greengadgets.ca,** where you'll pay $34 for the basic version.

 • To curb all that power sneakily leaking from your electronics when they're off, the answer is simple (and free). Just unplug them when you're not using them. That includes your microwave and coffee maker. To make things easier, put your entertainment centre on one **power strip** that you can readily flick off. Bits Limited makes some über-cool ones called **Smart Strips** that sense when something in the "Master Plug" has been shut off and automatically kills off all the peripheral devices plugged into "Slave Plugs." Belkin's **Conserve Surge Protector** lets you control your strip via remote switch and includes a few "Always On" outlets for your digital video recorder or router.

(lead, cadmium, mercury, hexavalent chromium, polybrominated diphenyl and polybrominated diphenyl ethers).

- **Get the extended warranty.** The longer the better. It costs more upfront, but if you have four years of complete-care service, you're less likely to ditch the thing for a newer, younger, kink-free model.

## TELEVISIONS

Generally, the bigger and sharper the image, the more juice your set needs to deliver it. A Samsung 32-inch LCD model might use only 2 watts on standby and 117 when actually on, whereas a 40-incher by the same company uses 16 watts on standby and 200 or so when on. Of course, getting your guy to watch the game on anything but his big-screen might be a losing battle, so at the very least make sure that the TV is as efficient as possible for its size. Philips's 42-inch **Eco FlatTV** (a.k.a. Philips 42PFL5603D) creams the competition by using less power than a 100-watt bulb when on (as little as 75 watts). And in standby mode? A teeny 0.15 watt. Too bad it's not available in Canada and seems to be vanishing from the U.S. market now that Philips has sold off its TV brand. Look for **Samsung LED LCD HDTVs** in the 6,000, 7,000 and 8,000 series, which all use 40% less energy compared to traditional LCD HDTVs of a similar size. As a rule of thumb, plasmas are the biggest energy vampire and rear-projection systems are the smallest. For a full breakdown of how much power HDTVs suck back, check out CNET's handy-dandy quick guide to the power consumption of nearly 100 sets (cnet.com).

Power-Saving TV Tips:

- No quickies, please. Turn off the quick-start button (it makes your TV use up to 50% more power in standby mode).
- Dim it down over there. The brighter your settings, the more juice gets used.
- Bigger ain't better. Smaller screens use less power (duh).
- Pass on the plasma. These bad boys use the most power of all the

## FLATSCREEN FIASCO

Those old cathode ray tube televisions seem so old-school, don't they, with their 1 to 4 kilograms of lead? Well, if you think flatscreens have less hazardous innards just because they're skinnier, you've got another think coming. Partway through 2008, news hit the stands that one of the gases used to manufacture LCD displays is actually 17,000 times better at heating up the atmosphere than $CO_2$. (Not an attribute you'd want to brag about.) Yet since nitrogen trifluoride ($NF_3$) was barely in use when the Kyoto Protocol was signed, no one's capping their emissions. The irony of all ironies is that a U.S. manufacturer of $NF_3$ was actually awarded a climate protection award. It seems, back in the day, $NF_3$ originally looked like a champ replacement for PFCs (a more common greenhouse gas).

Oh, what clarity a few years can bring. In fact, $NF_3$ will likely be folded into any post-Kyoto global greenhouse gas treaty by the end of 2009. Luckily, some electronics makers are starting to get the picture earlier—Toshiba has developed a process that uses zero greenhouse gases to manufacture its Matsushita Display Technology. Let's hope more manufacturers get on board. If you do buy a flatscreen, be sure to pressure the manufacturer to take action—and soon.

flatscreens (twice as much as your old TV). In fact, going from a 28-inch cathode ray tube TV to a 60-inch plasma could spike your bills by $100 a year.

- You have the power. Put all your electronics on a power strip and switch it off.
- Turn it off. The best reality shows happen when the TV's not on.

# COMPUTERS

I have to admit, I wouldn't have the patience to be a writer if I didn't have the easy, breezy editing functions of a computer. But why does the tech sector have to make it so difficult to keep one up and running for more than a few years? In early 2007, Greenpeace argued that, with the introduction of Windows Vista, "Microsoft could effectively hasten the obsolescence of half the world's PCs." Seems a study by SoftChoice Corporation found that 50% of personal computers in use at the time were "below Windows Vista's basic system requirements." Just another day in the life of upgrade culture and planned obsolescence.

Computer Tips: You may not have much control over the greed of software and computer companies, but you do get to decide which computers you sink your cash into, so make sure they're the greenest around:

- Pass on extras. If you're a simple home user, you definitely don't, for instance, need a fancy graphics accelerator, which hogs more juice, so don't get one.
- Lean on a laptop (most of the time). On top of being portable, a laptop uses way less power than desktop models—anywhere from 15 to 30 watts of electricity (desktops use anywhere from 80 to 160 watts). On the other hand, desktop computers are more readily upgradable, adding to their longevity, although you should be able to upgrade your laptop's memory and batteries no problem. With new high-performance laptops, you can also upgrade your graphics card if you wake up one morning and decide to become a major gamer or video editor.
- Search for Energy Star. According to the program, if all computers sold to homes and businesses in North America met Energy Star requirements, we'd save well over $2 million in energy a year and greenhouse gas emissions equivalent to those from 2 million cars (see energystar.gov for qualified computers).
- Peek at EPEAT (Electronic Product Environmental Assessment Tool): This online tool helps institutional buyers (and anyone

else, for that matter) assess computers on energy use, packaging, product longevity and the reduction of toxins. All EPEAT computers meet the Energy Star standard. South of the border, federal offices must buy EPEAT-registered products, but anyone can search EPEAT's product directory of bronze-, silver- and gold-ranked computers (some top scorers include Toshiba Porteges, Apple MacBooks, Dell Latitudes, and HP Elite Books; epeat.net). While it's an important tool, some critics say EPEAT isn't tough enough. For additional shopping criteria that go beyond EPEAT, go to etoxics.org and punch in just that: "beyond EPEAT."

• Use your computer's power-saving features. A laptop in hibernate or standby mode uses only 1 to 2 watts of power; on the other hand, graphics-intensive screen savers can cause the computer to burn twice as much energy as it would normally (plus, they can prevent a computer from going into sleep mode). Check your control panel's power options to make sure your machine's energy saving settings are switched on.

## CELLPHONES

I know, I know, you really want to upgrade to a new iPhone or whatever the latest and greatest is at the precise moment you read this. Truth is, most cell users get a new one every year and a half, and we spend a communal 2 trillion minutes on mobiles annually. Hurts my ears just thinking about it. Not so sure everyone would want to get so snuggly with their phones if they knew about all those brominated fire retardants in the plastic shells. And they probably wouldn't junk them so readily if they knew about the toxic arsenic, beryllium, cadmium, copper and lead leaching out of them into landfills.

Luckily, more and more companies are starting to remove the most persistent chemicals from their phones. In fact, cellphone

## UNPLUG THAT CHARGER!

So you're running out of the house and you grab your cell. Do you make sure to a) say farewell to your pooch before slamming the door? b) check to see there's no toothpaste on your chin before you exit? c) unplug your cellphone charger because you know it keeps trickling energy from the wall, even when your cellphone's away? That's right, that charger might seem unoccupied and lonely without a phone attached to it, but it's keeping itself busy by sucking power from the wall. According to the U.S. Environmental Protection Agency, if every phone sold in North America this year used an Energy Star–qualified charger, the energy saved could light 290,000 homes for a year; in addition, we'd save 430,000 tons of greenhouse gas emissions (just like taking 70,000 cars off the road). An easy way to duplicate those effects for free is if we all just unplug our chargers! Seriously. Most new cell chargers are Energy Star–qualified, but you can stop your old charger from draining power with a very simple act—unplug it.

manufacturers top Greenpeace's list of greener electronics brands. Nokia gets top scores on toxic chemical issues, having had PVC-free models since '05 and aiming to be totally free of brominated flame retardants and antimony trioxide by the end of 2009. Plus, all of its chargers meet or exceed Energy Star requirements by 30% to 90%. Samsung went totally PVC-free in 2008, its handsets are also BFR-free and its chargers are all Energy Star. Oh, and keep your ear to the ground for even greener phones, like Samsung's solar-powered phone made from water bottles. (For alternative ways to charge your phone, see the Solar and Crank Battery Chargers sidebar, page 153.)

Sony Ericsson, while PVC-free, lost points with Greenpeace for having "unreasonably high threshold limits for brominated flame retardants in products that are allegedly BFR-free." Still, they've taken the lead in banning antimony, beryllium and phthalates from new models launched since January 2008. LG jumped ahead to 6th from 16th place by the end of '08, by finally starting take-back programs and by committing to more recycled plastic content, as well as having all Energy Star–qualified chargers. It's also got halogenated flame retardant–free phones but won't be phthalate- and antimony-free until 2012. By early 2009, it had lost a few points for backtracking on its promise to have all its products free of PVC and BFRs by the end of 2010. See the latest-breaking news on cell companies at greenpeace.org/electronics.

**Cellphone Tips:** All right, so you've picked a phone that's green inside and out (well, it doesn't have to be green hued). Now what?

- End the infidelity and try a long-term relationship with the phone you already have.
- Recycle your old phone(s) gathering dust in a drawer. The non-profit Rechargeable Battery Recycling Corporation's Call2Recycle program has cellphone recycling drop boxes at most cellphone stores, as well as at Canadian Tire, Home Depot, Sears, The Bay, and countless other locales (for locations near you, punch in your postal code at rbrc.org/call2recycle). Warning: in big stores like Canadian Tire, the little drop boxes can be hard to find. Ask at the customer service desk.

## BRAND-NEW SECOND-HAND PHONES

Who needs to buy a brand-new cell, or, wants to, pay all the fees attached to brand-new contracts? Through **cellclients.com**, you can take over someone else's cellphone contract and get a free second-hand phone, avoiding the cost of a SIM card and activation fees associated with new phones. And if, on the flipside, you want to get rid of your old phone or plan without having to pay hefty termination fees, this is the place to do it.

## CAMERAS

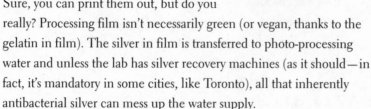

It took me years to let go of my old-fashioned film camera. I still yearn for the days when you'd race to the photo lab and every picture was a surprise. Now memories of that camping trip or Costa Rican vacation are locked in our computers. Sure, you can print them out, but do you really? Processing film isn't necessarily green (or vegan, thanks to the gelatin in film). The silver in film is transferred to photo-processing water and unless the lab has silver recovery machines (as it should—in fact, it's mandatory in some cities, like Toronto), all that inherently antibacterial silver can mess up the water supply.

Digital cameras, of course, don't create all that processing pollution, since there's no silver-laced film involved. Good thing too, considering over 30 million digital cameras are purchased in North America every single year. Trouble is, people are constantly upgrading them for new ones with more megapixels and slimmer lines.

Camera Buying Tips: If you are getting a new one, which should you pick?
- Make sure to get one with a **rechargeable battery**, none of that disposable stuff you toss every time your camera's drained yet another set. Cameras that run on AAs may seem convenient because you can find AAs everywhere, but they also don't hold a charge all that long.
- Ask for the most efficient camera that conserves batteries the best. **Sony Cyber-shots** and **Canon PowerShots** are considered good picks.
- If you're printing at home, get an **Energy Star–certified ink-jet printer** for your pics and be sure to refill or recycle your old ink cartridges.
- If you're shooting primarily family pics and printing standard 4-by-6 images, you don't need more than 6 megapixels. The more

pixels and added features your camera has, the more batteries it sucks up.

- Get a camera that also has an old-fashioned **viewfinder** option, in case you drop your camera and crack the digital screen. That way, you don't *have* to run out and buy a new camera.
- If you're really clumsy and drop everything you own (ahem), invest in durability above all. After breaking my first digi camera, as well as cracking the lens on my old film-based SLR, I was wisely given a shock- and waterproof Olympus for my birthday that can be safely dropped from up to 2 metres. Phew.
- Save power by turning off the flash when you don't need it.

## BATTERIES

What in life doesn't call for batteries? Even items as basic as a disposable plastic toothbrush or a tube of mascara demand an energy source if you want to get their full vibrating potential (that's right, they make vibrating mascara wands now). Sure, mercury might have been phased out, but that doesn't mean batteries are totally benign. So you might as well invest in ones that last.

Buying Rechargeables: Okay, so they cost more upfront, but decent rechargeables can replace up to 1,000 single-use batteries, saving you a hell of a lot of cash in no time. Just stay away from old-fashioned rechargeable nickel cadmium batteries. They're bad news for the planet. Most consumer rechargeables now run on nickel metal hydride (NiMH), which is much less hazardous. Least toxic are rechargeable alkalines, but they don't last as long. In terms of performance, the top-rated nickel metal hydride in 2006, according to Rechargeable Battery Review ( rechargeable-battery-review.com) were **Powerex, Sanyo** and **Energizer. Rayovac** was in fifth place of ten batteries ranked. Other things to consider:

- The higher the mAh (milliamp hours) number on the side of a nickel metal hydride battery (for example,

2,000 or 2,700), the longer it will last per charge (and the longer it generally takes to charge up).

- Ready-to-use models that come fully charged are a little less powerful, but they're perfect for consumer electronics that aren't heavy drainers or gadgets you use only here and there. They avoid the

## SOLAR AND CRANK BATTERY CHARGERS

$$\$\$$ Why bother charging your gadgets with dirty socket power when you can run your batteries on the sun's free rays? The **Soldius solar charger** will power up your cell, MP3 player or PDA in two to three hours on your windowsill—a little longer on cloudy days (**soldius.com**). Soldius even makes a solar backpack that can charge your gizmos while you're walking or biking around town. Freeplay makes a great little **hand-cranked FreeCharge charger** for times when your cell dies in an emergency and there's no socket or sunlight around (**freeplayenergy.com**). MINIWIZ makes a way cool handheld universal charger/adapter thingy that combines a micro wind power generator, solar panel and conventional plug-in power to recharge most 5V digital gadgets. It's called the **HYmini** (**hymini.com**). No sun or wind in sight? With only 1 minute of winding, the **wind-up Eco**

**Media Player** will give you up to 40 minutes of digital music, video playback and FM radio enjoyment. The thing holds a good 500 songs, it stores photos and reads text, and it comes with a voice recorder and flashlight! You can even use it to charge your cellphone (buy one through online sites like **terrapass.com** or **realgoods.com**).

Looking for more oomph? Freeplay also has a **non-spill, lead-acid gel battery** capable of jump-starting boat or car engines, as well as powering your GPS or cell. All you've got to do is step on the Weza's foot pedal to get it going (**freeplayenergy.com**). Talk about portable power!

**153**

"self-discharge" problem of regular NiMH batteries, which slowly lose their charge over time. That makes ready-to-use—a.k.a. precharged—batteries great for remote controls or anything you don't want to be constantly fiddling with. If you need big power in shorter bursts, stick with regular, higher-capacity options.

- Energy Star battery chargers use 35% less energy than conventional models. If North Americans got more energy-efficient battery chargers, we could save over 1 billion kilowatt hours of energy per year, pocketing $100 million annually and saving 1 million tons of greenhouse gas emissions from being released, according to the peeps over at Energy Star.

**Recycling Batteries:** So what happens when your rechargeables just won't hold a charge any more? Whatever you do, don't trash them! Rechargeables are much more toxic than single-use alkaline batteries, so a massive take-back program has been put in place for them. There are thousands of locations where you can take your old batteries from cellular or cordless phones, power tools, laptops, camcorders—you name it. Just stop by your neighbourhood Canadian Tire, Home Depot, Bay or Zellers and ask for the battery recycling box. Or call 1-800-8-BATTERY

### EVEN BETA TAPES GET ANOTHER KICK AT THE CAN

This has got to be one of the most common questions in the Ecoholic inbox: What do I do with my old Rick Astley tapes/Chevy Chase box set/undergrad diskettes/all of the above? If you can't give them a second life on sites like **freecycle.org**, and you've already called your municipality to make sure they don't recycle them, send them to **GreenDisk**. They take diskettes, zip disks, CDs, CD-Rs, CD-RWs, DVDs, video tape, audio tape, game cartridges, DAT, DLT, Beta or Digibeta and more. They're then reincarnated into things like new jewel cases, rewritable CDs or soft-shell cases for CDs and DVDs (**greendisk.com**). FYI, at this point Canadians have to pack their own box off to GreenDisk and fake a U.S. return address.

for the collection site nearest you (you can also visit rbrc.org). Warning: the drop boxes are quite small and hard to spot in big stores, so ask.

## LIGHTING

How many Canadians does it take to change a light bulb? Just one (come on, we weren't born yesterday). But how many light bulbs have to be changed before the greenhouse gas emissions saved equal taking 66,000 cars off the road? That's also easy enough—we just need every household in Canada to replace one solitary bulb. Actually, you've got till 2012 to get rid of all your old, inefficient incandescents, then you won't find any more on shelves, thanks to a federal ban. That's a move that should save us all a whopping 6 million tons of GHGs a year. Now there's a bright idea.

**Incandescent vs. CFL Light Bulbs:** Don't feel bad for Thomas Edison. His brilliant invention lit up our lives for well over a century, but now it's time to move into the future. Seriously, with incandescent, only 5% to 10% of the electricity goes towards lighting your living room; the rest is wasted as heat. Compact fluorescent light bulbs (CFLs), on the other hand, are 75% more efficient and they last 10 times longer than incandescent.

 Switching (almost) all your bulbs over to CFLs should save you about $60 on your electricity bills every year, saving Canadian

### WHEN TO FLICK OFF

Your father was right to nag you about turning the lights off when you leave a room. Regular incandescent bulbs are so wastefully inefficient they should always be turned off as soon as they're not needed. But your dad might have to update his nagging when it comes to CFLs and fluorescent tube lights. Most agree it's worth turning them off only if you're leaving the room for more than five minutes, since they take more energy to start up. That means CFLs aren't always ideal for bathrooms and closets (see Microbrite bulbs, page 157).

In early 2009, headlines across the country screamed, "Green light bulbs spark safety fears." Kind of unnerving, if you just made the switch to all CFLs. And yes, it turns out CFLs do give off some UV rays, but the final British government assessment just said you shouldn't sit closer than 1 foot (30 cm) away from bare light bulbs for more than one hour per day. And if you have a lamp shade on that light, you should be all good. Unless you have a photosensitive health condition like lupus, I wouldn't stress about it. However, CFLs flicker on and off over 20,000 times per second and could potentially aggravate migraines, photosensitive epilepsy and vertigo-plagued Ménière's Disease sufferers. Still, they flicker with much less frequency than old school fluorescents, which visibly flickered 100 times per second—so again, they shouldn't bother most people.

Others with electrical sensitivities worry about the radio frequencies (RFs) coming off many of these bulbs. The easiest way to see if your bulb is a culprit is to hold an AM radio close to the light while it's on. If the signal is affected, you've got "dirty electricity" (for more, see the Dirty Electricity Getting You Down? sidebar, page 274).

The Australian government, which is banning all incandescents by 2010, recommends that anyone with sensitivities try **240-volt halogens** (versus low-voltage halogens). They can look like traditional incandescent light bulbs and can be used in all the same fittings. Note: they're not as energy-efficient as CFLs or LEDs (which can also flicker).

households a total of $600 million a year, according to the Office of Energy Efficiency.

Now, you might have heard the media fuss about an early 2009 B.C. Hydro report claiming that homes that switch to CFLs could end up cranking up their thermostats in the winter (thereby losing CFLs' energy savings) because CFLs don't create heat the way incandescents do. Environmental orgs around the country were quick to point out the logical gaps in the argument. Sure, incandescents give off a little heat, but, for one, the David Suzuki Foundation countered that a lot of that heat hovers around the ceiling, where lighting fixtures are positioned. As well, the report didn't factor in the reality that, much of the year, lights are on when furnaces are off (making the heating argument moot) and, in fact, come summer, the presence of incandescents can actually increase air conditioning needs. Even B.C. Hydro reps clarified that, at the end of the day, when all elements are factored in, "[CFLs'] energy savings outweigh the amount of heating you are adding to your heating load." So leave those CFLs plugged in, people.

It is true that most CFLs don't perform well in enclosed indoor fixtures or on dimmer switches—unless you buy CFLs designed to work in those conditions. Check the labels. Otherwise, you'll shorten the life of the bulb dramatically. FYI, if bulbs keep burning out early in the same fixture, it could be a wiring problem with your old fixture. Also, cheaper CFLs don't always do well in fixtures where they're flicked on and off a lot for short periods of time (as in bathrooms). High-quality bulbs that use cold cathode CFL technology (like **Literonics' Microbrite bulbs**; turolight.com) shine in heavy on/off scenarios.

**Mercury in CFLs—the Controversy:** Do CFLs contain mercury? Yep, unfortunately they do, but only enough to fill up the dot in this "i" (2 to 5 milligrams, compared to the 25 milligrams in watch batteries and 500 in silver dental fillings). Do I think that's enough of a reason not to purchase them? No, but I do think every package of light bulbs should come with a big red warning label telling the purchaser that these should never, ever be thrown in the garbage. That mercury can be safely recycled into new bulbs if you bring your bulbs to a Home Depot, IKEA or municipal hazardous waste depot.

To put it all in perspective, the biggest source of mercury pollution in this country comes from coal plants, so the more energy we conserve, the more coal plants we can take offline and the more mercury we can save. That's why enviros will tell you saving energy with a CFL actually reduces the amount of mercury pollution in the environment. Energy Star calculated that every CFL bulb creates 70% less mercury pollution than a comparable incandescent bulb. Still, Environmental Working Group says the Energy Star CFL standard for maximum mercury content (5 milligrams) could easily be chopped down to 3 milligrams. A few companies have actually gotten it down to 1 to 2.7 milligrams per

> To put it all in perspective, **the biggest source of mercury pollution in this country comes from coal plants**

## HELP! I BROKE MY CFL!

If a fluorescent bulb happens to break in your home, don't panic: the tiny amount of mercury shouldn't make you sick. But here's what Energy Star says you should do:

- Open some windows, turn off duct heating or cooling and leave the room for 15 minutes.
- Carefully scoop any large pieces into a sealable plastic bag, use sticky tape to pick up smaller pieces and wipe the area with a damp paper towel.
- Put it all in the plastic bag and take it to your haz-mat waste depot, just as you would your burned-out CFLs.
- If you're dealing with a carpet, skip the paper towels and go straight to duct tape to clean up smaller shards.
- If you need to vacuum after (and only after) all the other steps have been followed, be sure to replace your vacuum bag immediately and seal it in a plastic bag.
- Wash your hands and you're good to go.

light bulb. Literonics' **Neolite** (which goes by **Genesis Fusion** in Canada) and **Earthmate** have by far the lowest levels, with only 1 milligram of mercury. (Too bad Earthmate isn't yet in Canada, though the good news is that the mercury in Genesis Fusion bulbs doesn't even vaporize when bulbs break! You'll find them at turolight.com.) **Sylvania's Dura-one and Micro-Mini, MaxLite** and Feit's **ECObulb Plus** are all under 2.5 milligrams. If you've got traditional tube-shaped fluorescents in your ceiling, you should stock up on **Philips's Alto lights**. They're the only fluorescent lamp granted non-hazardous status by the state of California. The **Alto Energy Advantage** bulb should save you nearly $40 in energy over its lifetime.

## Lighting Tips:

- Look for the Energy Star symbol, it guarantees that your light uses 75% less power than regular bulbs. And if your Energy Star bulb dies in under 2 years, call the company for a refund or replacement (that means you need to save your receipts).
- Check the "colour temperature." The lower the Kelvin, the warmer the light. The closest to the yellowy glow of regular incandescent bulbs is 2,700K. The higher the number, the whiter, cooler and bluer the light. Most "daylight" bulbs are about 6,500K. To be honest, I don't think they resemble the light you find outdoors by day in the slightest, but I'm a fan of the warm bulbs.
- Don't put a CFL on a dimmer switch unless the label says it's dimmable. Once you're in the clear, dim away, knowing that dimming a light by just 10% doubles the bulb's life.
- No need to leave your chandelier out of the energy savings. Chandelier-sized CFLs are now available, and some are even dimmable. Let the party begin!

**SOLAR HOLIDAY LIGHTS**

Oh, the weather outside is frightful, but the twinkle in your shrubs has you dreaming of turkeys and iPhones under the tree. Seems counterintuitive to power holiday lights with the sun's rays when there's so little natural light to be had in December but, yes, Virginia, solar Christmas lights do exist. The question is, do they deliver? It all depends on what type of fixture you're looking at. Canadian Tire carries only the outdoor kind, and a full day of sunlight should light up your trees for, oh, six hours after sundown. My set does well even on grey days. Some models come with a battery-powered option, complete with charger. For indoor use, you'll want to get yourself some regular LED light strings, which use 99% less power than those old-fashioned strands you have dangling from your porch/balcony/trees. Bonus: you won't be hunting for burnt-out bulbs that spoil the whole strand.

**Halogens to LEDS:** Sure, halogens have been the go-to lights for interior designers aiming for a slick, sophisticated mood, and yeah, they're more efficient and longer lasting than regular incandescents. But many halogens are serious fire hazards—the bulbs get sizzling hot. Torchières have been banned from many university residences because of their propensity to tip and catch fire. And in 2008, 58,000 halogen work lights were recalled, thanks to melting, fire and electric shock risks. Still, halogen lovers should keep their eye out for halogen energy saver bulbs, which come in the classic incandescent bulb shape but use 30% less energy.

The most exciting news to hit the lighting world is that LEDs (light-emitting diodes) are poised to swoop in and take over the market. Why the fanfare? For one, LED technology is so efficient, they beat out CFLs (they're actually 90% more efficient than incandescent). But while they'll last 20 to 25 times longer than halogens, they'll cost more too. Guess that's why they haven't broken through to mainstream hardware stores en masse yet. But the price should be dropping within a few years now that scientists have discovered a new way of making affordable LEDs that last, oh, 100,000 hours! In the meantime, Philips is bringing new **AmbientLED** bulbs to Home Depot as we speak that can take the place of 35-watt incandescent as well as 25-watt accent lighting. Yes, they'll cost you about $30 per bulb, but Philips swears that if you use them an average of 4 hours per day they'll last a good 20 years. Pretty impressive, no? You also can get snazzy LED accent lighting from high-end lighting stores near you and online shops (see ledlightingcanada.com, progresslighting.com, cooperlighting.com and allpurposeleds.com).

By the way, LED is the only technology that currently meets the Energy Star standards for decorative light strings. Oh, and keep your eyes peeled for **IKEA**'s new **solar-powered LED desk lamp**. The Sunnan light doesn't require messy cables or cords, "just a little sunlight now and then," according to IKEA.

**Full Spectrum and Natural Spectrum:** Want to cure all that ails you with the flick of a switch? Just turn on a full-spectrum light bulb. The lights are said to reduce fatigue, cavities and hyperactivity, while boosting neural function, improving grades, hell, even improving marriages. Sound too good to be true? The National Research Council of Canada says the research is too thin to support the claims. At the same time, if you feel it helps you with seasonal affective disorder or whatnot, there's no harm in trying. What we do know for sure is that these lights have spectral emissions in all parts of the visible

Full spectrum lights are said to reduce fatigue, cavities and hyperactivity, while boosting neural function, improving grades, hell, even improving marriages

161

spectrum and some UV properties. They come in incandescent and CFL varieties.

These differ from bulbs marketed as giving off "natural" or "daylight" qualities. Daylight bulbs filter out the yellows and greens that regular lighting has (so they tend to look bluish, which never feels all that natural to me).

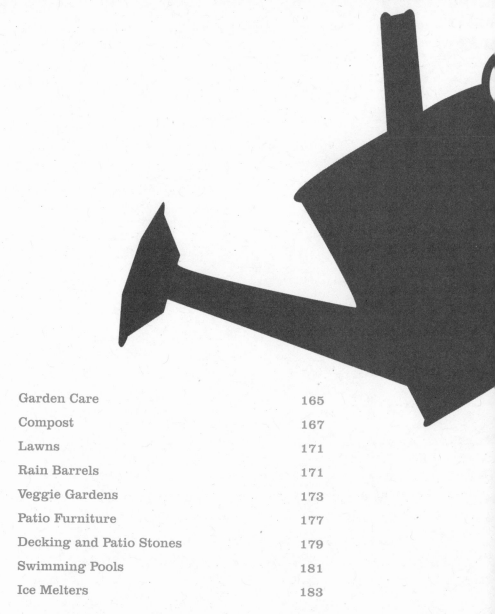

# GARDENING

## Digging for a revolution

## My favourite part of the house

—the garden! Come spring it's like your home suddenly
expands to include the most beautiful room, full of greenery,
with grass for carpet and sunbeams for light. Of course, our
relationship with the great outdoors gets a little twisted when
we start dousing it with chemical pesticides and filling it with
furniture made from chopped-up old-growth trees (not to mention those chlorine-filled lake simulators we call pools).
Whether you've got a wee balcony or sprawling backyard, it's
time to return those swaths of outdoor space to their earthly
origins—or at least as close to them as we can get.

## GARDEN CARE

You don't need a big yard to experience the joys of getting your hands dirty—even a 10th-floor balcony can help you get your green thumb fix. God, my old apartment had horrible AstroTurf on the second-storey deck, which only drove me to cover every square inch with as many flowers as I could. Of course, now that I have a whole yard to myself, I realize more space comes with more responsibility, and lots and lots of weeding.

**Fertilizer:** Mary, Mary, quite contrary, how does your garden grow? If it's with the help of synthetic fertilizers by Scotts, the company behind Miracle-Gro, I'd rethink your approach. Scotts actually lobbies against stricter environmental health policies on pesticides and fertilizers, according to Boston Common Asset Management, a Scotts shareholder. Scotts also works with biotech villain Monsanto on distributing genetically engineered lawn seeds (in fact, in 2007 Scotts agreed to pay a $500,000 fine for failing to prevent Roundup Ready genetically engineered bent grass for golf courses from contaminating surrounding lands during testing).

The best gift you can give your garden?

- Spread a layer of nutrient-rich **organic compost**. Either make your own in a composter or pick up a few bags from your local garden centre (a mix of composted manure, leaves, bark and the like). A good thick layer will suppress weed growth.
- For an added boost, look for **all-natural fertilizers** made from kelp, worm castings, or other nonchemical substances. **TerraCycle** sells certified organic, odour-free, squirtable liquid worm poop fertilizer in reused soda bottles (available at Home Depot, Zellers, Wal-Mart and more, as well as online at terracycle.net).

**Herbicides:** When did our societal war on weeds begin? Maybe when we started trying to grow impossibly perfect lawns with needy imported grasses. So we got the big guns out and shot ourselves in the foot. Case in point: we douse our lawns with potent chemical herbicides

like 2,4-D (in pretty much everything marked "weed 'n' feed" or "with weed control," including Killex and many Scotts products). Too bad it's linked to elevated rates of non-Hodgkin's lymphoma and prostate cancer in humans, not to mention malignant lymphoma in household dogs. Scariest of all, it's found in higher rates in the bodies of young children than adults, and California health officials list the stuff as a developmental toxicant. Marvellous. Good thing Quebec, Ontario and now New Brunswick have a ban on chemical herbicides like 2,4-D.

Make your peace with the pesky greens, and try these tactics.

- Who needs toxic weed killers when you've got straight vinegar or flat cola in your cupboard that you can pour on tricky weeds creeping out of concrete?
- Forget an apple a day, a native lawn keeps the weeds at bay. Sprinkle a little **compost** on your grass and throw down some **low-maintenance rye** or **fine fescue grass seeds** instead of water-sucking Kentucky bluegrass.
- **Overseeding and mowing high** (so you leave 5 to 7 centimetres of grass) minimizes weeds. Leave any grass clippings on your lawn (unless there's over a centimetre of the stuff, in which case, add it to your flower beds or compost pile); clippings break down into valuable nitrogen and make it harder for weeds to grow.
- **Aerating** your lawn will let it breathe and help nutrients and water reach the roots.
- Add weed-inhibiting **corn-gluten fertilizer**.

**Pesticides:** With long-banned pesticides lingering in 74% of homes and home pesticide use linked to childhood cancers, it's time to go natural. All you need is sitting in your kitchen. So what d'ya got?

- Oranges: Pour 2 cups (500 mL) of boiling water over the peel of one orange and let it steep for a day (repels ants, kills aphids, mealy bugs and fungus gnats).

- Baking soda: Put 2 tablespoons (25 mL) in 4 cups (1 L) of water, shake and spray every few days (works on fungal diseases).
- Soap: Mix 1 tablespoon (15 mL) natural dish soap or castile soap in 4 cups (1 L) of water (all-purpose pesticide).
- Spices: Any potent flavours like cayenne, horseradish and garlic work as excellent repellents. Boil one or more of the above in 4 cups (1 L) of water and let steep (it even works to keep deer and rabbits away).

**Beneficial Insects:** Release beneficial insects in your garden to chow down on unwanted guests.

| BENEFICIAL BUG* | ITS DINNER OF CHOICE |
|---|---|
| NATIVE LADYBUG | Munches on aphids the most, but also eats mites, scales, thrips, whiteflies |
| PRAYING MANTIS | Devours whiteflies, aphids, beetles, caterpillars, chinch bugs, colorado potato beetles, leafhoppers, hornworms, leafrollers, squash bugs, thrips |
| BENEFICIAL NEMATODES | Chows on root weevils, leather jackets, root worms, caterpillars, maggots, grubs, June and Japanese beetles and more (depending on the type of nematode) |
| LACEWING | Makes a meal out of mealybug, thrips, spidermites, whiteflies |

* For info and bug orders, see thebuglady.ca, natural-insect-control.com or thebugfactory.ca.

## COMPOST

Nova Scotians have it right. Out east it's illegal to throw an apple core or any other food scraps in the garbage, since there's a better place for them: the composter. Of course, if your town isn't as ecologically enlightened and hasn't started picking up compostables door to door (yes, they do that in other cities!), then you might want to set your own backyard example. A third of the trash we put at the curb is actually food waste: stuff that just ends up rotting and creating toxic gases in land-fill when it can easily be turned into nutrient-rich

Peat moss is a major component of most potting soils, since it's so wonderfully absorbent and water-retaining. Too bad peat bogs have been totally pillaged in Europe. No wonder conserving peat bogs (which store 455 billion tons of $CO_2$ worldwide) is, as the National Sustainable Agriculture Information Service says, "as important an issue as saving the rainforests." Canadian sphagnum peat moss is supposed to be less threatened at the moment—less than 1% of the total is harvested annually. Still, peat bogs grow only 1 measly millimetre per year and it takes hundreds of years for peat to fully grow back, so it's best to stay away. Instead, try using the super-absorbent coconut fibre called **coir**. It comes in bricks that, once soaked, expand to 10 times their size (ask for it at garden centres).

compost. Just get yourself a bin from your local garden centre, green store or hardware store (either a rotating one, a regular plastic one with a lid and air holes, or a wooden one), place it on a level spot in a corner of your yard, then get started.

- Feed me, Seymour: You'll want to feed your compost equal layers of green stuff (food scraps, coffee grounds, tea bags, houseplants) and brown stuff (dry grass clippings, dry leaves, straw, a few wood chips). Unless you want to encourage raccoon break-ins, keep meat and fish, dairy products, peanut butter and fats out. Diseased plants, cat litter and weeds (like crabgrass) should be left out too.
- Create a layer cake: Start by laying down a layer of twigs or coarse material, then a 10-centimetre layer of browns, followed by a 10-centimetre layer of greens, then a thin layer of soil. Continue alternating layers, stir it up every couple of weeks, and you should have good compost within a few months.
- Problem solving: Weird smells? Compost MIA? That means you've been putting in too much of one layer or another. For troubleshooting tips, check out Cornell's Department of

Crop and Soil Sciences' handy chart at compost.css.cornell.edu/trouble.html.

## GOODBYE CHEMICAL PESTICIDES, HELLO POSERS

Thankfully, pesticide usage is really starting to drop now that many municipalities and whole provinces (namely Quebec, Ontario and soon P.E.I., New Brunswick and possibly others.) are banning the cosmetic use of chemicals on lawns and gardens. Even Home Depot stopped selling traditional chemical bug and weed killers at all its Canadian stores at the end of 2008. Though you'll note that even so-called green pesticides and herbicides in some hardware stores still come with a skull-and crossbones warning. Green Earth's Bio-Mist spray, for instance, comes with a perturbingly lengthy warning: "Avoid breathing spray mist. Remove pets and birds and cover fish aquariums before spraying. Remove food and food utensils before spraying indoors. Product is toxic to fish. Do not contaminate lakes, streams or ponds." That's because its active ingredient, pyrethrins, might be naturally derived from chrysanthemums but it's also a serious neurotoxin and shouldn't be sprayed in the air. And yet it's sold as a mist. Oh, the irony. Also, be aware of landscaping companies that market themselves with terms like "natural," "eco-friendly" and "organic" but still use questionable chemicals. Ask for the names and brands of the pesticides they use and do your own research.

**Indoor Composters: The Naturemill vs. Worms:** If you're trapped in an apartment tower or condo, hauling your perfectly biodegradable food scraps to the garbage chute, knowing they're destined for a sad, wasteful life in landfill, can be pretty guilt-inducing. But envy doesn't have to be a sin if it motivates you into indoor composting! Option number one is vermiculture, the art of worm composting. Option two: an electric composter. Which is the right one for you?

| | WORM BIN* | NATUREMILL |
| --- | --- | --- |
| WHO | People who don't mind getting their hands a little dirty | Lazy people and/or anyone with a fear of dirt or earthworms |
| WHAT | Anything from a plastic recycling bin with holes in the bottom to a stacked worm hotel (see **cathyscomposters.com, allthings organic.com** and **vermiculture.ca**) | A 50cm x 50cm x 30cm recycled plastic plug-in |
| HOW MUCH | $20–$120 | $299–$399 |
| ACTIVE INGREDIENT | Worms | Heat and automated mixing (using 10 watts of power a day) |
| WHAT GOES IN IT | Food waste minus dairy and meat; 500 grams of worms will eat about 2 kilograms of food scraps per week | Food waste, including dairy and meat; takes 2 kilograms a day |
| BONUS | No plugging in. You're using pure unbridled nature power, baby. | • Claims to recycle its weight in waste every 10 days<br><br>• Can be kept under kitchen counter<br><br>• Optional vacation mode means composter can be turned off when you leave town |
| DOWNSIDE | If things go wrong, worms die. Also, worms can't be turned off when you leave town (although an established bin can go up to 2 weeks without new food if you give them a bunch before you jet). | You're buying a new electronic appliance, which will one day face the landfill. And some find it a little noisy (though it can be kept outdoors). |

*Vermi-virgins, take note: there's no need to fret that you'll end up with worms wiggling out into your kitchen unless you starve the little guys for weeks on end.

## LAWNS

Up there with inheriting a million-dollar cottage and getting two months' paid vacation, never having to mow the lawn again has got to be one of the top summertime daydreams. Many rye and fescue grasses make that fantasy come true. **Eco-Lawn** seed mixes, once grown, need to be mowed once a month at most, if you want that clipped suburban look. Left to their own devices, these fescue seeds will form a low, flowing turf that looks like a green golden retriever's coat. The grass's 23-centimetre roots go much deeper than those of regular Kentucky bluegrass, digging deep for natural nutrients and water instead of relying on external inputs (a.k.a. your hose and a bag of Miracle-Gro). And since it'll stay drier at the surface, you can say so long to grubs and the accompanying raccoons. You will have to water it frequently in the first year, but the next season you shouldn't have to pull out the sprinkler at all, except during serious droughts (eco-lawn.com).

Want strawberry fields forever? Well, you can get pretty close with the cool, drought-resistant, low-mow (not no-mow) **Fleur de Lawn** grass seed mix from a company in Oregon (protimelawnseed.com/about-us/fleur-de-lawn). No actual strawberries, but the mix will give you a yard full of nitrogen-rich strawberry clovers mixed with perennial rye grass (a good alternative to fescues), plus squat, pink English daisies and baby blue-eyes. Basically, a lawn so cute you'll want to hug it. The pretty flowers are annuals, so you'll have to reseed if you want an annual encore.

## RAIN BARRELS

Canadians are major water hogs come summertime, but just putting a rain barrel at the base of your downspout can help pull your reputation out of the mud. A hell of a lot of pitter-patter falls on that roof of yours every year (just 10 millimetres drizzling on an average bungalow creates 1,200 litres of runoff). And in a major storm, that runoff only helps flood basements as well as sewers, which can overflow and pollute nearby creeks and waterways. A rain barrel, on the other hand, can store hundreds of litres of free water for use on your property anytime you need it! Not only will you have lower water bills in July, but your plants will be much happier drinking chlorine-free water. Just keep in mind that some horticulture experts will tell you that, depending on your roofing materials, it's best to limit your rain barrel water to ornamental plants and lawns. There is no firm data on the topic but chemicals could potentially leach from pressure-treated wood shingles. Ditto for lead from painted metal roofs and petrochemicals from asphalt and tar roofs. A rain cistern, by the way, is just like a rain barrel only a lot bigger (typically holding 4,000 to 20,000 litres). You can store them above or below ground and, together with a good greywater system (see the Touch of Grey sidebar, page 220), you can then use that water to flush toilets and run washing machines.

- Install the barrel on a strong, level surface like a patio stone so it doesn't sink and tip.
- Elevate your barrel so gravity pushes the water down your hose into the garden (a very useful thing!).
- Look for a barrel with a diverter valve so water can be ushered away from the house when the barrel is full or when sub-zero temps arrive.
- Drain your barrel before a storm (duh).
- Get yourself a soaker hose that you can attach to your rain barrel spout and snake through your garden.
- Make sure you buy a barrel with a mosquito screen securely built in—my screen fell into the barrel two weeks in! If that happens to you, you'll have to build your own DIY screen.

## DRIPPING IN WASTE

Did you know running the sprinkler for 2 hours can use up to 2,000 litres of water? And households with automatic sprinklers use 50% more water than those that rely on manual sprinklers. Keep your sprinkler time to no more than one hour, once a week.

## VEGGIE GARDENS

As pretty as flowers can be, a pot full of petunias won't connect you to the land like a planter full of rainbow chard, which, sautéed with a little homegrown garlic, transforms you into the ultimate land-loving locavore. As long as you have a patch of outdoor space that gets a good hit of sunlight every day (at least three hours for shade-tolerant veggies like spinach, six for tomatoes, peppers and other full-sun lovers), the size of the plot doesn't matter. Veggies aren't biased. Here are a few ways to make the most of the space you've got as you join the legions of Canadians minimizing their food miles and maximizing their harvest, eco-style.

Front Yard Veggie Gardens: Who says vegetable planting has to be a secret backyard affair? (Unless, of course, you face a busy thoroughfare with lots of sooty auto emissions.) Now, that doesn't mean you have to sacrifice aesthetics and grow yawn-inducing (and neighbour-inflaming) rows of carrot tops. Veggies can be landscaped, too. The French have been doing so for years with what's called potager gardens (i.e., attractive kitchen gardens). Think of planting raspberry and blueberry bushes where you might otherwise put a hedge. Mix herbs, curly lettuce, tomatoes and your favourite veggies in with pretty indigenous flowers. And, so your garden looks ravishing long after harvest season, give it good bones

173

with evergreen bushes, maybe a recycled stone pathway, a trellised fence (great for growing vertically), even a little wooden arbour.

**Balcony Veggie Gardens:** Not everyone has room for row after row of sprawling squash. If your space is limited to a balcony/deck/fire escape (or you're stressed about pollutants like lead in your graden), get yourself a bunch of containers, and, really, any old ones will do, from vintage wooden crates to tin buckets with holes punched in the bottom. Of course, the bigger the pot the deeper the roots can roam and the healthier your plants will be, though I've seen veggie gardens take root in everything from plastic garbage bags to old plastic water bottles with drainage holes (though I can't promise that plastic won't leach).

What grows in a pot? Well, leafy greens like lettuce and spinach and hardy fall greens like kale. Peppers, eggplant, cukes, green beans—hell, even corn will thrive. And in my opinion, tomatoes are actually much tastier in a pot regularly laced with molasses water than they are planted in the garden. Avoid potting soils containing ecologically troubled peat moss (see the For Peat's Sake sidebar, page 168).

**Square Foot Gardening:** This technique hit it big right about when Hall & Oates were top of the pops, but it's still perfect for anyone with space limitations or those with crappy and/or polluted soil. To carry out this intensive gardening method, you build raised wooden beds in a 4-by-4-foot (roughly 1.25 m$^2$) grid, lay down cardboard or a plastic-free landscape cloth as a weed barrier, fill the frame with soil, then plant each square foot (marked off with string) with a different veggie seed, like, say, one big tomato or broccoli plant or 16 onion or carrot seeds. There's a whole breakdown in Mel Bartholomew's bible *All New Square Foot Gardening* (squarefootgardening.com).

You're supposed to fill your box with 15 centimetres of "Mel's mix" (one-third compost, one-third vermiculite and one-third peat moss), but stay away from the eco mess that is peat harvesting (see the For Peat's Sake sidebar, page 168) and try substituting coconut-based coir fibres instead. You can also replace vermiculite with perlite (a volcanic

## CLUCK IF YOU LOVE EGGS

Okay, urban/suburban hen-raising isn't quite legal in most jurisdictions, but if you live in Vancouver, Surrey, Victoria, Niagara Falls, Brampton or Guelph and have an itch for local eggs, you're in luck. (That's not to say dedicated egg lovers aren't doing it on the downlow in other cities.) Really, owning your own hens is the single most direct way to get fresh, organic, free-range eggs, and you'll never have to worry again about your brekkie coming from crowded battery cages. The little cluckers will also help you with your gardening by munching on weeds, grubs and all sorts of pesky insects. Plus, their poop makes excellent compost. For more info on coops, organic feed, winter care tips and more, peck around at **backyardchickens.com**, **torontochickens.com**, **urbaneggs.com** and **omlet.us**.

glass). Proponents swear these compact, veggie-dense eco-systems translate into less watering, less weeding, less space-wasting and zero added fertilizers. Just ignore dodgy suggestions like building your beds out of vinyl sheeting (unless you want to eat lead).

**SPIN (Small Plot Intensive farming):** Dreaming of pitchforks and farm life, are ya? Well, you don't need to move out of the city to live off your veggie-growing habit. If you've got a green thumb the size of a cornfield but nowhere to park your imaginary tractor, check out the wonderful world of SPINning, where the "back 40" is measured in feet, not acres. SPIN stands for Small Plot Intensive, and those small plots are basically rented ($100/1,000 square feet) or bartered from anyone in your 'hood who's open to you ploughing their land in exchange for fresh organic veggies. Serious SPIN farmers focus on high-value crops like heirloom beets and heirloom tomatoes that can spin out, oh, a good 20 to 30 weeks of income, but you don't have to be a full-on farmer to put their ideas into practice.

## 8 GREAT TIPS FOR A TRULY GREEN GARDEN

**#1** Plant native plants indigenous to your home province. They know how to grow on your home turf without the help of pesticides and excessive amounts of $H_2O$, plus you'll be attracting plenty of biodiversity to your garden (for a list of recommended trees, shrubs and plants native to your province, see **evergreen.ca**).

**#2** Ditch the water-thirsty lawn. If you do have grass, go with low-mow, low-maintenance rye or fescue (see page 171).

**#3** Get a rain barrel. Why waste rain-water when you could be feeding it to your plants all summer long?

**#4** Turn sprinklers on once a week max, and only in the morning or evening, when the sun ain't beatin' down, so you don't lose water to evaporation.

**#5** Grow your own organic veggies! You can't get a more local and nutritious food source (see page 173 for more). Any produce you can't eat yourself, donate to a shelter (**growarow.org**).

**#6** Preserve a piece of history by planting heirloom tomatoes, beets, flowers and more that haven't been genetically modified or hybridized. Check out Seeds of Diversity's annual heirloom seed swap (**seeds.ca**).

**#7** Ditch chemical pesticides and reach for homemade solutions.

**#8** Turn in your two-stroke gas mower and swap it for the push-powered kind or an exhaust-free electric mower (**mowdownpollution.ca**). You can even snag yourself a solar-powered mower for a little extra cash (**solarispowerproducts.com**). Home Depot's carrying them now.

So how do you incorporate SPIN into your private patch? Forget waiting for conventional frost-free dates (see almanac.com/ garden/frostcanada.php) to pull out the spade; you can plant cooler crops like arugula, chard, green garlic, spinach and more weeks before the frost lifts. You'll also want to fan out your planting so you can produce all summer long. Lettuce can be started mid-April, rotated with scallions (your "relay" crop), then planted again in mid-August. Max your growing space by converting your front yard, fence, hanging baskets, even rooftops and spare rooms (full of pea and sunflower shoots) to brimming harvest zones. For a full breakdown of the Canadian Prairies–born SPIN doctrine, check out spingardening.com.

## PATIO FURNITURE

So you're in the market for new patio furniture, are ya? Let me guess. Your old plastic patio chair has collapsed on you. Now, I hate to say I told you so, but that cheap vinyl stuff is not only toxic to produce and off-gasses hormone-disrupting phthalates, it lasts about as long as a Hannah Montana crush.

Exotic Wood: Ask around to see if anyone's carrying eco patio furniture and you're bound to be told, "Yes, we've got plantation teak." That's when your back should go up. Exotic wood brings you into dodgy, dodgy territory. According to the Rainforest Action Network, at least 75% of logging in Indonesia's rain forests is illegal. And even Indonesian "plantation teak" often comes from 200-year-old, rich second-growth forest. The word from the New York–based forestry watchdog Rainforest Relief is that Indonesia is starting to run low on teak and is now slyly importing Burma's disappearing trees. Too bad most manufacturers aren't keen on the quality of teak from Central America's much more sustainable (though much younger) plantations. Even a Forest Stewardship Council label, says Rainforest Relief director Tim Keating, won't guarantee a tropical table that's old growth–free (see the Chipping Away at the FSC Wood Label sidebar, page 90).

Rainforest Relief tries to pressure retailers like Pottery Barn to stop selling any patio furniture made of teak, nyatoh, kapur, balau, jatoba, garapa, ipê and other old-growth tropical woods altogether. The group's campaign has already pushed Wal-Mart, Linens 'n Things and Crate and Barrel to stop using nyatoh wood (Crate and Barrel now sells tons of FSC–certified options that are also old growth–free). IKEA's acacia wood outdoor furniture isn't certified, but the company does get the thumbs-up from Rainforest Relief for having responsible forestry policies.

**Eco-Options:** Just because a store might carry one or two FSC-certified patio sets doesn't mean it's not still selling endangered tropical woods. You'd be much better off parking your sweaty sun-kissed bod on the following:

- Pre-loved: Your very greenest bet is always the second-hand route. Craigslist is crammed with used patio sets of all shapes and sizes, including some in wrought iron and, yes, teak.
    - Milk jug Muskoka chairs: Plastic furniture is made of either PVC (vinyl) or cheap polyethylene, which is considered much more benign than vinyl. But both types tend to break suddenly after a couple of years. Better to get sturdier patio furniture made from old milk jugs and water bottles (sold under the name **PolyWood**). It's mostly centred on the Muskoka chair theme, though Sears has a broad collection of PolyWood bar and rocking chairs, lounge chairs, dining sets, benches and more. **Taylors** carries patio dining sets, benches, lounge chairs, planters and loveseats (taylorsplastic.com). It's nowhere near as cheap as the non-recycled stuff, but it's pretty durable and low maintenance too.
- Heavy metals: Yes, mining for metals is messy business, but **wrought iron** and **aluminum** win points for durability (especially wrought iron). Ideally, it would be made with high recycled content, but if you're having trouble finding some in

your area and you'd rather not ship from California, look for it
second-hand on sites like Craigslist.

- Wicker, rattan and willow: These are generally considered
sustainable and renewable since wicker and rattan both come
from rattan vines. And willow, a.k.a. twig furniture, is made from
hand-cut willow branches. The only problem is that rattan is
most often boiled in diesel and kerosene to make it more
durable and less prone to fungal attacks and boring insects (it
also gives it a tan, glossy surface). That's why new rattan furniture can off-gas diesel fumes for weeks or more. Unfortunately,
the main alternative, boiling it in palm oil, is not much better.
Palm oil is linked to serious deforestation woes in the South
Pacific. If you can find someone crafting rattan or wicker using
linseed oil or another vegetable oil, you'd be much better off, but
good luck. Otherwise, get your wicker or rattan second-hand.
- Plastic wicker (a.k.a. resin): Yes, it's durable and weather-resistant
and comes in all these sexy outdoor sofa shapes, but since the
plastic isn't from recycled sources, pass on it—unless you score
some second-hand.
- Reclaimed: This involves taking wood from old buildings, barns,
etc. and using it in new furniture. Kind of like high-end recycling. If you've got padded pockets, check out **Maku**'s slick
**reclaimed teak lawn furnishings** (makufurniture.com).

## DECKING AND PATIO STONES

Cracking open a beer mid-heatwave is just not the same if you don't
have a deck to do it on. I spent hundreds of dollars on tabs while patio-
hopping until I had a deck to call home. Of course, once you have your
own, you end up spending those savings on, well, decking it out. Which
brings us to the great summer dilemma: what's the greenest deck of all?

- Canada's big on making decking and fencing with **recycled
plastic**. It sort of looks like wood (complete with faux wood grain),
and you'll never have to worry about rot, termites, carpenter ants
or refinishing the bloody thing. To find out where you can get

Some things just seem so obviously idiotic, like building play sets with arsenic-laced wood. It wasn't so long ago (oh, around 2003) that Environmental Defence tested 58 kids' play sets made with pressure-treated chromated copper arsenate (CCA) wood and found arsenic (a known human carcinogen) leaching into surrounding soil at alarming levels. Soon playgrounds were being ripped out from schools nationwide, and yet all those CCA-treated play sets, decks and raised DIY veggie patches still sit in our backyards. (If you decide to toss your old wood, be sure to take it to your local hazardous-waste depot. Call your municipality for details.)

Do you have a greyish-green wooden play set, gazebo or picnic table? Chances are it's made with CCA-treated lumber (the stuff is still legally sold in stores, though it should be labelled). Health Canada says you should make sure to wash your kids' hands after they play on these surfaces and in surrounding soil, but I say toss it. Washington-based Environmental Working Group tested 263 decks, play sets, picnic tables and sandboxes across 45 states and found that arsenic levels on wood surfaces remain high for 20 years!

Cascades' Quebec-made decking systems, check its website, cascadesreplast.com. U.S. company **Trex** makes fencing, decking, railings and benches from 1.5 billion recycled plastic grocery bags a year, mixed with waste wood. Both Home Depot and Lowe's carry Trex products (trex.com). **Rona** has cool recycled plastic deck tiles for a good price (rona.ca).

- Not down with plastic? Again, beware of tropical wood, since it's hard to guarantee it's old growth–free. Except **FSC-certified eucalyptus deck tiles**, since eucalyptus is fairly fast-growing and far greener than native tropical stuff, says Rainforest Relief (though they still come from thousands of miles away). You can special-order them from **Green Design Studio** (greendesignstudio.ca).

- If you're on a budget, cheap, locally made concrete patio stones might be tempting, but concrete is incredibly energy-intensive to make. It's actually one of the single most greenhouse gas–intensive industries in the world.
- Flagstone slabs (often sourced locally and extremely durable) are a little greener because they don't go through the same energy-intensive processing. But you're still demolishing mountains to get them, according to Gravel Watch Ontario.
- Creative Bob Villa types would be smarter to whip up a deck with **second-hand lumber** from salvage shops like **Habitat for Humanity's ReStores** (habitat.ca). Or scour for sources of **FSC-certified Canadian wood**, particularly naturally weather-resistant cedar (certifiedwoodsearch.org).

Sealers: When it comes to sealing your deck or any of your outdoor wooden stuff, stay away from anything with a poison sign on it. I used Hempola's All Natural Wood Finishing Oil on my outdoor lounge chairs, but it didn't stop the wood from weathering in a hurry. For tougher natural wood sealants, check out **SoySeal Wood Sealer & Waterproofer** at soyclean.biz and **Deck Boss** at weatherbos.com. B.C.'s plant- and mineral-based **LifeTime Wood Treatment** is another good non-toxic option used on marinas, houses and decks, and the company swears it doesn't fade or need restaining (valhalco.com; special-order it through Home Hardware stores.) **AFM Safecoat** (afmsafecoat.com) makes some respected **low-toxicity stains and sealers** that you can special-order through organiclifestyle.ca, greenworksbuildingsupply.ca or AFM itself. Then you can seal the deal without smogging everything up for the rest of us.

# SWIMMING POOLS

Swimming may be a zero-emission sport if you're doing the sidestroke across a nearby lake. But maintaining a backyard pool won't win you

181

any green medals. Not when it sucks up 95,000 litres of (drinking) water to fill the average residential swimming pool every summer (enough water to take 2,375 showers with a low-flow shower head). And that doesn't even factor in all the topping up pool owners do as water evaporates during hot, dry months (when pools lose an average of 50 millimetres of water per week), not to mention the chlorinated filter backwashes that involve dumping pool water into the sewer system. And what happens when you get a leak in the vinyl lining? Why, you've got to drain the whole thing and start over. And creepy but true, when chlorine mixes with carbon-containing material like leaves, bugs, dirt and skin flakes, toxic trihalomethanes like carcinogenic chloroform can form. In fact, several studies have linked swimming in chlorinated pools to asthma. Even bromine (pushed as a chlorine-free alternative) has been linked to respiratory problems and skin irritation. Bottom line is, if you don't have one already, don't build one. Get to know your community pool. But if you've already got one sitting out back, well, I won't lie and tell you I wouldn't stop by and do a lap or two. Here are some thoughts on how to green your strokes.

**Chemical-Free Swimming:** Who needs chlorine when there are all kinds of cool alternatives that kill bacteria, like **UV light, ozone generators and hydrogen peroxide**? The most popular alternative is **salt water**. You just need a chlorine generator and about 23 kilograms of salt, and soon your skin and hair will thank you. The coolest eco-pools, though, have been around in Europe for over 20 years. They're called **natural swimming pools** and they work by mimicking a lake's ecosystem. Natural "regeneration zones," complete with water filtering plants, make them essentially self-cleaning.

**Solar Pool Heaters:** Like your pool bathwater-warm? Ditch the fossil-fuel-hogging pool heater and use the summer's best asset, solar rays, to warm your waters instead. Solar pool heaters are not only super-low-maintenance, but in most areas of Canada, they'll actually extend your swimming season by two to four weeks, especially if you pair one with a solar pool cover. And best of all, Natural Resources Canada says replacing a natural gas or propane heater with a solar one could save 3 to 10 tons of $CO_2$ from entering the atmosphere. For a directory of solar installers, check with the Canadian Solar Industries Association (cansia.ca).

## ICE MELTERS

It's hard to talk snow in a chapter on warmer seasons, but, hey, your outdoor access doesn't stop when a blizzard hits. Canadians know snow, ice and sleet can happen any time, and it's good to be prepared with a bag of whatever it takes to keep your mail carrier from slipping and suing you. Of course, if nature had a lawyer, she might file a class-action suit on behalf of all the plants and waterways harmed by most of the stuff on the market. While it's not like you're pouring battery acid on your driveway, it ain't good. You probably already know that basic rock salt (sodium chloride) isn't great for your grass, concrete and flower beds (never mind the trees around snow dumps), but did you know that salt can cause heavy metals like lead to leach into your soil's surface and into groundwater? And when it washes into our storm sewers and overflows into lakes and streams, we're talking long-term damage to aquatic life. Calcium chloride, often pointed to as a greener alternative, actually stresses the environment in the exact same ways, you just use less of the stuff. Not great.

**Alternatives:** Really, your first and greenest choice is always good old-fashioned shovelling. But if the freezing rains come and ice sheets form, here's a breakdown of some alternatives on the market.

- Organic Melt: This all-natural product is made with degraded sugar beets and sodium chloride, reducing rock salt applications by up to 50% and making it less corrosive. It works in temps as low as –30°C. Bonus points: you'll use up

to 30% less Organic Melt than rock salt to get the same job done. Not recommended on coloured or patterned concrete or concrete under one year old.

- EcoTraction: As the name suggests, it's less of a de-icer than a traction booster. It's made with a green volcanic mineral that has a honeycomb structure that sucks heavy metals and harmful toxins from the ground. Not sure that's a good thing if it gets shovelled into storm sewers, but the company suggests you sweep them up when the winter's done and reuse them the next season. EcoTraction is even useful at absorbing chemical spills, rehabilitating poor soils and, oddly, protecting your lawn from dog pee burn marks (ecotraction.com). It's available at Home Depot.

- Magic Salt: It might cost more than plain old salt, but you use about half as much of it. It's basically rock salt coated in a syrupy waste product of the booze biz (making good use of something that would otherwise be trashed) and mixed with magnesium chloride. It's also much less damaging to vegetation and concrete. It kind of smells like molasses, and it's biodegradable and water-soluble. Several American municipalities are even using the vodka by-product in spray form on municipal roads and have cut their salt consumption in half (magicsalt.info). Home Hardware and Zellers carry it.

- Calcium magnesium acetate: This non-corrosive, biodegradable de-icer found in products like Arctic Blast Ice Melter, is generally petroleum-derived but can be made from corn, whey or wheat. Unlike straight-up salt, calcium and magnesium actually improve soil quality, and acetate is biodegradable. The thing is, it doesn't really melt ice so much as turn it into a lumpy porridge, so you still have to shovel it away. But that's what you should be doing with all de-icers: use just enough to loosen the ice, then shovel. We pile way too much of the stuff on our walkways, hoping we won't have to do any manual labour.

- Paw Thaw: Available at pet stores, this stuff is a purportedly critter- and vegetation-friendly blend of calcium magnesium acetate and "fertilizer-grade ingredients." Too bad the manufacturer won't tell us exactly what those ingredients are. But two commonly used fertilizer/de-icers (potassium chloride and urea) can actually burn grass if you use too much (FYI, Get A Grip Natural Ice Melter contains potassium chloride and sodium chloride, a.k.a. regular salt). Urea can also release toxic ammonia and excess nitrates into groundwater.

- Sand: Some municipalities use sand on roads, but again, it does nothing to melt ice and can actually clog sewer systems. Plus, when crushed by car tires, the particles become fine enough to take flight, polluting the air and irritating asthma sufferers.
- Homemade Solutions: DIY solutions like sprinkling your walkway with kitty litter and ash, well, I have to be honest here, neither does anything to melt ice. They just provide a little extra traction. Plus, neither is particularly great for the earth, your plants or any waterways they may seep into.

Hard Labour: Hate to be the bearer of bad news, but the wisest, most conscientious option is also the most labour-intensive. That's right, shovelling. Get yourself an ergonomic shovel if you have back trouble, and a flat hoe to break up icy patches. Bend at the knees, not the waist—you know the drill. If you must, use a little de-icer to break up the surface, and shovel your snow towards the road, not your flower beds and bushes. You can even put a sprinkle of de-icer down as the storm starts, to prevent the snow and ice from building up. And if you can't shovel, pay a teenager to do it.

# RENOVATING
## Change you can believe in

## Ever daydream about TV crews

demolishing your kitchen and putting in reclaimed wood cabinets and solar panels on the roof? Sorry, that's me fantasizing again. Until **Extreme Makeover: Green Edition** comes a-knockin', it's best to take matters into your own hands.

But first things first. Be a responsible renovator. Don't just gut and build at will. If the existing wood floors work, leave 'em. Ripping them out to install imported bamboo because it's the new thing to do ain't the right thing to do. And if you do decide to purge the whole kitchen or bathroom, make sure you recycle all construction waste properly. Try donating usable pieces to Habitat for Humanity's ReStores or posting them on **Kijiji.ca** or **craigslist.org**, and while you're at it, look for second-hand materials you can use in your own home. And most importantly, do the stuff that'll shrink your energy use and, consequently, your home's greenhouse gas footprint, first. No polar bear will drown if you don't get new countertops installed.

# RENOVATION RESOURCES

I'm the first to admit that finding local sources of eco-friendly building materials used to be a nightmare, but the times they are a-changin' and by 2010, green remodelling should be a $39-billion business, says the U.S. Green Building Council. In all honesty, if you're living in Vancouver, you'll still have much more variety within driving distance than does, say, someone living in northern Saskatchewan; but if you can't find options in your hometown, you can always order online, though you should try to buy from sources closest to home. If you live in St. John's, scope out Halifax's and even Montreal's green scene before you book a shipment of recycled tiles from Calgary. And, hey, if you want to see more of these products at mainstream stores near you, pipe up and tell the manager. The store might special-order some for you. If it gets enough requests, it just might start carrying them. In the meantime, here are some websites that can help put you in touch with what you need.

**Hey, if you want to see more local products at mainstream stores near you, pipe up and tell the manager**

**EcoLogo (Environmental Choice):** Launched by the Canadian federal government in 1988, these guys now certify 7,000 greener products, including building materials like tiles, caulking, paint and insulation. Look for their logo when you're shopping around. ecologo.org

**Green Building Pages:** Though U.S.-based, Green Building Pages will pull up detailed background info on your product options, including living-wage policies, whether the product off-gasses fumes and how far the product is shipped to get to the manufacturer. greenbuildingpages.com

**Green2Green:** This website provides side-by-side chart comparisons, so a quick scan will tell you who's got the longest warranty, who has the highest recycled content and who'll take the product back for recycling at the end of its life, though again, it might be missing some Canadian options. green2green.org

**Greenspec:** The bible of green building products. You'll definitely want to get a copy of *Green Building Products: The GreenSpec Guide to Residential Building Materials*, either online or in print. It'll give you access to 2,000 listings for everything from adobe blocks and insulating blinds to solar shingles and wind turbines—including Canuck-made options. And they've all been screened by the authoritative publishers behind *Environmental Building News* (buildinggreen.com). An offshot of Greenspec is the highly useful GreenBuildingAdvisor.com, crammed with in-depth how-to advice, a blueprint library, a product database and more.

**Light House Sustainable Building Centre:** This enterprising west-coast non-profit functions as a "first-stop integrated service shop" that connects British Columbians to the info, services and skills they need to build and reno their homes sustainably. Its site has a good directory of green building material products and professionals in B.C. Why do BCers have to hog all the green resources? sustainablebuildingcentre.com

**Office of Energy Efficiency:** Natural Resources Canada's Office of Energy Efficiency website is full of tips on retrofitting your home, plus lots of deets on Energy Star and EnerGuide (two programs it runs) and regional energy-saving initiatives, as well as its main program of rebates for retrofits, ecoENERGY. oee.nrcan.gc.ca

**Raising Spaces:** This site connects to you a listing of mostly Canadian green home improvement products. It's not super well-organized (at this point it's just one long list of products), but it does have some interesting listings like recycled rubber bricks and paving for outdoor use. raisingspaces.com

For more green home websites, see Resources: Good Green Home Websites.

# CABINETS

They're the face of your kitchen, the ambassadors of your good taste. Cabinets can also fill your cooking area with lung-irritating volatile organic compounds (VOCs) like carcinogenic formaldehyde year after year, according to California's Air Resources Board, without you even realizing it. That's because most of us are living with laminate or veneer cupboards made with medium-density fibreboard (MDF) and particleboard made of wood shavings often bound together with urea formaldehyde. Now, you'd think all those shavings would come from recycled sources, but Green Seal says they actually use up to 80% virgin tree content. Be sure to ask. Definitely avoid MDF plywood and particleboard unless you know they're formaldehyde-free or have only trace amounts, like IKEA's cabinetry or that of smaller suppliers like B.C.'s **Raintree Cabinets** (raintreecabinets.com), as well as the **EVO line** offered by **Aya Kitchens and Bath**. Aya's cores are actually FSC-certified 100% recycled particleboard with no urea formaldehyde (at Aya locations nationwide; ayakitchens.com). All of these will be cheaper than full-on green cabinets because they come with conventional melamine (see Countertops [and Backsplashes], page 193) or wood surfaces. Just stay away from cheap laminates made from PVC. PVC is often stabilized with lead and softened with hormone-disrupting phthalates that can also off-gas.

**Green Options:** Looking for something in a deeper shade of green? You've got a few options. **Salvaged solid wood cabinetry** is your number one choice in sustainability (sticking to the first two Rs of environmentalism: reduce and reuse, of course). Small woodmakers specializing in reclaimed barnwood and the like can help you with custom work (like piecesfromthepast.com out west or infinitywoodcraftcreations.ca in central Canada). Although not all reclaimed wood is locally sourced. Toronto's **Greentea Design**, for instance, offers custom cabinetry made with wood taken from old buildings and floors in Japan, Korea and China (greenteadesign.com).

**FSC-certified wood** from North American sources is another good choice for cabinets. You'll find some through B.C.'s francislemieux.com, Ontario's infinitywoodcraftcreations.ca and premisys.ca, as well as Nova Scotia's **Windhorse Eco-Woodshop** (windhorsefarm.org/ecowoodshop.htm). Some green home stores like **The Healthiest Home** in Ottawa and **Green Design Studio** in Toronto offer a few choices for custom cabinetry, including solid certified wood, certified veneers or bamboo and cores made with no added urea formaldehyde or formaldehyde-free **PureBond** cores (see page 193) (thehealthiesthome.com) (greendesignstudio.ca). Both **Pentco** and **Merit Kitchen's Eco Plus** line of cabinets are built with FSC-certified particleboard made from 100% recycled wood fibre with no added urea formaldehyde (pentco.com and merit-kitchens.com). (Note: even certified exotic woods are questionable; see page 88 for more on tropical wood.)

Bamboo cupboards are far from local, but they can be eco-friendly if you make sure they're extra-sustainably sourced and formaldehyde-free (see page 201 for more on the bamboo debate). Toronto-built **Umbrella Cabinetry** is custom-made with FSC-certified wood and respected Plyboo bamboo as well as 100% recycled MDF (free of added urea formaldehyde) and water-based VOC-free finishes. The counters are made of quartz (umbrellacabinetry.com). **Teragren** is another trusted source for bamboo veneers and panels (easterners, try mcfaddens.com and westerners, check out pjwhitehardwoods.com)

In the growing-impossibly-hard-to-find category are **strawboard or wheatboard cabinets**. These are basically particleboard made of compressed agricultural waste (like wheat stems or rice husks) bound without formaldehyde. They're best when finished with FSC-certified wood veneers. Several of the retailers that used to carry wheatboard have discontinued their lines because the Canadian manufacturer has gone belly-up. Vancouver's **GreenWorks Building Supply** still offers **Dakota Burl** (made of sunflower husks) as well as some wheatboard, but these all come in sheets, so you'll need a cabinetmaker or good DIY skills (greenworksbuildingsupply.com).

Kirei board is made from reclaimed stalks of the sorghum plant and poplar wood bonded without formaldehyde. Plus, it's got a stunningly striated look to it. Though it's made in China, its light weight makes it more economical to ship than some others (west coasters, see greenworksbuildingsupply.com and easterners, see octopusproducts.com). It doesn't generally come ready-made. Again, you'll have to find a cabinetmaker or get out the saw yourself.

$$ The most affordable reclaimed cupboards are actually straight-up second-hand. Visit Habitat for Humanity's **ReStores** (habitat.org) and local salvage shops and **troll** sites like Craigslist or Kijiji for second-hand cupboards made of solid wood.

**Formaldehyde-Free Cores:** Keep an eye out for cabinets with a PureBond core—a formaldehyde-free plywood that's bound together with a soybean-based glue. It's extra-sustainable when you pair it with FSC veneers or bamboo veneers (as greendesignstudio.ca does). Check columbiaforestproducts.com for distributors near you.

**Stains and Paints:** Always ask for water-based finishes, no- or low-VOC stains or paints, or natural oils. Otherwise, get unfinished cabinets and stain them yourself.

## COUNTERTOPS (AND BACKSPLASHES)

What is it about countertops that gets reno-ers so revved up and rarin' to blow their budgets? Maybe it's because we spend so much time chopping and chatting around them, they become the nexus of our daily activity. Still, you'll find cheapy laminate countertops in 55% of kitchens because they're so damn affordable. Even if your wallet is taxed, you want to make sure you stay away from laminate options backing onto pressed wood that's been bound together with carcinogenic and allergy-aggravating urea formaldehyde. Melamine Formica and Wilsonart use phenol formaldehyde resin, which doesn't off-gas as much once the material hardens but there are greener options on the table.

## IS YOUR GRANITE COUNTERTOP RADIOACTIVE?

 You always wanted your kitchen to be sleek, sophisticated . . . and radioactive? As quick as you can say "Jumpin' Jack Flash," radon gas is back, and it's freaking out homeowners continent-wide, especially those installing fancy stone slabs in their kitchens and bathrooms.

What the hell is radon anyway? It's a gas that comes from decaying uranium in the soil and rock under your feet. Yep, uranium isn't just found in massive deposits in northern Saskatchewan; it's scattered pretty much everywhere, just in smaller quantities. Outside, not a big deal, but trapped in your house? Well, it depends.

We all have a little radon gas floating around the recesses of our homes, especially the basement. It's just that some of us have more than others. And when we start bringing great hunks of rock into our pads to tart up our counters and floors, we're potentially carting in even more radiation. One physics prof at Rice University in Houston found that all 55 granite slabs he sampled had higher-than-background levels of radiation. Most were still considered "safe," but a few were 100 times above background! The worst offenders included striated granites from Brazil and Namibia.

But there are a whopping 1,600 varieties of granite on the market from 64 different countries. Even if 85% are safe, as the Marble Institute of America points out, what about the rest? The only way to know whether your counters are hot is to get them tested. (FYI, the Marble Institute is supposedly setting up a testing protocol as we speak. Renovators should start pressing their suppliers for certified proof that their slab isn't hot.)

If I found high levels, personally, I'd rip it out. Better safe than sorry. Still, in a well-ventilated kitchen, you're generally exposed to less radon and radiation than many basement dwellers. And if you eat out a lot, even better. Kidding. Just keep your windows cracked open.

- A **vintage** slab of wood won't just add serious character to your kitchen, you'll also have the greenest counters around. Antique bureaus can also make for gorgeous islands. Get creative. Think outside the countertop.
- Recycled **glass** is a gorgeous stain- and scratch-proof choice. Look for products with a high recycled content. **Interstyle** sells a few gorgeous recycled glass options primarily for backsplashes or accent tiles, but their **Aquarius tiles** would make stunning countertops and are 80% scrap glass (interstyle.ca). **Bio-Glass** is a stunning solid surfacing for countertops, walls or anywhere else you want to slap it down, and it's made of 100% recycled content (coveringsetc.com, distributed in Canada through sipdistribution.ca).
- Want something with a bit more pizzazz? Check out **recycled terrazzo** (terrazzo is a smooth multicoloured surface made of chipped stone or glass bound in concrete). **Vetrazzo** is a stunning brand of terrazzo made with chipped recycled glass from old traffic lights, windshields, stemware, old Heineken bottles— generally glass that can't be recycled elsewhere. Plus workers are paid a living wage (vetrazzo.com). **IceStone** is a somewhat less flashy option made with 100% recycled glass (for a list of dealers across the country, see sipdistribution.ca). **Eco-Terra** is a ter-razzo made with 80% post-industrial and 10% post-consumer recycled stone and concrete. It comes in tiles and slabs.
- Dig the cool aesthetic of cold hard metal? **Eleek** makes slick metallic counter tiles out of 100% **recycled aluminum** (eleekinc.com or through Ontario's ecoinhabit.com or B.C.'s greenworksbuildingsupply.com). **Coverings Etc.'s Biolu-minium** surfaces are made from old airplane fuselages (cover-ingsetc.com; again, see sipdistribution.ca).
- Sounds a little loony, but you can also get counters made with **recycled paper** that can actually stand up to kitchen use; **Paper-Stone** makes some (check sipdistribution.ca for dealers across the country). **Richlite** also makes a paper-based countertop, but

Love a good bath? Well, if you've got a porcelain enamel tub, you're probably soaking in lead. In fact, according to one sample, 62% of porcelain tubs were leaching the stuff. Older bathtubs long scrubbed with abrasive cleansers leach the most. It's not really a big problem unless you've got young ones swallowing bathwater on a daily basis or if, like one older gentleman, you're making vats of red wine in your tub (no joke—the guy got severe lead poisoning!). Worried? Order a lead testing kit from **leadinspector.com**.

Maybe you have no lead woes at all but just a really old, nasty tub. Either way, what do you replace it with? Rather than throwing the baby out with the bath water, have it refinished (look up "bathtub refinishing" in the Yellow Pages). Your main option is to get an acrylic tub liner installed. You could get a porcelain or cast iron tub refinished with a glazing done by a pro, but to be honest, the urethanes they're bringing into your bathroom to do this are quite heavy in VOCs. I hear there are new low-VOC options on the market, especially in the DIY market, but you'll have to ask around. At the very least, refinishing keeps a giant tub out of the trash, and you always want to minimize renovation waste wherever you can.

If you're building a shower stall from scratch, however, best to steer clear of fibreglass and acrylic, since they're polluting to manufacture. Glass or ceramic tiles, especially the kind with high recycled content, are a good clean option for both walls and floors.

Caulking can be an air-polluting job, thanks to all the VOCs they give off, but luckily you can get the job done with low-VOC options by companies like **AFM Safecoat** (**afmsafecoat.com**).

Warning: You'd be a fool to go with solid wood, bamboo or cork in this room. Even natural linoleum isn't recommended. And don't start tempting fate by putting up wallpaper. That's just asking for punishment. FYI, if your washroom's got vinyl flooring older than Van Halen, it could be backed with asbestos-heavy paper. Don't rip it out without professional consultation.

it doesn't contain much recycled content (it uses paper from "certified managed North American forests" and has FSC-certified options; richlite.com).

- Get the look of limestone or soapstone without carving up mountainscapes or old riverbeds. **Squak Mountain Stone** is a warm, rugged concrete surface made of recycled paper, recycled glass, coal fly-ash and cement. It comes in slabs (squakmountainstone.com).
- Chefs yearning for more prep room might consider butcher block surfaces made with **reclaimed and local FSC-certified wood** (thehealthiesthome.com or windfalllumber.com). Just note that many will tell you wood doesn't hold up as well over time, and durability is a cornerstone of sustainable renovations.

- Look into low-maintenance **Marmoleum** as a countertop. It's made with a blend of linseed oil, jute, ground cork, wood flour and pine resin (themarmoleumstore.com or Home Depot stores).

## FLOORING

Starting from the ground up, you've got lots of options for what falls beneath your feet, and everyone seems to be pushing an eco-friendly choice these days. So which will keep you well grounded on the road to sustainability?

**Reclaimed:** The greenest of the green is definitely reclaimed wood floors harvested in Canada (the closer to your home the better). The wood is taken from old barns, lake floors and construction sites and not only saves a new tree from the chop but revives a little piece of history in your living room. Some, like **Coast EcoTimber**, tap into a network of beachcombers who salvage trees from landslides and storm-ravaged coastal areas (coastecotimber.com). Others, like Toronto's **Urban Tree Salvage**, stick to timber plucked from abandoned factories, demolition projects and felled city trees (urbantreesalvage.com). The "Rethink" floorboards at Winnipeg's **Wood Anchor** are created by carefully removing wood floors from one building, de-nailing it and installing it

197

in your home (woodanchor.com). **Woodland Flooring**, from B.C.'s interior, makes gorgeous floorboards salvaged from trees killed by the mountain pine beetle (woodlandflooring.com).

Buyer beware: flooring labelled "vintage" can actually be new wood that was distressed to make it look old. Suppliers should tell you as much if you ask.

**FSC-Certified:** If the reclaimed stuff is too pricey for you (it doesn't come cheap) and you want to stick with wood, be sure to look for FSC-certified flooring. Though not without weaknesses (see the Chipping Away at the FSC Wood Label sidebar, page 90), it's the most respected wood certifier around and beats out the Sustainable Forestry Initiative and others in terms of cred. Still, even FSC-certified tropical woods could come from old-growth forests so avoid them. Ideally, your FSC-certified floorboards would be sourced from Canadian forests, as Toronto's **Nadurra Wood**'s maple floors are (nadurrawood.com). Montreal's **DuroDesign** also carries FSC-certified Canadian maple and oak flooring (duro-design.com). Out west, Nelson's **The Building Tree** carries FSC-certified unfinished fir milled from a local community forest (buildingtree.ca). You might find FSC-certified options at Home Depot, RONA and Lowe's home improvement centres, though they're likely to be imports and aren't consistently in-store.

**Engineered Wood vs. Laminate:** Tight budgets might shift homeowners away from solid wood floors to more affordable alternatives. So what's the difference between engineered and laminate? Well, both are floating floors that can be easily snapped in place above concrete since they're nail-free. But beyond that, laminate is basically a picture of wood grains coated with melamine (say cheese!). Engineered floors actually use real wood in thin stacked layers (a.k.a. veneers). They're considered stronger, harder and more warp-resistant than solid wood floors (and can, unlike solid wood, be used in higher moisture rooms like bathrooms and basements). They can also be sanded and refinished a few times, so that adds to their durability. They're the only wood flooring option that can be used with radiant floor heating. Many also consider them more ecological since they use less wood—though that doesn't guarantee the wood they do use is anywhere near sustainable. One of the main concerns with engineered flooring is that those veneers are bonded together using carcinogenic urea formaldehyde, which can off-gas VOCs into your home. Warning: You'll need luck finding an engineered flooring product that's formaldehyde-free, FSC-certified and made of North American wood. They're few and far between, so you might have to settle for two of the three. A head's up: FSC engineered options aren't usually cheaper than FSC solid floors.

- Make sure you're buying ultra-low-formaldehyde or formalde-hyde-free. All Columbia Flooring uses formaldehyde-free **PureBond** glue as a binder (the wood isn't certified FSC, but it's U.S. grown; columbiaflooring.com). **Mohawk**'s U.S.-grown hardwood engineered floors are also PureBond (its exotic woods aren't; mohawkflooring.com). Nadurra Engineered Click Bamboo Flooring is low VOC. (nadurrawood.com).

- Keep your eyes peeled for FSC certification, especially North American–sourced stuff. Your best choice for Canadian-made, FSC-certified, engineered floors is probably **DuroDesign**. It comes in over 12 shades of wide plank engineered oak (duro-design.com). **Qualifor Harvest Green** floors are FSC-certified, but they're made with tropical old growths like ipê, which Rainforest Relief and others warn us to avoid. **EcoTimber** sells exotics as well as FSC-certified engineered floors made with American wood and bound with formaldehyde-free adhesive (for dealers across Canada, see ecotimber.com). BC-based **West Wind Wood Hardwood Inc** offers North American–grown FSC-certified Douglas Fir engineered floors (flooringbywestwindhardwood.com). But they're not totally formaldehyde-free (they use lower-emitting phenol formalde-hyde); in addition, the engineered options come with the FSC Mixed Source label (see the What's FSC Mixed Source? sidebar, page 200).

If you spot the FSC Mixed Source label on shelves, that basically means 30% of the wood involved can be non-FSC (before 2009 it could actually be 50% non-FSC). With FSC Mixed Source engineered floors, the FSC label might just apply to the outer veneer and not the substrate, or vice versa. Best to ask.

- Consider reclaimed options. These are tougher to find in engineered form, but Shelburne, Ontario's **Country Wood Floor Finishers** offer some made of gorgeous old elm, hemlock, salvaged Queen's Wharf pine and more. They use ultra-low VOC glues and the plywood backing is bound with lower-emitting phenol formaldehyde (historicwoods.com). In the "no added formaldehyde" category, Mohawk offers some of the few reclaimed hardwood engineered floors I've come across. The veneers in its Mohawk Artiquity and Zanzibar Reclaimed products are made of antique heart pine salvaged from old southern U.S. textile mills, a distillery in Kentucky and ancient structures in China (these are manufactured in China).

- There is one green laminate option for those of you with wallet woes. **Eco Floors laminate flooring** is bound with natural tannins, any wood involved is FSC-certified, and the floors are essentially formaldehyde-free. Plus, that decorative image that makes it look like wood is printed with water-based dyes with a wear layer made with aluminum oxide and tree resin. Pretty damn good for laminate (eco-floors.com). Of course, it won't be as cheap as conventional laminate flooring made with zero concern for the environment, but it is still more affordable than solid wood floors and it's great for basements, rec rooms and the like.
- If you're looking for a sound control underlayment to slap beneath your engineered or laminate floors, Eco-Floors also makes a totally natural woven **Jute High Performance Sound**

**Control Underlayment** (eco-floors.com). Ecotimber's **Floating Floor Pad** is synthetic, but it has 92% recycled content (ecotimber.com).

Bamboo: Bamboo floors are shooting up faster than you can say "Kung Fu Panda," but is that a good thing? No doubt bamboo is a miracle fibre. It can be used like wood but is actually a grass that grows so quickly it can be harvested every few years. Its intricate root structure can help prevent erosion when it's planted on hillsides and riverbanks. Plus, bamboo forests are impressive carbon sinks and detoxify land by sucking heavy-metal pollutants into its shoots. Really, the plant deserves the Nobel for most sustainable resource of the year.

But whether it gets to keep that trophy depends on a few factors. One is deforestation. Up to a third of the world's 1,200 bamboo species are on the brink of extinction, according to a report funded by the UN and the International Network for Bamboo and Rattan. And their loss is threatening rare animals like giant pandas, Madagascar's golden lemurs and Africa's mountain gorillas. Luckily, manufacturers don't generally lust after pandas' bamboo (it's less than 3 centimetres in diameter and is now relegated to remote parts of China). And these days, most bamboo product suppliers get their bamboo from plantations. Problem is, the past couple of decades have seen diversity-rich natural forests axed to make way for monoculture bamboo plantations. The dodgy practice is supposedly slowing (now that the dirty work is done). Still, there are no guarantees.

The next point-docker has to do with how you process the stuff. Most cheap bamboo imports are bound by carcinogenic urea formaldehyde, so you have to do your research. And lastly (and this one you can't get around), bamboo has to be shipped over 10,000 kilometres from China to get here. All this to say, bamboo shouldn't, generally, be your first choice in flooring. But if you are determined to get it, here are a few things to keep in mind:

- Make sure you look for bamboo that's formaldehyde-free (or ultra-low in it) and comes with a low- or no-VOC finish so it's not polluting the air in your home. **Silkroad**'s flooring is certified by Environment Canada's EcoLogo program and offers both ultra-low- and formaldehyde-free options (silkroadflooring.com). **Teragren** is another reputable source for ultra-low-formaldehyde bamboo flooring, both solid and engineered (teragren.com). Cheaper brands may tell you they're low-VOC, but ask them if they have third-party certification to prove it. Also, ask if that testing is done here in North America.
- Now that the Forest Stewardship Council is certifying bamboo, look for the FSC seal. Those with the seal are basically the cream of the green crop. **Smith & Fong** (makers of **Plyboo**) offered the world's first FSC-certified bamboo plywood and flooring (plyboo.com; check taproot.ca for Canadian sources).

## LOVE THE LOCAL: SAY NO TO TROPICAL WOOD

I'll say this again and again: we need to stop buying tropical wood. I know it's pretty and exotic, but unless your definition of beauty involves the destruction of old-growth rain forests, stay away. Everyone will tell you their wood comes from responsible plantations, but orgs like Rainforest Relief will tell you illegal logging is rampant in countries such as Indonesia. WWF says 85% of Africa's rain forest has been destroyed. Enforcement practices are weak, and even monitoring by trusted orgs like the FSC gets spotty deep in the belly of Brazil's rain forest and elsewhere. No wonder Norway banned tropical flooring in public buildings in 2007. Maybe it's time to start your own ban. Unless it's reclaimed or salvaged, stay away.

Plyboo is always ultra-low in formaldehyde, but you can also pick the PlybooPure upgrade if you want to go totally formaldehyde-free. Silkroad's sister flooring company Nadurra should also be offering FSC-certified bamboo options now (nadurrawood.com).

- Keep in mind that cheaper bamboo floors might dent more easily and carbonized bamboo is softer than regular bamboo.
- Look for brands that come with a lengthy warranty, to give you a sense of their durability.

**Cork:** Looking for something with a little give? Check out warm and cushy cork. I know peeling the bark off a 600-year-old tree sounds like a bad thing, but don't cry, tree huggers! Not a single cork tree is axed to get the cork. In fact, environmental organizations like the World Wildlife Fund (WWF) say that precious Mediterranean cork forests, and the endangered animals that dwell in them (like the Iberian lynx), will actually be threatened if we don't continue to buy cork. There's no denying it's not local and has to be shipped in, but at least it travels 50% fewer miles than bamboo from China. You can find cork floors in nearly every flooring shop these days, but you should really check out Quebec-based **DuroDesign**'s gorgeous cork tiles and click-together cork floor planks. They're made of 100% post-industrial recycled content from wine-stopper production and coated with four protective coats of low-VOC urethane (duro-design.com). Stay away from cork treated with antimicrobial products: Natural Cork brand floors come with triclosan-heavy Microban. Not good when triclosan is turning up in breast milk and is feminizing frogs.

$$ **Linoleum vs. Vinyl:** Faux tile, faux wood, faux marble. If a flooring style exists, they can fake it with vinyl (PVC). Even though people often refer to vinyl floors as linoleum, real linoleum floors (invented in the late 1800s) were quietly replaced by vinyl in the '50s. Too bad vinyl is considered super-polluting to manufacture, and the hormone-disrupting, plastic-softening phthalates used to soften it can build

up in household dust as the floors erode. Disturbingly enough, a 2009 Swedish study originally designed to connect the dots between the phthalates in vinyl floors and the allergies and asthma in children ended up finding, quite by accident, that infants or toddlers who lived in bedrooms with vinyl flooring were twice as likely to be diagnosed with autism five years later as kids that lived in bedrooms with wooden or linoleum floors. The same risks that kids of smoking moms have.

And note that until the '80s asbestos was commonly used in vinyl flooring, which means sanding this stuff is definitely a big no-no. If you're worried, order an asbestos testing kit online. Many say you're better off just covering it up with a new layer of flooring, but if you decide to rip it out, be sure to call in an asbestos abatement expert.

Naturalists will be relieved to learn that genuine natural linoleum is making a comeback, but don't worry, it doesn't look anything like the stuff in your mother's kitchen. Just check out all the funky patterns natural linoleum now comes in, making it a bit hit in the green scene thanks to brands like **Forbo Marmoleum** (themarmoleumstore.com, available at Home Depot stores). The extra-tough flooring is made of pine rosin, cork flour, jute and, yes, linseed oil (hence the "lin" in "linoleum"). And just like the good old days, a quality linoleum floor should last you, oh, 40 years.

Tiles: If cool is what you're going for, keep your eyes peeled for ceramic and glass tiles made with high recycled content, like **Coverings Etc.'s Eco-Terr** terrazzo tiles, made from up to 80% post-industrial recycled material and 10% post-consumer recycled content (coveringsetc.com and sipdistribution.ca). **EcoCycle** tiles by Crossville (crossvilleinc.com) have 40% recycled ceramic content, and **Terra Green Ceramics** tiles are all at least 55% recycled glass (terragreenceramics.com). **Interstyle** offers some beautiful recycled crackled glass tiles in gem-like hues (interstyle.ca). For more of a mosaic look, check out **Eco-Body** (quarrytile.com) and peruse all kinds of cool tile patterns in 100% recycled glass through **Sandhill Industries** (sandhillind.com). You'll find recycled glass terrazzo and

You want to overhaul your home but, who are we kidding, green reno materials don't come cheap. Here's where Habitat for Humanity's ReStores come in. It's like the Value Village of the home reno world where you can score second-hand items, including lumber, sinks, doors, windows, chandeliers, tiles, mantles and even nails and hooks for about half the retail price. They also get donations of unwanted extras from builders, contractors and do-it-yourselfers, as well as scratched and dented items, customer returns and discontinued stuff from retailers and manufacturers. If you're gutting your home or trashing parts of it, you can call them for free pick-up and get a charitable donation receipt in exchange. They have locations across the country, and all the money goes to the great cause of building homes for the less fortunate. For more info, go to **habitat.org** and follow the link to ReStores.

a full range of other flooring options at Ottawa's **The Healthiest Home** (thehealthiesthome.com), Riva's **The Eco Store** in Calgary (rivasecostore.com), Vancouver's **GreenWorks Building Supply** (greenworksbuildingsupply.com) and Toronto's **Green Design Studio** (greendesignstudio.ca) and **The Zero Point** (thezeropoint.ca).

**Concrete:** The pinnacle of modern loft-style flooring has got to be plain, hard **concrete**. It can seem pretty cold (especially when you consider that its main ingredient, cement, is one of the single most energy- and greenhouse gas–intensive industries in the world), but poured concrete floors are commonly used in über-green, passively heated homes since they absorb solar warmth so damn well. And, really, that concrete is already going to be there as a foundation under your wood/cork/bamboo regardless.

Ask around about concrete with recycled content. The only poured concrete with recycled content is the stuff that's cut with, say, 25% fly ash left over from a local coal plant (which technically adds "recycled" content to the concrete). **Eco-Cem** concrete tiles are made of 20% post-consumer and 40% post-industrial recycled content (coveringsetc.com; Eco-cem is available in Canada through Green Design Studio and the Zero Point). Green Spec lists several low-VOC concrete underlayments, sealers and more.

## CARPETS

All that soft, cushiony goodness feels so nice on your toes it can't be bad for us, right? Well, it depends. There's no denying that a few major players in the carpet industry have gone to great lengths to green themselves over the past decade. Some, like **InterfaceFLOR**, have even become posterboys for corporate sustainability (since '96, InterfaceFLOR's greenhouse gas emissions have purportedly plummeted 82%, its water use has dropped 75%, waste to landfill has fallen 66% and its energy use has also been scaled back; interfaceflor.com).

But by and large carpets are still mostly made of virgin petroleum-based fibres that require a massive amount of energy and water to make, not to mention all the hazardous air pollutants and VOCs released in the process.

Then, once you get them home, carpets act as a giant dust trap, pulling in all sorts of allergens. Now, industry players will say that's a good thing, that carpets are actually beneficial for wheezy children because they lock in particles and keep them from being kicked up into the air. Of course they don't tell you that carpets also lock in chemical contaminants given off by crumbling couches and dirty shoes — stuff like heavy metals, pesticides, fire retardants, even long-banned DDT (according to testing by the U.S. Environmental Protection Agency, University of Southern California and others). One researcher said you'd have to vacuum 25 times a week for several weeks to bring the level of those contaminants below safety standards! A little OCD, I know, but even the carpet peeps say you should vacuum twice a week to keep basic allergens down. If you've got

**You'd have to vacuum 25 times a week for several weeks to bring the level of contaminants below safety standards**

carpeting already, one thing's for sure: check your shoes at the door before you drag the dregs of the world onto your carpet.

Disposal: Wanna talk landfill clogging? A whopping 2 million tons of carpeting is trashed every year in North America. Luckily, most major carpet companies now have take-back programs. Some manufacturers, like Milliken, Shaw and InterfaceFLOR, have figured out how to make old carpet parts into new ones (the ideal scenario). Most, like DuPont, downcycle them into car parts, soundproofing and other products, though even DuPont is starting some carpet-to-carpet recycling now. Still, since the Carpet America Recovery Effort (CARE) was created in 2002 to help the industry meet carpet recycling goals, only about 5% of carpets get recycled. Some installers will take your old one away and recycle it for you. Though, admittedly, many will just toss them, since few recycling facilities exist here in Canada and carpets have to be shipped to the U.S. (there are six depots across Canada that act as holding and sorting centres for carpets on their way to the U.S). Be sure to press for details and ask about proper carpet recycling. And if you've moved into a home with an old mystery carpet of unknown origin, ask your municipality about your recycling options. Or call carpet companies like Beaulieu and ask them to recycle it for you. Of course, they'll charge you roughly $2.50 per square yard of carpet, but they should arrange a pick-up for you through a local dealer.

## CARPET BUYING GUIDE

Here's a four-step guide to buying your next carpet in a green way.

☐ 1: Figure Out What It's Made Of
  • Nylon: Nylon carpeting is considered the most durable, but it can be incredibly polluting to manufacture. The good news is that nylon 6 and even nylon 6,6 are now recyclable, and manufacturers like **Mohawk** (mohawkflooring.com) and **Shaw** (shawfloors.com) include up to 50% recycled content in some products. Milliken carries carpeting with as high as 80% refurbished post-consumer

nylon, but it's not available to residential customers. Annoying but true, many carpeting companies keep their greenest products and services for the office crowd.

- **Olefin (a.k.a. polypropylene or polyethylene) and polyester (a.k.a. polyethylene):** Although polypropylene (PP) and polyester (PET) rugs are more environmentally friendly to produce, they aren't as durable, and you can't always recycle them into new carpets when you're done with them (though that's starting to change). Mohawk's **EverStrand** line is made of 100% recycled pop bottles (PET), which at least gives your old cola bottles a second crack at life. Quebec-made **Beaulieu's Bliss** carpets all contain some recycled pop bottle fibre, turning roughly 1.6 billion plastic bottles per year into its Get Smart PET fibres (blissflooring.com). Their **Enviro Select** line is coming out with carpeting that's 100% recycled pop bottles. Over 35 pop bottles will go into every square yard of that carpet. Plus, Beaulieu's Enviro Select collection is manufactured with hydro and wind energy.

- **Corn Fibre (a.k.a. Bio-Fibre):** If you've spotted corn listed as one of the ingredients on new carpet, don't worry, you haven't wandered into the food aisle by accident. A few carpet manufacturers are starting to blend fibres made of corn sugar into the mix. In fact, corn sugar is being used to make all sorts of biodegradable plastics these days, including that biodegradable cup your smoothie may have come in if you purchased it from an eco-conscious juice bar. DuPont's corn polymer is now going into everything from car parts and cosmetics to, yes, carpets, including Mohawk's **SmartStrand** carpets. Being made of up 37% corn fibre, the rugs are touted as renewable, and they say one gallon of gasoline is saved for every seven square yards of carpet. Also, the company says greenhouse gas emissions from the production of Sorona are 63% lower than typical nylon carpet manufacturing. It all sounds fabulous, but corn-based materials do have their critics—loud ones. For one, using food for fuel and other non-essential products became a less welcome concept as basic crop prices began spiking (the skyrocketing price of corn sparked riots in Mexico in early 2008). Also, most companies won't guarantee that their fibres are made with corn that hasn't been genetically modified (not great, since enviros consider GMO crops to be serious ecosystem disruptors). **InterfaceFLOR** says its corn fibre–blended rugs are indeed GMO-free (interfaceflor.com). Best to ask.

• **Natural Fibres:** Skip the whole petroleum-heavy quagmire by resting your feet on carpeting made with fibres sustainably plucked from natural sources. **Jute** is one of the cheapest and strongest plant fibres nature has to offer (hell, we use the stuff to make rope), and this South Asian plant is commonly woven into durable, contemporary area rugs. **Sisal** is essentially the Mexican version of jute, now harvested all over the world, with much of it coming from Brazil, followed by Africa. Just note that wall-to-wall sisal is often synthetic because of complications with installing the natural kind in this format. You'll also see rugs made of woven dried **seagrass**, which is a flowering underwater plant. But you don't want seagrass harvested from the wilds on a mass scale, since the plant is threatened in many parts of the planet and the grasses offer important habitat for all sorts of fish. Many companies are now sourcing from China instead, where seagrass is being cultivated inland in flooded rice paddies.

**Merida Meridian** offers a stylish selection of rugs made with **hemp**, jute and **abaca** (a cousin of the banana plant) for everywhere from sleek living rooms to playful kids' rooms. They even have sexy shag rugs (meridameridian.com). **Fibreworks** has **coir** (coconut fibre), jute, sisal and more (fibreworks.com), as does **Interface** (interfaceglobal.com).

**Wool** is a classic natural material for carpeting. But most of the wool rugs and carpets hanging in flooring stores are treated with harsh moth-proofing chemicals, including the possible carcinogen naphthalene (for more on naphthalene, see Moths, page 47). To go chem-free, you'll have to check out the green design stores nearest you (see Resources: Green Home Storefronts). Or head online. **Nature's Carpet** sells insecticide-free wool area rugs and carpeting with jute and natural latex backing (naturescarpet.com), as does **Earth Weave** (earthweave.com). Contact the companies for local dealers.

If you're buying an Oriental rug, make sure it's fairly woven and free of child labour by looking for the **RugMark** logo. For a directory of retailers near you who offer **RugMark-certified rugs**, punch in your postal code at rugmark.org. **Ten Thousand Villages** also has 100% pure wool or silk-wool blends that are all sweatshop-free. Some of the rugs are dyed with natural pigments — just ask to be sure (rugs.tenthousandvillages.com).

## ☐ 2: Green Your Backing

Over half of a carpet's weight comes from the backing, so make sure to look into what it's made of.

- **PVC:** Stay away from PVC backing; although, as backing, it can be recyclable, it contains phthalates that could off-gas harmful chemicals throughout the life of the carpet. Plus, it releases persistent toxins when it's incinerated after you trash the carpet (or during a house fire, god forbid). Popular polyurethane backing, the main PVC-free alternative, is still quite polluting to manufacture but shouldn't give off any fumes inside your home.

- **Natural materials:** **Wool** and **jute** backings are your ideal alternatives, but can be a little tougher to find. **Eco Floors** (eco-floors.com) carries Jute High Performance Sound Control underlayment, as well as matting made of coir fibre (harvested from coconuts).

- **Recycled content:** Carpet padding is way easier to make out of recycled content than the carpet itself, so you should insist on high recycled content. Shaw makes 100% recycled Endurance II carpet cushioning using about 25 million pounds of carpet waste from its production each year. Milliken's backing system for carpet tiles contains 35% recycled content.

- **Low VOC:** Home Depot carries Eco Foam carpet and rug cushioning with a closed-cell water-, odour- and mould-repelling polyethylene fibre that eliminates the three VOC chemicals common to carpet cushions, but it's got zero recycled content.

### ☐ 3: Request No-VOC Glues
Glues and seam sealers can all give off smog-inducing, lung-irritating VOCs. Be sure to ask the person laying your carpet to use water-based, no- to low-VOC products that comply with the CRI IAQ testing program (that's the Carpet and Rug Institute Indoor Air Quality program to you). Peel-and-stick carpet tiles also minimize the amount of glue used on-site, although they do get their stick from somewhere. Keep windows cracked for a few days after carpets have been installed.

### ☐ 4: Ask About Finishes
Given all the stain-, soil- and microbe-repellent finishes that come with carpets these days, you'd think your rug is life-proof. Find out exactly what's in them before you decide whether you want these finishes in your home.

- **Antibacterial:** Sure, no one likes the sound of bacteria and mould breeding under your toes, but are antimicrobial finishes the answer? Well, the prime ingredient in Microban-treated floor pads is triclosan, that antibacterial chemical turning up in rivers, streams and breast milk, and linked to reproductive changes in frogs. Best to just avoid putting carpeting in areas prone to dampness like basements, washrooms and kitchens.
- **Stain repellents:** Thankfully, 3M, the maker of Scotchguard, decided to phase out its shockingly persistent liver-damaging signature ingredient, PFOS, in 2002. Thank god, too, because it was sticking to the blood of humans, polar bears, dolphins, birds—you name it. 3M is still using fluorochemicals to make its

211

trademark Scotchgard products, though it claims "3M's 'next generation' formulation has low potential to bioaccumulate." Notice they haven't said there's no chance that these will build up in your blood—just a low chance.

And what about Teflon-based finishes like Stainmaster? Well, they're made with and/or break down into PFOA, the very carcinogen being found in polar bears and bald eagles and now

## SQUARE TO SPARE: CARPET TILES

Who needs wall to wall when you can go square to square? Carpet tiles are the most sustainable option around because you need only replace heavily worn squares, not the whole carpet. Most, unfortunately, have no recycled content, including Milliken's Legato tiles. However, Milliken is a "carbon negative" manufacturer (thanks to its small hydro-electricity plant and 138,000 acres of forest), plus all of the carpets sent back to the company either go into new carpeting, get donated to charity, are recycled into new products or fire up kilns.

Your prime choice when it comes to recycled content is Interface's **FLOR Fedora** carpet tiles, which are made of low-VOC, 80% post-consumer recycled polyester (**flor.com**). FLOR also has amazing natural modular tiles made of

coconut-husk fibres (a.k.a. coir), dye-free wool or 35% GMO-free corn-based plastic. As long as you pick the non-vinyl backing option, you should be in the clear. When you've worn through a square, don't toss it—call Interface's customer care for info on recycling. By the way, FLOR tiles are secured with non-toxic adhesive dots in each corner, so you won't have to worry about fumes.

You can, theoretically, request carpet squares from Beaulieu's commercial line called Nexterra, with a backing that's 85% recycled pop bottles, automotive glass and computer screens. (Though the face fibre itself has only 25% recycled content at this point, there's more backing than face fibre by weight in commercial carpets, so it balances out.)

in 95% of North Americans. Unlike PFOS, PFOA-linked prod-ucts are still on shelves and will only be fully phased out by 2015. Of course, it's virtually impossible to get a new carpet that hasn't been treated with some sort of stain-repellent finish. Even those who aren't overtly using PFOAs in their finish anymore are find-ing trace amounts of PFOA as a by-product. Interface's Bentley Prince Street line reps say they're close to "a PFOA-free"

## WHAT'S THAT COMING OFF YOUR CARPET?

Carpet industry PR is chock full of contradictions. They'll tell you carpets have been formaldehyde-free for, oh, 20 years, but the other volatile organic compounds (VOCs) still in use are enough to warrant the Carpet and Rug Institute's quiet warning that exotic birds be removed from the area until any new smell is gone. They'll tell you any air-polluting, lung-irritating VOCs coming off your new carpet should dissipate within 48 to 72 hours, after which your floor covering is "essentially" VOC-free. Yet they also backhand-edly acknowledge that odours could actually linger for weeks, and if opening windows and vacuuming doesn't help, "try to have a hot water extraction done on the new carpet." Carpet brochures tend to, well, gloss over these kinds of details.

Rugs that meet the Carpet and Rug Institute's emissions standards have a Green Label logo on the back (for more details and a list of compliant products, check out **carpet-rug.com**). However, the national coor-dinator of the *Healthy Building News* openly dissed the industry-run program as greenwashing. The Green Label Plus program is relatively more hard-core, analyzing carpets for "chemicals of concern" (which aren't otherwise tested for), and there are 24-hour and 14-day emissions limits for dodgy chemicals like benzene, toluene and vinyl acetate, as well as moth-proofing naphtha-lene. It makes sure carpets meet California's stringent indoor air–quality standards for low-emitting commercial settings. The catch is, Green Label Plus is less commonly available to homeowners. Still, you can always ask if your rug meets Green Label Plus standards. All Beaulieu rugs do.

breakthrough. In the meantime, at the very least refuse any extra stain-repelling services (including Teflon Advance sprays). And if your carpet was treated with Scotchgard in 2002 or earlier, you might consider yanking it out, especially if you've got young kids crawling around on it.

- **Odour-absorbing:** Beaulieu makes a built-in odour neutralizer called Puralex that it claims will absorb and break down cigarette smoke/urine/fishy odours. In addition, it says independent tests using EPA-approved methods show that Puralex reduces total VOC emissions from, say, painted walls or furniture by 25% to 40% by absorbing odours from the air. Company reps say they're not at liberty to reveal the chemistry of Puralex, since it's proprietary, but they claim it's "similar to salt" and that's its "completely inert and harmless." Hard to give it the Ecoholic thumbs-up without more transparency from its maker.

## COOL CARPET FOR A WARM PLANET

Every phase of your carpet's lifecycle—from harvesting raw materials and manufacturing to shipping, vacuuming and finally recycling—contributes to global warming and Interface knows it. Which is why they've calculated the carbon footprint of all that and offset it all by funding clean wind farms through Native Energy and clean train technology. The carbon offsets come standard on all InterfaceFLOR products sold in North America (**interfaceflor.com**) and can be requested when you buy Interface's Bentley Prince Street line (**bentleyprincestreet.com**).

# PLUMBING

Okay, so not every retrofit is quite as ooh- and awe-inspiring as new countertops or floors, but the changes you make to your home's water systems are critical to your green cred. Some changes are quick and cheap, like swapping your shower head; others require a call to your plumber (like putting in a new low-flow toilet or drain water heat exchanger). But any and all water- and energy-conserving moves you make in this domain will be thoroughly appreciated by the planet. Plus, they should bring you pleasant surprises on bill payment day.

**Showers:** It's morning. You're standing in the shower and belting out the Bee Gees/Britney/Bowie like there's no tomorrow. While you're whiling away the time, any idea how many 1-litre bottles' worth of water are pouring on your head? If you've got an old shower head, anywhere from 15 to 30 bottles' worth each and every single minute. That's like 300 to 600 bottles for all you soakers taking 20-minute showers! A family of four can save 160,000 litres of water a year just by putting in low-flow shower heads. Truth is, in many parts of Canada, local plumbing codes and bylaws make low-flow heads mandatory, so you'll be hard-pressed to find a new shower head that's over 9.5 litres per minute, though many are closer to 5.

**Shower Spray Types:** Just because your shower head is low-flow doesn't mean you have to give up on water pressure. You just need to decide which pressure-boosting low-flow head you prefer.

- Atomizing shower heads: These push the water through at higher speeds, making for an invigorating shower without using more water. Warning: They get your shower curtain billowing and can also be a little harsh on the skin.
- Aerating shower heads: Same as above, but these use air to boost water pressure. The main complaint is that water cools faster.

## WATER-HOGGING SHOWER FEATURES

Not everyone's looking to save the planet when they get ready in the morning. That's why you'll see showers with 10 heads and why one salesman gave me a little nudge nudge wink wink and told me I could remove flow restrictors from my shower head if I wanted to beef up the pressure. Shocking, I tell you. But I know you would never do such a thing, dear *Ecoholic Home* reader, so here's a list of features to avoid.

• Removable flow restrictors: Some companies still make shower heads with removable flow restrictors so homeowners can boost their flow rate. Do not, I repeat, do not take advantage of these.

• Oversized shower stalls with multiple shower heads: The growing trend towards multiple jets is a way of getting around building code restrictions on flow rates. While oh so spa-like, you're doubling, tripling, even quadrupling your water consumption every single morning!

• Recirculating showers: These sound like a good idea because they cycle the water kind of like a fountain would (combined with multiple shower heads you get a full-body carwash-style shower), but the Kohler recirculating BodySpa uses a mind-blowing 300 litres of water per minute! And you're not allowed to lather up or use soap of any kind when it's on, so you still have to do your sudsing before or afterwards. It takes water wastage to a whole new stratosphere. At least the Quench brand uses only 4 litres of water when it's in its recirculating mode. It's designed for the person who likes to just zone out in the shower after washing—but with less guilt (although it comes with a mysterious sanitizer for the excessive Sanitize-Rinse cycle).

**Valves:** There are a few other ways to make sure your shower isn't wasting water, all through the valves. Some can be tacked on to existing shower heads, others come built in.

• Built-in volume-control valve: Allows you to increase or reduce the amount of water you're using so your shower isn't always on to full-blast.

• Shut-off or "lathering" valve: Lets you turn the water off while

## ITCHY SHOWERS? TRY CHLORINE FILTERS

All that chlorinated water is enough to make your skin itch. If you've got dry skin, eczema or anything of the sort, the chlorine will often make it worse. You could also be inhaling harmful trihalomethanes (a dodgy by-product of using chlorine in water). And, of course, there's the lead. Best to get a good carbon shower filter so you can breathe easy. You'll find these at green home stores—for listings, see Resources: Green Home Storefronts.

you're sudsing; can come built into the head or you can easily install one yourself. These aren't recommended in pre-1987 homes where no scald protection valve is installed, especially when it comes to the elderly or those who can't jump back quickly, since the water temperature can suddenly spike when you flick it back on.

- Built-in heat sensors: Does your water take forever to heat up? Feeling guilty about wasting water while you wait? **ShowerSmart** technology will slow your $H_2O$ to a trickle when it reaches the right temp. Press the resume bottom when you're ready and jump in. Flick the valve again when you're lathering up (evolveshowerheads.com).

**Showers vs. Baths:** I know, I know, you're either a shower person or a bath person. Bath people tend to get slapped across the face for their habits (sorry, but you can waste a lot of water in there), yet when does a bath become more sensible? (Besides when you're sharing it with another warm body.)

- Five-minute shower vs. bath: You're dealing with the champ of water conservation here, so clearly the 5-minute shower wins.
- Ten-minute shower vs. bath: Hmm, tough call. What are your specs? A typical half-full 80-litre bath would beat an old shower head and tie with a 9 litre/minute one (but not an

217

- Listening to a dripping faucet isn't just an excellent torture technique for the earth-conscious, it wastes over 20,000 litres a year! If a wrench won't stop a sniffling faucet, call a pro.
- A leaking toilet can silently spill a good 2,800 litres a month. Test your toilet by putting food colouring in the back tank. If it seeps to the bowl, time to call a plumber, pronto.
- Plug your tub before you start running the water for a bath.
- Okay, so this doesn't qualify as a leak, but turning off the taps while you brush your teeth will save you around 10 litres of water per minute!

ultra-low-flow head). If you've got a boat for a tub and a relic of a shower head, you're tied for last place.

- Fifteen-minute shower vs. bath: If you like a lot of water time, ' stay out of the shower and commune with the H$_2$O molecules while lying down.

**Toilets:** Fine, so low-flow toilets didn't always, ahem, get the job done. You ended up flushing twice just to whisk everything out of view. Well, the times they are a-changin', but not every discount low-flow toilet on the market will earn your trust. So which latrines actually keep everything out of sight and out of mind without flushing away our water supply? Here are a few winners and losers.

- The cheapest low-flows are often the poorest performers. No need to break the bank, but you'll want to spend at least $200 to $300.
- Homeowners and expert plumber reviewers like Terry Love (terrylove.com) are absolutely over the rainbow about the **TOTO** brand, regardless of the model. Though you will have to fork out a little more cash.
- Overall, pressure-assisted toilets (ones in which water is forced out with the help of compressed air) are the way to go if your home has

decent water pressure. But be warned, some of these high-pressure, low-flow toilets are a little louder as they flush (kind of like a quieter version of an airplane toilet). *Consumer Reports* gave top marks to the **Kohler Highline Pressure Lite K-3493** as well as the **Gerber Ultra Flush 21-312**, while the Eljer Patriot totally tanked.

- Standard gravity models are good for homes with low water pressure, but you'll have to spend a good $300 for top-performing low-flow gravity models, says *Consumer Reports*. Skimp on a cheap low-flow gravity and you might regret it.
- Many municipalities have low-flow toilet rebates, including North and West Vancouver ($50), Calgary ($50), Ottawa ($60 to $75), Toronto ($60 to $75) and Cape Breton ($100), as well as whole provinces like Saskatchewan and Manitoba ($50). Check

## IS YOUR WATER GIVING YOU A *HARD* TIME?

Having hard water (high in calcium and magnesium) can be a real headache—shampoo doesn't lather, detergent deposits build up on your clothes, soap scum rings form on tubs and, worse still, limescale deposits can clog hot water pipes. But you shouldn't get a water softener unless you really need one (and tests prove your water hardness is above 121 mg/litre). Why? Well, water softeners not only waste a lot of water (545 litres of water for every 4,500 delivered), they add a lot of salt to the system. Not good for anyone with kidney problems or high blood pressure and not good for farmers who might use municipal waste water to irrigate crops (which explains why many U.S. states have partial bans on softeners).

If your water is so hard you can barely get clothes clean, look for fully automated water-efficient softeners like **Aquamaster** that sense the hardness of the water and use less salt and water in the processing. FYI, some offer potassium chloride as an alternative, but it can still come with health risks for those with kidney disease or diabetes. Better to have a separate line running to your kitchen tap so you're not drinking softened water. P.S. Magnetic softeners have little scientific backing.

Take all that fresh, filtered H$_2$O you wash with, then banish it down the drain forever. No wonder Canadians are the second-biggest water consumers in the world, right behind the U.S. Now, let's back up a moment and imagine what the world would be like if you saved that water that runs down your shower, your sinks and your washing machine and used it instead to flush your toilets and nourish your garden. Greywater systems do just that—and they'll save you 35% to 40% on your annual water bill. Price will depend on your storage capacity (from 150 to 450 litres) and how many people you have consuming water in your house. Montreal-based **Brac Systems' Greywater** pumps were voted one of the top 10 green building products of 2007 by *Sustainable Industries Magazine* (**bracsystems.com**). The system will cost you $1,800 to $2,800, plus installation. An average family of four could save over 80,000 litres every year. That's a whole swimming pool's worth! New water supply lines for your toilets will need to be installed, and some of your drains will need to be rerouted. Unless you're Bob Villa, call a pro. Oh and by the way, not all building codes permit greywater systems, so it's best to check with city hall before you start ordering.

with your home town and province. Also, the federal ecoENERGY Retrofit program is now offering $65 for low-flow or dual-flush toilets.

 • Renters take note: you can reduce the flow of your loo by adding a cheapy toilet dam (available at hardware stores) to the tank— or just fill up a 1-litre water bottle and place it back there. But be sure that it doesn't obstruct the flushing mechanism or you're going to start having problems.

# HOT WATER HEATERS

Like Joni said, you don't know what you got till it's gone, and when hot water dries up we mourn the loss immediately (especially if you're halfway through lathering your hair). Canadian households suck up more energy washing dirty hair, dirty dishes and dirty socks in warm water than almost anything else. But if your showers are running cold, the tank is leaking or your hot water looks rusty, it might be time to send that water heater packing, especially if it's electric. Besides, if your water heater is over 10 years old, it's only half as efficient as it was in its prime.

> If your water heater is over 10 years old, **it's only half as efficient** as it was in its prime

Conventional Storage Water Heaters: In the market for a new water heating system and going with a traditional storage tank model? Know that you're wasting a ton of energy keeping a tank full of water scalding hot day and night. No wonder a whopping 20% to 25% of your energy bills goes towards heating water. If you're browsing for a new water heater, here are some tips on shopping for a greener model. (Just know that all electric water heaters are inherently inefficient, and are particularly guilt-inducing if you live in a coal-heavy province.)

- Natural gas models should come with electric ignition (so you can skip having a pilot light on all the time) as well as condensing heat exchangers.
- Look for factory-installed heat traps, which prevent unwanted flow of hot water through inlet and outlet pipes (these can be added to old tanks for $30 if they don't have 'em).
- Condensing storage hot water heaters are about 40% more efficient than basic models.
- Energy Star is just coming out with water heater standards, so keep your eyes peeled.
- Remember: the cheapest storage water heater might be the most costly to maintain over its lifetime.
- Dump your dusty old domestic hot water heater and trade it in for a condensing hot water heater with an Energy Factor (EF)

of 0.94 or better and the feds will dole out $375 under their ecoENERGY Retrofit program. Some provinces, like Ontario and B.C., will match that, so check. Note that rebates are subject to change. (EF indicates a water heater's overall energy efficiency over a typical day. In Canada, EF is determined by Canadian Standard Association test methods.)

**Solar Hot Water:** see Powering, page 265.

**Tankless / On-demand / Instantaneous Hot Water Heaters:** You know that bulky hot water storage tank hogging up all that space in your basement? Well, that is just so 1989. These days, hot water heaters are the size of a large briefcase (say 10 by 6.5 centimetres). Instead of a bloated tank of water heated up to 60°C every minute of

---

## CHEAP 'N' EASY WAYS TO SEE HOT WATER SAVINGS

If you've got an old electric storage tank–style heater that heats water 24/7, and you can't afford to switch to tankless or you're a renter, you can save up to 12% on your bills by installing a timer that turns off your heater at night and when you're not home (this won't be as effective on natural gas heaters).

Regardless of whether your tank is electric or natural gas, be sure to add a cheap water heater blanket around your tank to help insulate it. Unless your water heater's storage tank already has a hard-core layer of insulation around it (at least R-24), adding some insulation can seriously reduce all the heat that's wasted while it sits there in standby mode, waiting for someone to take a shower. For less than $20, buy a water heater blanket from your local hardware store and save another 4% to 10% on your water heating costs.

P.S. Installation is a little tricky on natural gas modes, so you might need the help of a pro.

P.P.S. Once you've got the extra insulation on there, don't set the thermostat above 54°C on an electric water heater—the wiring could overheat.

the day, tankless systems heat water when you ask for it, on demand. And they use up to 50% less energy doing so. Plus, these small wall-mounted systems should last twice as long as tank systems, since they're at low risk of corrosion. There are just a few things you need to figure out before you shed your tank.

- Gas-fired tankless heaters generally put out more water per minute than cheaper electric models, making them better for families; just make sure to pick one with an electric ignition device so you don't waste energy keeping a pilot light lit.
- If you go for gas, make sure your current gas line will meet the requirements of your new gas-fired tankless water heater. You might need a bigger flue to vent it.
- Smaller tankless heaters won't necessarily cut it if you want to take a shower and run the dishwasher at the same time. Depending on your heating needs, you might want to ask for larger whole-house tanks (or just stagger your showers and dishwasher load, for goodness' sake). Some householders also add a point-of-use tankless system under the kitchen or bathroom sink so they don't have to wait 30 seconds for hot water to come up through the basement pipes.

- Get $375 back from the feds' ecoENERGY Retrofit program when you replace your domestic hot water heater with an Energy Star instant gas-fired tankless water heater that has an Energy Factor of 0.90 (ditto for Ontario, and B.C. will give you $310).

**Drain-water Heat Recovery (a.k.a. Heat Recovery Water Preheaters):** Ever think about how much energy is pouring down the drain every time you take a hot shower? Well, 80% to 90% of the energy used to heat water in your home ends up glugging away. Enter drain-water heat recovery systems/exchangers. They basically capture the heat in shower, bath, dishwasher and/or washing machine water and transfer that warmth to incoming cold water by adding a super-conductive copper drainage pipe that coils around in incoming cold water line. It's easily installed in about 50% of homes, according to

Wondering which retrofits and upgrades will bring you the most energy and cash savings? Just call up a green home auditor. They'll suss out everything from your heating and hot water system to your windows and walls. They do a "blower door" test that depressurizes your house to track down drafts and leaks. Then they'll send you a checklist of recommendations on how to improve your home's energy efficiency, along with a list of federal and provincial rebates to help you pay for those changes. You can choose to do as many or as few of them as you like, but at the end of the day you can qualify for up to $5,000 in rebates through Natural Resources Canada's ecoENERGY Retrofit program (and an additional $5,000 from provinces like B.C. and Ontario). Rebates are subject to expiry, so act fast. For more info on federal and provincial rebates, see Resources: Rebates and Incentives Guide.

Montreal's Eco-GFX Heat Exchangers. Basically, you just need access to at least 105 to 112 centimetres of vertical drain pipe, anywhere below your shower (a floor or more down). The majority of people find it in the basement. They can even be installed centrally in condos and apartment buildings if anyone's interested in lobbying their building for green changes.

These simple copper coils should increase warm water output from 25% to 50% by preheating the water. And all y'all with solar hot water systems crying about overcast skies, you'll be happy to know that these systems should extend the days a solar system can provide hot water by 100%. These are also great if you have a small hot water tank, tankless water heating or a geothermal system.

FYI, these babies are totally passive, so they require no added energy to run and they have a maintenance-free life expectancy of 50 years. Plus, they extend the life of your water heater by taking some of the burden off it. Prices for drain-water heat recovery systems range from $600 to $1,000 installed. Installation is cheaper in new homes. They should pay for themselves within two to six years. Canadian brands eligible for a federal rebate can be found at gfxstar.ca, watercycles.ca, retherm.com and renewability.com.

$$ Install one of these handy heat suckers and get up to $165 back from the feds. Ontario will match that, B.C. will give you $80 towards it, Saskatchewan will give you $150 and Quebec's Gaz Métro clients will get up to $400 back through its energy-efficiency fund. Plus, installing one of these devices should slice your water heating costs down 30% to 50%. Considering water heating hogs up a quarter of your home's energy bills, we're talking one seriously good deal.

## WINDOWS

Imagine a house without windows? I think they call that prison. Even a view of a brick wall is better than no view at all. Studies show that patients who get to look out a pane onto greenery recover way more quickly than those who don't. Not that windows are all about looks. A good window shields you from winter chills, summer swells, drafts, con-

> A good window shields you from **winter chills, summer swells, drafts, condensation and street noise**

densation, street noise—the works. If yours ain't cuttin' it and you've got the budget to move beyond weatherstripping and caulking guns, consider this: switching to high-performance windows can cut your heating bills by up to 18%. Overnight. And since these suckers should last you over 20 years, you'll want to make sure you invest in some good-quality ones with all the right features.

Frames: Aluminum frames seem to be vanishing from cold climes since more efficient vinyl swooped in to dominate sales. Vinyl frames are considered more efficient than aluminum (though less durable). But really, aluminum and PVC both tank cradle-to-grave life-cycle assessments (see The Problem with PVC sidebar, page 228), and vinyl can

225

Who can afford all new windows? Here are some affordable tips on for-
tifying what you've already got.

- Let there be light: Leave south- and west-facing windows uncovered during the day to let in the warming sunlight, and batten down the hatches
with insulating double- or triple-celled honeycomb blinds at night (if you
want something really hard-core, check out **cozycurtains.com** or
**windowquilt.com**).
- E-talk: Low-E coating (see below) doesn't just come on new windows. You
can get the invisible polyester film version to apply yourself. Just make
sure you don't get the tinted kind designed for office buildings in sunny
climes.
- Caulk and strip: A good caulking and weatherstripping job will taper your
heat loss by 25% to 50%.
- Be a storm trooper: If you can't afford new high-performance windows,
then look into the cost of storm windows.

seriously vary in quality. Classic wood frames have excellent insulating
value, but the high-quality wood needed is harder to come by. Go for the
FSC-certified kind by **Loewen** (loewen.com) and **Paramount Windows**
(paramountwindows.com). Your greenest pick, though, is probably
durable and energy-saving **fibreglass**, which does especially well on the
energy front if hollow sections are filled with insulating foam (accurate-
dorwin.com, duxtonwindows.com, inlinefiberglass.com and ther-
motechfiberglass.com, which has 15% recycled content, are good
Canadian sources).

**Low-E Coating:** Low-E coating is a thin, invisible metallic layer
applied directly to the windowpane. This is important because it allows
the sun's rays in but doesn't let heat pass, keeping the warmth locked
in come December and locked out come July. In fact, just adding a
low-E coating to a double-glazed window gives you the same insulation
value as a standard triple-glazed window.

**Gas-filled:** They sound like villains Superman might have battled, but argon and krypton are actually inert gases that fill the space between sealed panes, preventing heat loss. Argon is the most affordable upgrade. Krypton is a little more effective and works best with triple-glazed windows.

**Glazed:** Glazes are just another word for panes. Most Canadians have double-glazed, a.k.a. double-pane, windows. Single-glazed windows are just so 1889 and should be updated pronto! A triple-glazed window with regular glass and no added features reduces solar heat gain in summer by a good 20% compared to a single-glazed window.

**Fixed Windows:** Fixed windows (that don't open) are better sealed, but you definitely want to have at least one window that opens per room, in my opinion, so you're not stuck relying on air conditioners just because you can't get a breeze. With two open windows on opposite ends of the room, you should get a decent cross-current.

$\$ Energy Rating:** An Energy Rating (ER) number tells you how efficient your whole window is, not just the glazing or the frame (Natural Resources Canada's Office of Energy Efficiency says 11 is a good number for operable types—a.k.a. windows that open—and +2ish is good for fixed windows).

## SCREEN PLAY: PATIO DOORS

You don't have to rip out an old patio door to beat the cold. If it's in decent shape, dampen any drafts by adding weatherstripping and replacing the gaskets. If you don't even open the thing in winter, shut 'er down with a removable sealant. $\$ Swap your existing patio doors for Energy Star–qualified ones and you should get $40 per unit through the feds' ecoENERGY Retrofit program.

## THE PROBLEM WITH PVC: DEBATE UPDATE

You cannot find a plastic much more maligned than PVC (vinyl). Okay, fine, polycarbonate baby bottles heavy in estrogen-mimickers aren't winning popularity contests either. Still, PVC has had its share of bad press: PVC blinds shed lead dust (since lead is used as a stabilizer). PVC shower curtains give off hormone-disrupting phthalates (used as a plastic softener). And PVC toys? A little bit of both. But what about building materials (which make up over half of all vinyl purchased)? There's no denying that the building block of PVC, vinyl chloride, is not only a known carcinogen, but also creates dangerous bioaccumulative dioxins in the manufacturing process and when incinerated at low temperatures (as in crappy municipal incinerators).

Industry and enviros have been having a war of words on this front for years now and it's getting messy. Lots of greener homes are built with energy-efficient vinyl windows, and many argue that the energy savings they offer are worth the eco-price tag (plus, the hard vinyl should be relatively innocuous in this form/location). When the U.S. Green Building Council, which runs the LEED program, first put out a draft stating as much, its conclusions disappointed many anti-PVCers, who subsequently questioned the USGBC's methodology and source selection. They demanded a recount of sorts. Well, the council issued its final report on the matter in 2007 and it stuck by its stance that vinyl windows, for instance, are more efficient than aluminum frames and don't create enough of a hazard to homeowners to warrant a switch (unlike the case with vinyl floors, which they trashed). Too bad they didn't use the opportunity to remind people that there are greener choices than both vinyl and aluminum to pick from (like insulated fibreglass windows). Regardless, the public isn't digging PVC's dodgy potential—especially as studies have emerged linking vinyl flooring to autism in children (see page 204) and PVC piping to lead in drinking water. No surprise, then, that more and more companies continue to phase out PVC from their product line. For vinyl-less building materials, head to **healthybuilding.net/pvc/alternatives.html**.

## NEW WINDOW CAUTION

I've heard a few tales of woe from troubled homeowners who forked out for new windows only to find their home quickly grew colder than it was before. What happened? Well, for one, you have to keep in mind that not all new windows are good windows. And very importantly, quality windows can also be poorly installed, leaving you with unwanted drafts. Make sure to get references from your window installers before you give them the go-ahead.

Before you empty your bank account redoing all your windows, the good people at Green$aver recommend doing a heavy round of draft-proofing (see page 239), as well as insulation boosting (see Insulation, page 253) before you decide on whether you still need new windows (although single-pane windows should go, asap).

Energy Star windows, doors and skylights will save you money by reducing your energy costs up to 12%. They often come with longer warranties. When you pick Energy Star–qualified windows, you'll typically save up to $500 a year in utility bills when replacing single-pane windows or $100 a year over existing double-pane, clear glass windows. Not only that, but the feds will give you back $40 per Energy Star window; Ontario will match that; Quebec's Gaz Métro will give you up to $500 in rebates towards those windows; and BCers will be happy to know Energy Star windows are PST-exempt. Check with your home province and utility for grants.

## SIDING

There comes a time in every building's life when a major overhaul is needed and a paint job just won't do the trick. If you're looking to re-side your home, there are dozens of options to choose from, but which are actually green? For one, forget vinyl. It may be the most popular material around for siding, but it's also made with the most scorned plastic of all: PVC (see the Problem with PVC sidebar, opposite).

The full life-cycle cost of manufacturing this stuff just isn't worth it, even though it's probably your cheapest bet. Know that most siding has minimal insulation value (with R-values of less than one). If you're redoing the siding on your home, you might want to pick an option you can throw rigid foam board insulation under, like metal or wood siding, which can turbo-boost your insulation's R-value from 1 to 50 in no time. **Cedar Ridge** makes the only siding certified by Energy Star, and it has an insulating value four times that of most other sidings. Trouble is, it's impossible to find in Canada. Sorry!

**Polypropylene (a.k.a. Faux Wood/Stone/Brick):** If you're looking for something comparable to vinyl, polypropylene (PP) is a somewhat better option. PP doesn't have the same bad rap that PVC does, although it's still made from petroleum-based plastic. It's said to be more durable than vinyl and can be moulded to look like wood or brick shingles. (**Nailite** makes some and claims to be green since they're tree-free: nailite.com). I couldn't find a brand that had any recycled content though.

**Solid Wood:** Solid wood siding shingles can be a sustainable (though higher-maintenance) option, but only if you find a brand that gets its wood through the Forest Stewardship Council. Quebec-based **Maibec** sells quality spruce siding made with some FSC-certified content. But if you want 100% certified wood, you'll have to special-order it (maibec.com). By the way, it comes with a 50-year warranty.

Reclaimed wood siding is made from high-quality timber salvaged from the inside of old barns and other buildings. Don't worry, they're not giving you the weathered exterior stuff, unless you want that look (wood-source.com, secondwindtimber.com or logsend.com).

**Metal:** Old-fashioned aluminum or steel can be really energy-intensive to make and polluting to mine, but most of the new stuff is high in recycled content, so it's actually lower in embodied energy (energy used to make a material) than vinyl or composite wood. Plus, it can be recycled should someone choose to tear it down in 50 years. If you go for metals, ask about recycled content.

**Stucco/Concrete:** Traditional stucco lasts a hell of a long time and is very low-maintenance, but, again, concrete is an extremely energy-intensive material (and synthetic petrochemical-based stuccos can be dodgy upkeep-wise, so I'd stay away).

**Fibre Cement:** Fire-, insect-, weather- and mould-resistant fibre-cement siding (a mix of cement, sand and up to 10% wood fibres) is a decent choice, despite the energy- and greenhouse gas–intensive cement content. It wins green points for super durability, plus it looks like wood and is reasonably priced. Look for brands with some recycled content, like **CertainTeed**'s fibre cement siding with 30% post-industrial recycled fly ash (certainteed.com).

**Brick and Natural Stone:** Clay brick and stone are beautiful and durable choices but also involve digging up the landscape (a.k.a. quarrying), which isn't always welcomed by environmentalists. Reconstituted bricks and stone (made of a mix of silica, aggregate and concrete) minimize the quarry problem but replace it with woes associated with energy-intensive concrete.

**Paper:** Hard to believe, but you can clad the outside of a building with a slick product made of 50% post-consumer paper and FSC-certified wood. Just check out **Rainscreen** by **PaperStone**. PaperStone Certified is made of 100% FSC-certified, post-consumer recycled paper and is bound with a proprietary water-based resin with cashew shell (paperstoneproducts.com).

# ROOFING

Having a roof over your head is about as fundamental a human need as you can get. Now, a good roof can go unnoticed for decades. But if things go south, the quality of the materials used on top of your house can degrade the quality of life inside that home faster than you can sing "Raindrops keep falling on my head." If it's time for a new roof, I'd suggest staying away from typical asphalt shingles. Not only do these black tar slabs bake your home come summertime (subsequently cooking whole cities through what's known as the "urban heat island effect"; go for lighter shades like grey instead), they have serious durability issues. That explains why 11 million tons of these petroleum-based flaps end up in landfill every year in North America. Why bother when you can take your pick of sustainable options?

## HEY ROOFER MAN, CAN YOU RECYCLE MY SHINGLES?

Got a new roof coming in? What are you planning on doing with your old one? Bet you haven't put too much thought into it. Well, shredded asphalt shingles can be used in gravel road dust suppression, hot-patch road repairs, even for paved paths in nature reserves. Tell your contractor you'd like to help keep Canada's 1.25 million tons of asphalt roofing out of the landfill and recycle it if possible. Sure it costs more, which is why Nova Scotia compensates construction and demolition companies to divert that junk from municipal landfills. Your province may not be so wise, but it's worth asking if your shingles can get a second shot at life instead of clogging the dump forever.

**Recycled Plastic/Rubber:** Ontario-made **EnviroShake** shingles are made of 95% recycled plastics, wood waste and rubber from old tires. They kind of look like cedar shake, they're maintenance-free and you can install them yourself, if you're handy (otherwise, a contractor can do it for you). And they come with a 50-year warranty. You can get them from $3.50 per square foot (see enviroshake.com for retailers). Calgary-based **Euroshield** roofing products are made with up to 70% recycled tire crumble, come in a wide range of colours and also have a 50-year warranty (euroshieldroofing.com).

**Steel Roof:** Why have a black, matte, heat-absorbing roof when shiny **galvalume steel** sheets reflect the sun so beautifully? Steel is made with at least 25% recycled content (interestingly enough, all steel is made with some recycled steel), it'll last you a good 50 years, and in its dying days, it can be recycled. Plus, you can install it directly over your old asphalt roof (consult your roofer about this first). Green home builders/designers like **Solares** are big fans. Expect the installed cost to be around $3 to $5/square foot. If you don't like the look of smooth galvalum, plenty of Canadian companies put out pretty steel shingles. Just google for dealers near you.

**Green Roof:** If you've got a relatively flat roof and a few extra grand, forget shingles, baby, and go for drought-resistant, low-maintenance sedum grasses or ready-grown grass tiles. A green roof keeps your house cooler than a black roof, lowers your power bills and pumps clean oxygen into the air. You'll definitely need a pro to figure out if your roof is structurally sound and to prep it for planting. **ELT Easy Green** will do it from $15 a square foot, but they also have DIY options for about $10 (eltgreenroofs.com). **Verticiel** does green roofs as well as moss roofs and living walls (verticiel.ca). **Natvik Ecological** offers both green roof design services and pre-grown vegetated mats (roofgarden.ca). **ZinCo Canada** does a more landscaped green roof/roof garden (zinco.ca).

**Solar Shingles (a.k.a Building Integrated Photovoltaic Panels):** These look sort of like roofing tiles (they sit flush with your roof) but act like solar panels, feeding electricity into the house whenever the sun shines. **UNI-SOLAR** discontinued its roof shingles and is now making flexible lightweight laminate rolls that get glued onto your roof (uni-solar.com). They look slick and should be more durable and weatherproof than conventional panels, which are often coated with glass. The thing is, they cost a good deal more than regular solar panels (which are pricey to begin with) and unlike conventional solar panels, they can't be mounted over existing shingles. But hey, if you have a good south-facing roof and you're planning on redoing your roof anyway, these might be for you.

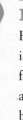

## APPLIANCES: REPAIR OR REPLACE?

From sewing machines to stoves, appliances don't grow into a ripe old age like they used to. (Hence your grandfather's mutterings.) Nonetheless, any appliance that's been around since bell-bottoms first lost out to skinny jeans should be in a museum. They're power relics, sucking back more than their fair share of energy. But other than scrapping appliances that come in avocado, teal or dijon, how do you know when it's time to stop repairing and show your stove the door? Here are some simple signs. (P.S. When your appliances are beyond repair, call your municipality to find out how you can have them recycled.)

**Washing Machines:** Show toploaders the door, no questions asked. Even newer ones are serious eco-laggards.

**Clothes Dryer:** If it ain't broke, don't toss it, especially if it's got a moisture sensor. Otherwise, technology hasn't changed that much. If it breaks down, call the repair guy. Or just start line-drying full-time.

**Fridge:** Anything from another millennium and you should consider upgrading to a much more efficient model. There were major efficiency rule changes in 2001, so anything older than that should be placed on the high-priority replacement list. You're wasting between $120 and $150 per year in electricity. Many utility providers/municipalities/provinces have offered rebates on new Energy Star refrigerators if you turn your old one in, so be sure to ask.

**Dishwasher:** No blue and white Energy Star logo on yours? Show it the door. Until a few years ago 92% of dishwashers came with the Star of approval, so yours is clearly behind the times. Replacing a dishwasher manufactured before 1994 with an Energy Star–qualified dishwasher can save you more than $30 a year in utility costs. Check for rebates on new Energy Star models in your area.

**Stove:** These loyal servants last us 18 years on average. If it's got convection and self-cleaning features, I'd stick with it till it croaks.

**Air Conditioners:** If it's kept you cool for more than 10 summers, it's starting to lose its cool. Make sure this baby gets taken to the hazardous waste depot so coolants don't seep into landfill. If you swap your old central a/c for a new Energy Star one, you could qualify to get a $250 rebate from the feds, plus your home province might have additional rebates (Ontario, for instance, offers an additional $250 for such a swap). A window a/c swap would slip an extra $25 into your wallet.

## TOP 8 RETROFITS

It can be hard to figure out what retrofit to do first. So here are some suggestions:

**#1** Draft-proof your house.

**#2** Add extra insulation, first in your attic, then everywhere else (like wall cavities and crawl spaces).

**#3** If you need to replace leaky old windows, check out new triple-glazed gas-filled ones (or any high-performance windows). And make sure they're installed properly.

**#4** Replace your 10-year-old fridge (the biggest energy-sucking appliance in your home) with an Energy Star model; upgrade your appliances based on trusty repair or replace advice, opposite.

**#5** Swap your old, dying water heater with a tankless or solar model.

**#6** Get yourself a good low-flow toilet(s) and other water-saving devices.

**#7** Turn in that 20-year-old furnace for a new high-efficiency one.

**#8** Repair your old fireplace (by adding a heat shield to old chimneys and flue pipes), replace it with a high-efficiency wood stove, or just remove the whole drafty thing by sealing up your chimney.

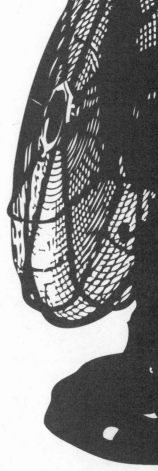

# HEATING & COOLING

## Oh baby it's cold outside
### (or inside, if you've cranked the a/c)

## Don't ask me how those early

pioneers made it through the seasons with little more than a basic roof over their head and a furry hat. But you can bet few of today's Canadians have the hardiness to suffer from January to July without a good heating and cooling system (even if that cooling system is nothing but a fan and a cold shower). So how do you keep your home's temperature stable without burning up the planet? Read on.

# HEATING BASICS

Remember when you could play all day in the cold, wet snow and not even realize your pants were soaked and your toes were glued to your socks? Clearly, Canadians tend to lose that robustness as we age. Just look at the way we crank the hell out of our heating systems come winter, helping to secure us a top spot as one of the world's largest energy users. Well, folks, it's time to take it down a notch and prove that we can weather our winters without melting the ice caps.

**Programmable Thermostat:** If you have forced air, there's no excuse not to have a programmable thermostat (in fact, they even make some for electric baseboards). Still, only 4 in 10 Canadian households with a thermostat have the programmable kind, according to StatsCan. You know what that means for the other 60% of you: time to go shopping! You can set yours so that your furnace kick-starts in the morning before you get up, cools down when you're gone and warms up again before you come home from work. You can get a good one for around $40, and it'll easily pay for itself within a year

$$ According to research by the Canadian Centre for Housing Technology, just reducing the temperature at night to 18°C from, say, 22°C will mean a 6.5% savings in natural gas, while dropping it down to 16°C at night and when no one's home during the day can add up to a 13% savings in gas use. Not bad for three minutes spent programming the thing.

- Energy Star–qualified thermostats have weekend and weekday settings and at least four possible temperature settings (wake, day, evening, sleep). The thermostat should arrive with pre-programmed settings if you're too lazy to do it yourself.
- As a general rule, you can save 2% on your heating bill for every 1°C you turn down the thermostat.

$$ **Weather Stripping and Caulking:** Now, you could call in a pro to perform a blower door test to track down leaks, or just turn off the furnace, close all windows, pull out an incense stick and go

hunting. It's not as thorough and won't count as an "official" energy audit if you're gunning to get in on the federal rebate program (see Resources: Rebates and Incentives Guide), but if your incense smoke shifts when you hold your stick in front of windows, doors, baseboards, electrical sockets and switches, and/or plumbing fixtures, you need to get moving on some super-simple (and affordable) insulation techniques.

- The cheapest weatherstripping is made of felt or foam, but unfortunately it ain't so hot at blocking cold winds.
- Weatherstripping tape is perfect for the tops and bottoms of windows, door frames and random cracks, and is especially handy for low-wear areas. It gets the job done for a rock-bottom price. Plus, you can just remove it come spring.
- Silicone caulking should be applied to all joints in a window frame and the joint between the frame and the wall (not the moveable/sliding parts).
- Stop gaps under your doors with an aluminum door shoe or door sweep.
- Electric outlet seals will cost you under $5 for a set of two and will seal up the drafts coming from around your plugs and switches.

## FURNACES

If your conventional furnace keeps switching on and off all the time, it's probably way too big for your purposes (in fact, that's a sign it's not running at peak efficiency). According to the Canada Mortgage and Housing Corporation (CMHC), a properly sized conventional or mid-efficiency furnace should run almost continuously during the coldest days of the winter if it's going to operate at peak efficiency. Sounds counterintuitive, but the truth is most Canadian furnaces are just too big for their houses. Although that's not the case with high-efficiency condensing gas furnaces.

**If your furnace is more than 20 years old, it's time to save up your pennies and invest in a new one**

If your furnace is more than 20 years old, it's time to save up your pennies and invest in a new one. Seeing as a modern condensing gas furnace is, oh, 33% to 38% more efficient than your old beater, you'll save money in the long run and your toes will thank you. Natural gas is definitely the cleaner and more efficient option (when you compare it to oil furnaces or dirty electric heat), but it's still a polluting fossil fuel that has to be dug up and piped in across sensitive northern habitats. That means it shouldn't be squandered by cranking up your thermostat to tank-top temperatures!

### Tips for Furnace Shopping:

- Look for furnaces with the Energy Star label—they're up to 15% more efficient than other models in stores. That means they cost more upfront, but you'll be making that money back when it comes time to pay your bills, plus they increase the resale value of your home and, naturally, reduce your greenhouse gas emissions.
- Pick a furnace with a long heat exchanger warranty, say, 20 years or more (the CMHC says if the manufacturer is willing to back this expensive part, it's a good sign).

- Get yourself an Energy Star gas furnace and the feds will give you anywhere from $375 to $750 in cash back (through their ecoENERGY Retrofit program), depending on how efficient it is. (You'll also get up to $750 back if you buy a good Energy Star boiler.) Many provinces and municipalities will also give you a rebate on a new furnace—check Resources: Rebates and Incentives Guide for details.

**Filters:** Look, a furnace filter won't magically rid your house of dust, but it does help reduce the amount of airborne particles kicking around. But if you don't change it regularly, your airflow could be reduced to a trickle. Furnace filters should be replaced or, if you have washable ones, rinsed out, every three months at the very least, though once a month is ideal. Dirt build-up here will mean your furnace can't do its job as well.

- Look for the MERV (Minimum Efficiency Reporting Value) rating on your filter; the higher the rating, the better.

• Some filters work better than others. The best-performing filters, according to CMHC testing, were 5-millimetre premium media filters and HEPA bypass filters. Actually, when *Consumer Reports* rated air purifiers, it also tested a few furnace filters and found **3M Filtrete 1700** (around $20) and **3M Filtrete Ultra Allergen Reduction 1250** (around $16) did almost as good a job at removing dust as expensive air purifiers!

---

## THE NEO OF FURNACES

Take the blue pill and you can go back to your regular old furnace. Take the red pill and you'll learn all about **The Matrix**, the complete furnace, water-heating and ventilation system from New Brunswick's NTI (NY Thermal Inc.). What is it exactly? The all-in-one appliance folds in a gas-fired furnace and boiler, an on-demand (a.k.a. tankless) water heater and a heat-recovery ventilator (which sucks heat out of stale air being ventilated to the outside and transfers it to incoming fresh air), plus it's pre-wired for air conditioning. Really, it's ideal for use in houses built from scratch, as well as retrofit jobs where owners are hoping to put in radiant floor heating. The boiler element will heat the water for use in the floor pipes, and the furnace components can still blow air through your ducts in areas where you don't have radiant heating. It also doubles as a pool heater in summer (if you've got a pool). The award-winning system was voted top 10 building material of 2008 by the respected peeps at Building Green (**buildinggreen.com**). And it's no wonder when it uses less energy and creates fewer greenhouse gases than equivalent systems (**nythermal.com**).

---

**Ducts:** So someone's trying to convince you to get your ducts cleaned. Seems like a good idea, since you can't check for yourself, but is it really necessary? In the 1990s, the Canada Mortgage and Housing Corporation and the U.S. Environmental Protection Agency tested houses and duct performance before and after a round of duct cleaning.

And surprise! There was pretty much no difference to airflow or dust reduction. Don't waste your money unless you have a mould problem or serious blockage.

## RADIANT FLOOR HEATING

Got cold feet? Radiant floor heating systems will keep them warm by running electric or hot-water-filled pipes encased in concrete beneath your floor surface. The concrete flooring is either left bare or you can overlay it with cork, tile or engineered hardwood (FSC-certified, of course). Note: while radiant floor heating is definitely comfy and quiet (there are no loud on and off gusts as with forced air), don't believe everything the salespeople will tell you about this system. Namely that it's so efficient at heating that you can turn your thermostat down a notch more than regular heating systems. The Canada Mortgage and Housing Corporation put that claim to the test and (cue Debbie Downer sound effects) they found that homeowners with radiant floor heating systems do not, I repeat, do not, set their thermostats lower than most homeowners with other types of heating systems. Sorry. Though CMHC notes, "Energy savings are still possible through zoning of in-floor systems." Translation: not all your floors need to be heated.

But what if you used the light hitting your roof to keep your toes toasty come November? If you run water heated by the sun through those in-floor pipes, you can get up to half of the energy required to heat the home from the sun gods instead of the utility gods. Keep in

**What if you used the light hitting your roof** to keep your toes toasty come November?

mind that solar-heated systems work best with concrete-slab floors, since hotter water is needed if those pipes are covered by wood. And, of course, backup heat is still required, but the cool thing is that a radiant floor heating system can also double as a domestic hot water source. Companies like Nova Scotia's **Thermo Dynamics**, for instance, can set you up with a system (thermo-dynamics.com). Check with the

Canadian Solar Industries Association's Member Industry Directory to find certified solar hot water system installers in your area (cansia.ca).

## ELECTRICAL HEATING

Like rain on your wedding day, Alanis Morissette should be crooning about the ironies of electric baseboard heaters. Namely, that they're so damn cheap to install but so bloody pricey to run (not to mention useless). And yet 25% of Canadians put up with them. Their rock-bottom price tag makes them extra-appealing to landlords, especially those who make you pay for your own heating bills. But what ends up happening in most homes with baseboard heaters is you can crank the bleep out of those babies and still shiver till you're blue in the face.

You nutters who are still thinking of buying new baseboard heaters know that cheaper models are noisy (if they have a fan) and offer crappy temperature control. Better ones have wall-mounted thermostats and quieter fans. Convectair makes larger (and notably pricier) recessed heaters that come with Energy Star–certified, programmable thermostats so you can automatically lower the temp when you're at work or asleep.

Tips for Using Baseboard Heaters (If You Must):
- If your heaters don't have fans built in (or their cheapy internal blowers are just too noisy), try placing a 15-centimetre fan nearby to help circulate warm air. (Make sure not to let electrical cords come in contact with your heaters.)
- Buy a programmable thermostat made especially for baseboard heaters. You'll save up to 10% on heating costs. If cash is really tight, start by putting them in your living room and main bedroom and turn the rest of the rooms down manually. The feds will slip you $40 if you install five of them through their ecoENERGY Retrofit program (see Resources: Rebates and Incentives Guide).

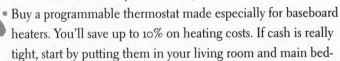

## RENTERS' TIPS: STAY WARM WITHOUT ROASTING YOUR WALLET

$$ We here at *Ecoholic Home* know renters have it tough. Hell, I *am* one! If your apartment gets your teeth chattering, here are a few ways to get toasty in a hurry with minimal out-of-pocket purchases. Keep in mind, of course, that even if you don't pay for your heat, your apartment is still likely wasting a lot of energy, whether you live in one of those super-drafty pads or one with rads cranked up so high you're wearing tank tops in January.

- Before lobbying your landlord for new windows and insulation, you can take care of most drafts very cheaply. Really, all you need is basic caulking and a caulking gun (available at any hardware store from $5 each; **AFM Safecoat** makes a non-toxic, ultra-low-VOC caulking compound), some $5 rubber weatherstripping tape and maybe a door sweep. You'll notice the temperature rise by a few degrees in no time.

- Yes, a new furnace might be nice, but furnaces also work much better if their filters are clean, and most landlords don't replace them more than once a year. If you have access to the furnace, figure out how to clean or replace them yourself every couple of months in winter (about $10 or so each).

- Three-quarters of those living in rented dwellings have access to a thermostat. Sure, most of you don't have the programmable kind, but that doesn't mean you can't ask your landlord to fund the switch. For only, like, $40, you can program the settings to save everyone money.

- While I'm not crazy about covering windows in plastic film, it is your cheapest route for keeping out drafts.

- If you do resort to portable space heaters (see Portable Heaters, page 246), have them running only in the room you're in.

- If your apartment is sweltering in February to the point that you're cracking open windows, alert your landlord to the energy wastage.

- Got a ceiling fan gathering dust overhead? Run it on low, in the opposite direction, so it pushes the heat down.

- Close doors to cooler rooms you seldom use (like a spare room).

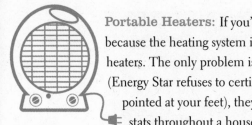 **Portable Heaters:** If you're a renter and wearing scarves indoors because the heating system is so crappy, you'll have to resort to space heaters. The only problem is that they're serious energy leeches (Energy Star refuses to certify them), but if used right (like, say, pointed at your feet), they can keep you from cranking up thermostats throughout a house filled with useless baseboard heaters,

## GET SMART: REMOTE-CONTROL UTILITY METERS

If you still have a real human being coming over to manually read your electricity meter now and then, let's face it, you've got a dumb meter. Especially when you compare it to the fancy new meters more and more utilities are handing out. Most just wirelessly transmit your hour-by-hour energy use to utility providers, which hope to, in time, apply different electricity prices to different times of the day, thereby encouraging residents to curb their energy hogging in peak periods. Some utilities actually give residents remote control access to their homes, so that you can, say, start your a/c half an hour before you get home.

With smart meters in place, a smart grid can track electricity use and predict peaks and blackouts. In fact, if a blackout is imminent, utilities could theoretically power down a/cs throughout your area to avoid losing the lights entirely. Something similar is already happening through Ontario's peaksaver program, in which residents sign up for smart programmable thermostats they can control remotely. On the hottest days of the summer, peaksaver sends a message to your thermostat to ease up by 2°C for up to four hours (but never on weekends and holidays). Ontario and B.C. are bringing in basic smart meters province-wide. If you haven't heard a peep about this from your local utility, call them and tell them you'd like to try smart metering, too. You can also always order yourself a wireless Blueline Innovations **PowerCost Monitor**, which tells you from moment to moment how much electricity your home is using. With real-time feedback, testing in Ontario has found that people are motivated to reduce their electricity use by 5% to 20% (**bluelineinnovations.com**).

potentially saving energy. Warning: portable heaters powered by a combo of electricity and natural gas or kerosene emit dangerous carbon monoxide and sulphur dioxides either into your living room (if they're unvented) or into the great outdoors (if they're vented). Both are bad, bad, bad.

Electric radiant heaters are supposed to be more energy-efficient, and since they don't use fuel they don't emit any nasty fumes, but they warm only the person they're pointed at, not the room.

The Portable Furnace is supposed to heat up to 800 square feet. It uses infrared light energy (and fans) to quietly toast up your environs (without the fire hazard risks of other space heaters) and uses 35% less energy than a baseboard heater and "less energy than a coffee maker." Is it worth the $500 price tag? Not sure. But Portable Furnace has one of those slick 30-day free trial things if you're curious (portablefurnace.com).

## FIREPLACES AND STOVES

Keeping the home fires burning through the coldest, darkest months of the year sounds like a snuggly Canadian tradition. But it ain't so heart-warmin' when you consider all the climate-changing carbon dioxide, greenhouse gas–precursor carbon monoxide, and other smog-forming pollutants that can end up clouding the air both inside and outside your home. Be it a real fire or fake, you're flame-broiling the planet from the inside, darlin'. It's time to get that blaze under control.

Wood Fires: Who doesn't love a crackling wood fire? The smell alone makes me want to put on a reindeer sweater and buy a bag of chestnuts. Well, that fire might smell like winter to you and me, but it smells more like trouble to anyone suffering from asthma, angina or bronchitis. In fact, residential wood burning is a major contributor to winter smog, says Environment Canada (which also points out that residential wood burning is responsible for a whopping 25% of fine particulates found in Canada's air pollution, 15% of volatile organic compounds and 10% of carbon monoxide).

Studies found that air quality in the wood-burning burbs outside Montreal was way worse than the downtown core. No wonder the town of Hamstead, Quebec, has given residents till 2015 to extinguish any and all fire burning. Truthfully, they might have gone a little far in stomping out all wood burning, including the lighting of cleaner pellet stoves (see Pellet Stoves, page 251). Montreal is simply banning the installation of new wood stoves to tackle its winter smog problems, while okaying pellet stoves. B.C. knew it couldn't ban wood stoves altogether (try taking wood stoves away from B.C.'s mountain dwellers—my sister being one of them—and you'd probably have a riot), so it wisely banned the sale of non-certified wood stoves.

Really, the problem is all the dirty old fireplaces and ancient wood stoves sitting in Canadian homes—not today's cleaner burning flame boxes (see below). I think the smartest policy would be a combo of B.C.'s sales restriction on crappy stoves and a bit of San Francisco's new fireplace ban (which slaps a fine on any city dweller sparking a fireplace/wood stove/pellet stove on Spare the Air alert days with poor outdoor air quality). If your municipality hasn't banned the burn altogether, here are some shopping tips to keep you smouldering cleanly.

- Get an **advanced-combustion wood stove** or **fireplace insert** approved by the EPA (U.S. Environment Protection Agency), the CSA (Canadian Standards Association) or the ULC (Underwriters Laboratories of Canada). These babies burn 90% cleaner than older models and use a third less wood. They even reburn smoke to create heat.
- If you've got a drafty old inefficient fireplace space, you can pick between a certified hearth-mounted wood stove (that basically sits in front of your fireplace opening) or a certified insert that's essentially a wood stove designed to fit inside and fill out your traditional masonry fireplace. Back in the '80s, inserts had a bad rep, but that's turned around. The EPA-certified **Quadra-Fire** brand has an insert that claims to heat a 3,500-square-foot home for up to 12 hours on one fuel load and a beautiful, though pricey, hybrid wood fireplace model with automatic combustion

control that promises "16 hours of uninterrupted, hassle-free fire-place performance" (quadrafire.com).

- Check square footage capacity. The label might say it heats any-where from 1,000 to 2,000 square feet, but what it really means is that it could heat 2,000 square feet in the central U.S. but only 1,000 in chilly Canadian climes. Plus older, drafty houses will get even less coverage. Better, says the Wood Heat Organization, to buy based on size—i.e., small for one-room homes or small cottages, medium for small to medium-sized houses and large for larger or drafty homes.

- Make sure split wood has been well seasoned (dried for six months or longer) and cut to the correct length (see woodheat.org for details) so toxic smoke is reduced. Start your

## GREENER LOGS

If you can't afford a new ultra-efficient wood stove insert just yet (and trust me, if you're a fire burner, you should indeed be saving up, since traditional fireplace setups lose a tremendous amount of heat through their chimneys), be sure to fuel your conventional fireplace with sustainable logs like **Java-Logs**, made of recycled coffee grounds, wood and vegetable by-products (**java-log.com**). They emit about 10 times less carbon monoxide and 6 times less particulate matter than firewood does. **Eco Log**, from Quebec, uses leftover sawdust from the flooring biz and is certified by Environmental Choice (available at Canadian Tire and Home Depot). Ditto for **SmartLog**. And remember, not all artificial logs are green! Most starter logs are branded as non-toxic, but they basically consist of sawdust and petroleum-based wax. **Duraflame** logs are now petroleum-free and use plant-based waxes instead. **Pine Mountain** also offers a "natural" version made without petroleum. Unless they specify otherwise, most fake logs should be burned only in traditional fireplaces, not in wood stoves.

fire with softwoods like pine and fir, then keep it going with longer-lasting hardwoods like maple or oak.

- Track down a sustainable source of firewood. The average homeowner not relying on wood as their primary source of heat should look for cases of **SmartLog's High Performance Energy Logs** and **Ecolog's Ecological Wood Logs**. They're made of 100% pressed recycled hardwood and are safe for all EPA-certified fireplaces and wood-burning stoves (unlike other pressed logs that contain coffee grounds or waxes). Because of how they're compressed and super-dried, they're said to produce more heat and fewer emissions. They both also get Environment Canada's EcoLogo seal of approval. FYI, SmartLogs are available at RONA and Ecologs are available at Canadian Tire and Home Depot (smartlog.ca; ecologcanada.com).

- Buying wood in bulk? Of course if you have a few acres of forest, you can stay warm with nothing but fallen logs. And if you live near a sawmill, you can always ask them if they have any unwanted slab wood they're willing to give you (or sell you for a bargain). Otherwise, you bulk buyers will have to press for details from local wood suppliers. Toronto firewood delivery service **University Firewood** swears all of its wood comes from plantation wood/sustainably managed forests/salvage operations/manufacturing leftovers (universityfirewood.com). Without a national certification system in place for firewood, you'll just have to take their word for it.

The feds will, under the ecoENERGY Retrofit program, give you $375 back if you swap your old wood stove for one certified by the EPA or CSA, or a pellet stove. Also check with your home province or territory. In the Northwest Territories, for instance, you can score $500 towards a new pellet stove and $400 towards a certified wood stove. New Brunswick gives $500, Ontario will match the feds' $375, and B.C. will give you $300.

**Pellet Stoves:** Who knew you could heat your home with rabbit feed? Or at least that's what those little compressed sawdust nibs that fire a pellet stove look like. Despite a minor 2008 kerfuffle created by a smear campaign (funded by the oil-furnace industry south of the border, no less), pellet stoves are still selling like hotcakes. Why wouldn't they when the EPA says they burn more cleanly than EPA-approved high-efficiency wood stoves, don't involve chopping trees and are super-cheap to run (which is why the oil furnace peeps feel so threatened)? Pellets are generally made of compressed sawdust or agricultural waste like dried switchgrass. FYI, some pellet stoves get certification from the EPA, but even the EPA says it's really not necessary since "they pollute so little, pellet stoves do not require EPA certification." Isn't that refreshing? Here are a few Canadian sources for pellet stoves: pelletstove.ca in B.C., naturalheat.ca in Ontario and Canadian Tire locations.

A few points to keep in mind:

- You may have trouble accessing pellet supplies, depending on where you live, so check hardware stores near you for jumbo 10- or 20-kilogram bags of pellets.
- Like wood stoves, pellet stoves aren't an automated heat source. They require a little extra attention (you know, loading, lighting, tending, cleaning).
- Unlike wood stoves, they don't need a whole chimney to vent, they just need a narrow pipe to the outside, which means they can basically be installed in any room.
- Bottom-fed models don't require premium high-grade, low-ash pellets like top-fed models do, because of design issues. But you will want to look for a big ash pan you don't have to empty as often.
- Most pellet stoves require electricity, so if you're buying one to get you through blackouts à la Quebec's ice storm of 1998, you'll want battery backup. At the same time, you'll love models that come with automatic ignition so you don't have to pull out a match each time.

**Gas Fireplaces:** Imagine how freaked out cavepeople would be to see you spark a fire with one flick of a finger. You'd be crowned some sort of demigod, for sure. Truth is, gas fireplaces actually produce way less carbon monoxide and lung-irritating particulate emissions than wood fireplaces. You just have to make sure you pick 'em right. Stay far, far away from "vent-free" or "ventless" natural gas fireplaces, which can vent dangerous carbon monoxide emissions into your home. They're approved in most (but not all) U.S. states, but they're not approved for use in Canada. Natural Resources Canada's Office of Energy Efficiency says, quite unequivocally, these types of fireplaces "can cause serious indoor air-quality and moisture problems, particularly in airtight Canadian homes."

If you have no way to vent a fireplace, then look into super-slick, natural-gas-free, alcohol-based fireplaces, which are cleared for sale on the Canadian market. Check out the massive array of faux fireplaces and inserts offered by Toronto's **InFlame** that run on **Sunjel**—the only alcohol gel to be certified by the ULC (Underwriters Laboratories of Canada) and the EcoLogo program for unvented fireplaces (inflame.ca). **EcoSmart Fires**, which run on denatured alcohol, have several ULC-approved products (ecosmartfire.com, available through Canadian stores like greendesignstudio.ca and vangasfireplaces.com).

**Vented Natural Gas Fireplace Features to Consider:**
- Make sure your model is rated to over 70% FE (Fireplace Efficiency) on the EnerGuide label, which appears on every fireplace.
- Ask for an automatic starter. Continuous pilot lights can suck up as much as half the natural gas used by your fireplace every year, according to Natural Resources Canada.
- A built-in fan will help ensure that all that toastiness spreads out across the room.
- An efficient natural gas fireplace will have a secondary heat exchanger. Ask for it.

For information on geothermal heating and cooling, see page 276.

# INSULATION

You need a quality coat to keep warm in winter, don't you? Well, your house does too. Without a good layer of insulation covering every nook and cranny, you might as well send your poor little home out into a blizzard wearing nothing but a T-shirt. Actually, adding insulation is probably the number one thing you can do to make your home more energy-efficient, which is why, even if the material itself ain't all that eco, green-conscious building experts will say all insulation is eco-friendly. And yes, if your walls are properly sealed with airtight insulation barriers and the like, that should keep dodgy insulation materials from leaking into the home air environment. Nonetheless, can't we have insulation that works well and is a little easier on the planet? Here's a breakdown of your insulation options, and whether they're green on the inside or not.

Fibreglass: Most Canadians outfit their homes with the pink (or yellow) fluffy kind, namely fibreglass insulation. This stuff became shrouded in controversy in the '90s, when it was listed as a possible carcinogen south of the border (a classification that was later revoked, and Health Canada insists it's totally in the clear). Truth is, if you wear safety gear when installing it and it's sealed up in your wall properly, it shouldn't be a problem. Still, fiberglass isn't considered the greenest building material of choice because most of it is still bound with formaldehyde (albeit lower-emitting phenol formaldehyde versus the really bad stuff, urea formaldehyde). A few companies are making formaldehyde-free options.

## SIGNS YOU NEED MORE INSULATION

- ☐ My place is way too hot in summer and cold in winter.
- ☐ Walking on my floors requires two pairs of ski socks come December.
- ☐ My heating and cooling bills are through the roof.
- ☐ My house is menopausal: one spot's sweltering while another spot's freezing.

- Make sure it has high recycled content. These days, manufacturers tend to fold in at least 30% recycled glass content for a dash of green cred. If you're going to reach for fiberglass, go for something like **Ottawa Fibre L.P.**'s product made from 65% recycled glass (ofigroup.com).
- Ask about formaldehyde content. **Johns Manville** makes some that's totally formaldehyde-free and at least 45% recycled (jmhomeowner.com).

**Mineral Wool:** This batting used to win popularity contests in the '50s until fibreglass took it out. The cool thing about this insulation, made of molten slag (a waste product of steel production) and/or natural rock like basalt, is that it doesn't need any added fire retardants and it won't melt in a fire like fibreglass would. Plus, it's more soundproof than fibreglass. Thanks to the slag content in **Roxul's** Canadian-made **Flexibatt** and **Safe'n'Sound**, it's got a recycled content of at least 40% and comes with Environment Canada's EcoLogo seal of approval (roxul.com). The downside is that it's bonded with urea extended phenolic formaldehyde (although Roxul's insulation is GreenGuard Indoor Air Quality–certified under its more stringent Children & Schools standard), and mineral wool does share the same health issues as fibreglass, so you'll need to wear eye, skin and lung protection when working with the stuff. And while it's less energy-intensive to make than fibreglass, turning rock into fluffy insulation is a very energy-hungry process. Still, mineral wool is a very durable option.

**Natural Wool:** If you're looking for genuine wool insulation (I'm talking the stuff sheared off sheep), there is one Canadian company out in Rocky Mountain House, Alberta, making it. The product's called **Good Shepherd Wool Insulation**. It's naturally fire-retardant and moisture-regulating and is so free from health warnings it can even be installed with bare hands. The only additive is boron (a.k.a. borax), there to repel vermin and pests and to boost wool's inherent fire-retardant properties (goodshepherdwool.com). The U.K.'s *Independent* newspaper voted sheep's wool insulation one of the top 50 best ideas for the 21st century.

**Polyurethane, Polystyrene and More:** Stuffing fossil fuel–based fibres, heavy in questionable flame retardants, into your home's cavities seems like a serious green violation until you speak to green home builders. They'll tell you that polyurethane foam gets into every little pore of a wall so well, reducing a homeowner's energy use so greatly, that it outweighs any negatives. Not surprising when polyurethane insulation has the highest R-value, followed by extruded polystyrene foam board, or XPS. Still, there are a couple of cautions to keep in mind about this stuff. Luckily, the most persistent flame retardants (namely über-toxic PBDEs, which formed the basis of up to 30% of polyurethane foam insulation by weight until a few years ago), have been phased out of use. But alternative fire retardants are not without critics. Hexabromo-cyclododecane, for instance, used in pretty much all extruded polystyrene foam, is building up in wildlife and waterways the world over, and Europeans are trying to have it banned. And extruded polystyrene is still, until 2010, installed with an ozone-depleting HCFC blowing agent in North America (though polyurethane has long been blown

## WHAT'S R-VALUE?

The R (which stands for resistance) basically tells you how well the material keeps heat from moving through it. All you need to really know is this: the higher your R-value, the comfier you'll be in your home. If a material has a lower R-value insulation, you might just want to use a thicker layer, depending on the material. Oh, and don't be thrown by labels listing different values: R-value is imperial (U.S.) and RSI values are metric (Canadian/British). FYI, if you don't install your insulation right (e.g., you're leaving air gaps or compressing the batting), you'll lose some R-value, and that means you'll not only be wasting money, but you'll be letting valuable energy slip out of your grasp.

with non-ozone-depleting pentane). Luckily, there are some manufac-turers trying to green up insulation from the plastics family.

- Ask about renewable and recycled content. Montreal-based **Heatlok Soya** insulation is made of 18% soy and 40% recycled plastic (each barrel of insulation reclaims about 1,000 plastic bot-tles). Plus, it's the first Canadian spray polyurethane foam to meet the requirements of the Montreal Protocol, with Zero Ozone Depletion Substance (heatlok-soya.com). **BioBased 501** is also soy-based (about 40% soy oil) and the rest is conventional polyurethane. It was voted outstanding eco-friendly building product of 2003 by the National Association of Home Builders' Green Builders' Conference, and it emits very few VOCs (biobased.net).

- Find out what it's blown in with. Make sure it's HCFC-free. **Icynene** spray foam insulation is made with an open-cell, water-blown form of polyurethane called polyicynene, free of formalde-hyde, VOCs and harmful blowing agents, including HFCs and HCFCs. According to the experts at Building Green, polyi-cynene doesn't have an R-value quite as high as closed-cell poly-urethane, but it uses as little as a quarter of the material used for a comparable volume of closed-cell polyurethane (icynene.com).

**Cellulose:** I can hear the paperboy now: "Extra! Extra! Old news-papers make it big in the insulation world." That's right, old newspapers get a crack at new life as **cellulose insulation**. No wonder the blown-in or loose-fill fibres made with at least 80% recycled content are a hit with green crowds. If done right, it'll keep cold air at bay better than fibre-glass, and it takes as little as a tenth of the energy to manufacture, according to California-based EcologyAction's Green Building Materials

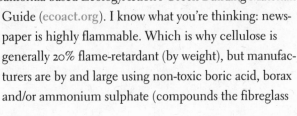

Guide (ecoact.org). I know what you're thinking: news-paper is highly flammable. Which is why cellulose is generally 20% flame-retardant (by weight), but manufac-turers are by and large using non-toxic boric acid, borax and/or ammonium sulphate (compounds the fibreglass

## UH-OH INSULATION: THE KIND YOU DON'T WANT TO FIND

Sometimes an idea that was once great (like spraying dirt roads with DDT) loses its lustre over the years. The same applies to certain forms of insulation.

**Urea Formaldehyde Foam Insulation (UFFI):** Sales of UFFI really took off when the energy concerns of the '70s were at their peak. But by 1980, mounting complaints about off-gassing formaldehyde led to a full-on ban.

What to do if you find it: After 25-plus years, the formaldehyde should have off-gassed and you should be in the clear. Unless it gets moist—then it could start breaking down. FYI, this stuff is generally avoided by house hunters, and homeowners with UFFI have to declare as much when they put their house on the market. By the way, one company, RetroFoam, recently snuck UFFI insulation onto the market, telling unsuspecting homeowners it was a green choice (ha!), but in early 2009, Health Canada warned consumers that RetroFoam of Canada had been illegally importing and selling long-banned urea formaldehyde–based thermal insulation. It was yanked from the market.

**Vermiculite:** This mineral-based insulation was pure gold, thanks to its natural fire-retardant properties. Too bad about the asbestos in some of it. Don't panic. Not all those little Captain Crunch–shaped nobs of vermiculite contain super-harmful amphibole asbestos fibres. Just most of the stuff mined in Montana between, oh, 1920 and 1990, which accounts for the majority of the world's vermiculite insulation during that time.

What to do if you find it: To be sure, send a sample away to get tested. In the meantime, don't disturb it. If it's totally contained within the attic, you should be fine, though asbestos could fall through cracks in the ceiling, so make sure to caulk up any holes or cracks in the rooms below. And Health Canada says you shouldn't let kids play near open vermiculite. Never try to remove it yourself. Remodellers should call in a pro. Proper remediation could cost several thousand dollars so many choose just to cover it with new batting. Search for testers near you at **ziplocal.com/find/asbestos-testing-in-canada**.

industry tried unsuccessfully to smear). You certainly wouldn't want to eat the stuff or inhale it while installing it (the dust it creates is a nuisance dust, not a carcinogen, so make sure it's well sealed behind walls and ceilings and a respiratory mask is worn during installation). FYI, cellulose comes in loose-fill (for horizontal surfaces like attics) or injected/sprayed (for walls and ceilings). Good Canadian brands include **Can-Cell's Weathershield Insulation** and **Climatizer Plus**, which both contain 85% recycled paper content and are certified by Environment Canada's EcoLogo program (can-cell.com; climatizer.com).

### Cellulose Insulation Features to Consider:
- The higher the recycled content the better; 85% is ideal.
- You might want to ask around for brands like Can-Cell that use only boric acid or borax as a flame retardant, since ammonium sulphate can have odour issues if it's not installed exactly right.
- If you're chemically sensitive and are affected by the inks in newspapers, ask around for loose-fill cellulose made with cardboard instead of newsprint, though this may be hard to find in Canada.

**Cementitious Foam:** One of my favourite insulation products is **AirKrete**, a blown-in shaving-cream-like cement foam made from magnesium oxide (extracted from seawater) and ceramic talc mined in Ontario. This isn't your usual dead-heavy cement. AirKrete is extremely light, totally non-toxic, nonflammable and rodent-proof. There's no off-gassing, and it doesn't have the same dust problem as cellulose, mineral wool and fibreglass, so that means installers don't have to don special suits and breathing masks. It dries within 24 hours, and residents don't even need to leave the house while renos take place, since no irritating dust is created. Bonus: it costs about the same as polyurethane foam (airkretecanada.com).

**Cotton Blanket:** If you're a DIYer who would rather avoid blown-in types, or if you aren't all that comfy with the respiratory worries associated with inhaling fibreglass or mineral wool blanket insulation, you have to check out insulation made with recycled textiles. **Bonded Logic's recycled denim insulation** is so safe there are zero health warnings for installers. Its non-toxic panels are fire-treated with benign borax and can be easily cut with a sharp utility knife (bondedlogic.com).

You can score federal rebates for adding insulation in every corner of your home (up to $750 for your attic, up to $1,875 for your exterior wall, up to $1,250 for your basement and up to $1,000 for crawlspaces). Ontario will match that. Check with your home province to see if they offer similar rebates. Keep in mind that in a reno job, the attic is generally the most cost-effective place to add insulation first, since, as BC Hydro says, a well-insulated attic can knock your year-round energy use down by 20% to 60%, saving you a nice wad of cash. (See Resources: Rebates and Incentives Guide.)

## COOLING BASICS

While hiding out in air-conditioned movie theatres and making sure your new BFF has a pool might be wonderful short-term solutions to beating the heat, they ain't gonna get you through summer's hot, sweaty nights. Now, before you cave and crank up the a/c, consider some ways of keeping cool without giving the planet a fever.

**Window Dressing:** Sure, windows let in all that pretty summer light, but 40% of your home's hellish temperatures come in through those windows. If you work your windows right, they can be a cooling ally.

- Leave your windows open at night and shut them early in the morning. This will keep the hot air out as temperatures outside climb. No need to let a scorching afternoon gust in.
- Draw all the curtains. Without a good set of blinds you're basically cooking your home in a deep fryer. Honeycomb blinds are more effective than most at blocking out rays. Just stay away from PVC blinds, which can erode and create a

harmful lead dust (especially scary if you have young kids sucking on them).

- Shut 'er down. These are a bit more of an investment, but outdoor shutters and awnings keep the sun's rays from touching the glass.

## FANS

Honestly, you don't really need an air conditioner if you've got air moving across your skin. It's in your grade 9 biology textbook. A breeze helps dry your sweat, letting your body cool itself like a good circulatory system should. And besides using 90% less electricity than air conditioners, fans also let you enjoy the seasons for all they're worth. Do you really want old man winter around 365 days a year? No? Well, they say the next ice age will be kick-started by global warming, so let's try to prevent both by keeping the fans on and the a/c off.

Fan Features to Consider:

- Get the right fan for your needs. Don't get a jumbo turbo fan for your tiny bedroom (you'll just end up with a sore throat from the gale force winds). Stick it at the foot of your basement stairs instead (if you have a basement) so it can shove cool air from subterranean levels up to the main floor. It's my dad's trick and it works like a charm. Speaking of turbo fans, the ultra aerodynamic **Turbo-Aire** purportedly delivers 100% more air at 300% greater efficiency than the competition while being "whisper quiet at all speeds" and well reviewed (available through Canadian Tire).
- Energy Star ceiling fans move air up to 50% more efficiently than standard models. If your ceiling fan has a light, make sure it's an energy-saving compact fluorescent bulb (one that's suitable for enclosed fixtures, if need be).

## FANS COOL PEOPLE, NOT ROOMS

If no one's in the room, flick the fan off. It's not like your furniture appreciates the breeze.

**Solar-Powered Fans:** I'm still waiting for the day when every fan is fed by solar panels propped in our windows. Until that day comes, renewable energy junkies who can't afford to mack out their roof with panels will have to head online and track down **solar-powered fans** from sites like solarwholesales.org. Can't tell you how well they work, though.

**Reversible Window Fans:** These fans rock since they can help create a mucho-refreshing cross-current by pulling air from one window and pushing it out another.

**Whole-House Fan Systems:** These systems aren't all that common in Canada, but they should be. They use about a tenth as much power as air conditioners but send cooling gusts of air throughout your house in seconds flat. They're especially useful if your summers are not outrageously humid, though my in-laws have one in muggy southern Ontario and it really does push out the day's hot stagnant air in a flash. These babies actually suck air from open windows and pull it up through your home into a vented attic. They're ideal for use at night or in the early morning, when the air outside is cooler. The only hitch is they actually contribute to heat loss in the winter, so you'll definitely want to install an insulated cover over the fan when it gets cold outside. Check out broan.ca or Calgary's canadawholehomefans.ca. If you're handy, you could plausibly install it yourself.

**Attic Fans:** These sometimes get confused with whole-house fans because they both vent hot air out of your attic. But that's all attic fans do. There's no refreshing wind created in living areas, just the cooling that occurs when your attic isn't so hot you could broil burgers on the ceiling. They're cheaper than whole-house fans, and for about $500 you can get a super-duper cool **solar-powered attic fan** from sunrisesolar.net. Again, you can install it yourself if you're good with your hands.

## AIR CONDITIONERS

Sure, our summers seem to be getting hotter (Al Gore likely has something to say about that), but does that give Canadians cause to crank the a/c all season long, regardless of what it's like outside? Turn it on only when you really need it (i.e., to stave off heat exhaustion) or right before you go to sleep on a sweltering night. And definitely turn it off (or at the very least raise the temperature on the thermostat) if you're leaving a room or your house for more than four hours. Air conditioners might not be filled with CFCs any more, but it turns out CFC replacements weren't all that green either. Many air conditioners now pump ozone-depleting and climate-changing HCFCs (like R-22) through their coils. The relatively greener alternative, HFCs, don't mess up the ozone layer but they're still a potent greenhouse gas. You can't win for losing. If either HFCs or HCFCs leak or escape from your system somehow, it's really bad news.

### RAISE IT UP

Turn your thermostat up to, at the very least, 25°C. I'm not kidding. Each half-degree below 26°C ups your energy consumption by 8%. Besides, it's the least you can do, considering the Japanese have instructed government departments to set the a/c to 28°C, and China's Jiangsu Province told municipal government offices not to turn on air conditioning until the thermostat hits 33°C!

Air Conditioner Features to Consider: If you are going to buy a new unit, here are some tips to being a cool shopper:

- Never buy used. Newer models are much more energy-efficient.
- Always buy Energy Star. Energy Star room/window units use at

## LEAKING TROUBLE

Is your a/c acting up? Are the coils frozen over? You could have a coolant fluid leak, baby—which means you might be spewing either ozone-depleting or climate-changing gases into the atmosphere in a bad way. Shut it down and call a repairperson pronto. Even if you don't detect any funny behaviour, have your central a/c unit inspected periodically by a pro.

least 10% less energy than other new models. And Energy Star central-air systems use about 20% less power.

- Let EnerGuide lead you. The higher the number on the label, the more efficient your unit.
- Stay ozone-friendly. Make sure your a/c is free of ozone-depleting HCFC refrigerants (which are being phased out south of the border as of 2010). Their replacements (HFCs like Puron) aren't perfect—both HFCs and HCFCs are greenhouse gases—but they're considered the greener option.
- Get the right unit for your space. Why buy a window unit with the ability to cool 1,000 square feet when you need to cool only a 12-by-10-foot bedroom? Same goes for your central system.
- If you have central air, get a programmable thermostat. You can start chilling your space about an hour before you get home.

## SOLAR AIR CONDITIONING

Imagine cooling your home with the sun's rays. Depending on your vantage point, it sounds either absolutely insane or incredibly logical. The day has yet to arrive when air conditioners everywhere run on solar power, but **Solcool One** makes an Energy Star–certified air conditioner that can run on DC power and can thus be used by off-the-gridders. It uses up to 50% less energy than regular air conditioners use, and it has a backup battery that can run for up to 12 hours on steamy nights (**solcool.net**). Now that's cool.

It's a handy-dandy tool that'll keep you cool while saving you money and energy.

$$ If you've got an old a/c unit you're looking to replace, the feds will give you $250 towards a new Energy Star–qualified central air system and $25 per Energy Star window unit, through their ecoENERGY Retrofit program (see Resources: Rebates and Incentives Guide). Stores like Home Depot have also been known to offer rebates on new, more efficient models if you bring in your old clunker for proper disposal or recycling. Be sure to ask.

## 5 STRATEGIES FOR COOLING YOUR SUMMER

**#1 Dig in.** Plant a cooling garden and trees to shield your house from the sun. Okay, so this one takes a while to grow into its own, but that's all the more reason to hurry up and get gardening! If your yard is paved over, reduce the heat-island effect of concrete and get landscaping.

**#2 Insulate yourself.** I don't mean stop meeting new people, I mean bump up the insulation in your attic. It'll help prevent your home from cooking from the attic down. If you can't afford to go whole hog, just add a radiant barrier (a thin sheet of aluminum, often lined with craft paper or cardboard) inside your roof to help reduce cooling bills.

**#3 Lighten up.** Black roofing materials turn your attic into a scrambled egg. Look for light-coloured tiles or roofing materials next time you're redoing your roof.

**#4 Get low.** Invest in high-quality low-E windows (with an argon or argon-krypton gas fill). These will help keep all those rays from charring your pad.

**#5 Combat global warming.** Reduce your carbon spew by biking to work and unplugging the a/c.

# POWERING
## Who needs Red Bull?
### Energize your home naturally

## You come home at the end

of a long day and, without much thought, flick on the lights, maybe put in a load of laundry, fry up your dinner, start the dishwasher, then sit down to watch a little telly, all by the power vested in the utility gods. Now, all that zapping, flicking and sautéing relies on a hell of a lot of coal burning, nuclear-waste dumping, land flooding and fossil fuel digging, all in all making electricity account for a shameful 20% of Canada's climate-cooking greenhouse gases. But there is a light at the end of the dirty electricity tunnel: a burgeoning world of green power getting its strength from the sun, wind, earth, tides . . . hell, even decaying cow poop. Right now it makes up only one humble percentage point (this number is growing) of Canada's grid, but that doesn't mean you can't access a piece of the renewable energy pie right in your home. What's realistic? What's suitable for your home? How much will you have to invest? And how do you get started?

# ASSESSING YOUR POWER NEEDS

**Know Your Load:** First things first: you'll need to assess the energy load of your pad to figure out how many kilowatt-hours you use on average. On top of gathering your monthly electricity bills to get a good sense of your consumption patterns, you can check out online calculators to give you a clearer picture of where your power's going (nspower.ca/en/home/energyefficiency/Energy-Calculator.aspex). You'll be shocked when you start to add up all the energy-sucking devices in your life, down to the minutes per day you use your toaster, coffee maker, TV, dehumidifier and alarm system, as well as devices you only occasionally use, like circular saws and electric lawn mowers. On average, Canadian homes consume 700 to 1,500 kilowatt-hours of basic electricity a month.

> **You'll be shocked when you start to add up all the energy-sucking devices in your life**

**Waste Not, Want Not:** Why waste renewable power on a leaky, wasteful house? Before you finalize your green power system, you'll probably be asked by your renewable energy consultant/supplier to make your home as energy-efficient and insulated as it can possibly be and invest in highly energy-efficient appliances (like top-of-the-line Energy Star types). Ditto for water-saving devices. The lighter your home's energy needs, the more value you'll get out of your solar panels, geothermal system, etc., and the less clean, green energy you'll be spilling out your windows.

**Consider Your Size:** Are you outfitting a little shack in the woods or a downtown townhouse? Do you want to go all the way off the grid or just reduce your conventional power usage by, say, 20%? Is your budget bottomless or is it restricted to a specific dollar amount? All of these factors will determine just how far you can go with green energy and what type of system suits you best.

## BASIC POWER OPTIONS

**Off the Grid:** A true off-the-grid home has no water lines, no natural gas lines and no power lines connecting it to the world beyond. So if you've moved to the middle of nowhere or you've got a cottage that runs on a generator, it's definitely worth your while to go green. Autonomous renewable energy systems are especially popular and affordable for cabins, where powering a few direct current (DC) lights, a DC fridge, a DC water pump and radios can cost maybe $3,000 in solar panels, but the bigger and fancier your cottage, the more you'll fork out (with $20,000 being more likely for a typical cottage). These make especially prudent fiscal sense if there are no power lines near you and the nearest utility provider wants to charge you tens of thousands of dollars to get hydro lines to your home.

Hybrid off-the-grid systems combine multiple renewable systems, like maybe solar panels with micro-wind turbines and some sort of generator. Geothermal still requires some electricity to run, so it might not be wise for off-the-gridders, unless you want to run a generator. Note that renewable energy systems require some maintenance, and off-the-gridders are likely doing it all themselves.

**Grid-Connected:** Are there power lines running to your home? Then you're grid-connected, baby. Even if you do swear off hydro bills forever, there's no point in getting dramatic and cutting down those power lines. Chances are you'll want a little of that regular coal-, big hydro-, nuke-fired power when the sun ain't shining, but you'll still reduce your overall reliance on dirty energy.

**Net Metering:** (Off-the-gridders can bypass this one.) If, thanks to your new renewable energy system, your home ends up putting out more power than it uses on any given day, thereby feeding the grid, you'll want to know about it. And net metering helps you do just that. Essentially, it lets your utility provider audit how much energy your home created this month and if, say, your home's renewable energy systems created more energy than you needed in July, net metering acknowledges that you fed that excess energy back into the general grid and you'll get a credit. Basically, any excess power your system bankrolls earns you credits with your utility supplier, so when your green systems aren't putting out much power you can still come out ahead. In Ontario, you have 12 months to use those credits. BC Hydro pays out 5.4 cents/kWh for any net export of power into its system. And don't be shy: if there's no net metering (a.k.a. standard offer contracts) in your area, call your representative in your province's legislature and your local utility supplier to complain.

$$ **Cash Rebates:** Get a grip on financial incentives for green power; for instance, Ontario, P.E.I. and B.C. offer a tax rebate on the purchase of solar, wind energy, micro-hydroelectric and geothermal energy systems. Through the Renewable Energy Loan Program, P.E.I. also provides loans up to $10,000, with max monthly payments of between $90 and $150 regardless of the loan balance (see Resources: Rebates and Incentives Guide for more).

## NET ZERO HOMES

If your home's renewable energy systems produce as much (or as little) energy as you consume over the course of the year, you can proudly call yours a net zero house. Realistically, this concept is more feasible in new homes designed to be highly energy-efficient, but that doesn't mean renovators can't aim for net zero status!

# SOLAR ENERGY

All right, so sunshine might not be the first thing that comes to mind when the world thinks of Canada, but, hey, we get our fair share of rays (well, at least those of us living outside of Vancouver). Yes, we're a little behind other countries (like Germany, Japan and the U.S., which hold the majority of the world's installed solar panels), but the market for solar power is growing at about 13% per year. It's an exciting area, though I gotta be honest with you here: you shouldn't expect solar to take your home off the grid unless you have a very small house or very deep pockets. Mounting solar photovoltaic (PV) panels will help reduce the amount you rely on traditional utility providers, which is positively fantastic. But this is Canada; it doesn't rain sunshine all day, every day, so keep your expectations in check. At the same time, unless you have lots of room for a wind turbine or have a waterfall on your property, solar panels are really your best and only option if you want your lights and toaster to run on clean, Gaia-given power instead of that dirty stuff your utility company gives you. Hell, if you can power your TV with the sun's rays, you might even be able to sneak in episodes of *Canada's Next Top Model* or *Are You Smarter Than a 5th Grader?* with less shame.

You can buy basic solar panel modules from hardware stores and install them yourself—but unless you're exceptionally handy, don't do it. You'll need to do fancy stuff like install an extra two-way utility meter (it costs several hundred dollars) and a power cutoff switch (so you don't electrocute the people working on power lines on your street), and you'll have to hire an electrician for a final stamp of approval. If you've got a yard with lots of sunlight, you'll want to look into backyard panels, since these can actually be more effective than roof-bound ones. For one, they can be shovelled off if it snows, plus they can be shifted seasonally to optimize the sun's rays. Also, panels can be mounted on a fence or on a pole. If you have a bigger budget, you can even get a PV tracking system to track the sun as it moves across the sky.

Getting Started: Whether you do it yourself or hire a pro, before you proceed you'll have a few questions that need to be addressed:

- How much sun does your region get? For maps of Canada's solar potential, google "solar map Canada" (the url's just too long and messy).

- What's your right to light? If your city/town/village gets lots of sun, consider how much sun your own home gets. Is at least part of your roof south-facing? How exposed is the roof? Not much point in buying a whack of solar panels if you've got big old trees or a building blocking the light from hitting your rooftop most of the year (and/or a shadowy yard if you're considering ground-mounted panels).

- What size system should you get? This one depends on a few basic factors, like whether you're off the grid or grid-connected, what percentage of your electricity you'd like to get from solar, how deep your pockets are and how much space you have. The size of your roof and yard will restrict the amount of panels you can hoist.

- How much will it cost you? According to CanSIA (the Canadian Solar Industries Association), the average cost for PV panels dropped from $11.09/watt in 1999 to $5.36/watt in 2006 (that's a good 50% drop in just seven years). So what will your grand total be? I hate to be cryptic, but it's impossible to say without having someone come out to your house, size up your power-hogging ways and assess how much energy you want to get from solar. Plenty of people start with a $12,000 to $14,000 system (which should buy you what's known as a 1-kilowatt system, giving you 11,000 kilowatt-hours of electricity per year). That will cover most of your needs if you live in a small cabin, or a tiny fraction if you live in a McMansion. In a highly efficient semi-detached urban space with room for $25,000 to $30,000 worth of panels on your roof (a.k.a. a 2-kilowatt system), that could cover up to 15% of your energy needs, says Go Solar, a program of the Clean Air Foundation. It all really comes down to how efficient your house is and how energy-conserving the people that live in it are. The average Canadian might find better value going for solar hot-water heating for $5,000 or so, where the payback is 8 to 10 years instead of 20 (see Solar Hot Water, below).

- Are you up to code? You'll want to make sure your roof is in good shape to handle the weight of the panels, plus you want it to be leak-free before you raise panels. Also, check with your municipality about getting the necessary building permits for those PVs. A good solar installer should work with you to get all the necessary electrical safety stamps of approval for the wiring changes that will take place.
- How do you get started? For help finding a pro, check out the Canadian Solar Industries Association's site (cansia.ca). Be sure to pick a dealer that offers a 25-year warranty on parts and labour.

## COMMUNITY SOLAR

Pining for solar power but can't afford the price tag? Talk to your neighbours about signing up for solar too and you might just be able to negotiate a good group discount. **Our Power** offers advice and resources for starting community-based solar projects for homeowners (**ourpower.ca**). **SolarBC** is offering a limited time $375 grant to groups buying solar hot water heaters in bulk (**solarbc.ca**).

## SOLAR HOT WATER

I call this the segue drug for renewable energy enthusiasts. Your budget doesn't allow you to smother your roof in solar panels, so you start small. You start with a solar hot water heater. Good news:

solar hot water (a.k.a. solar thermal) gives you way more value for your money than a roof full of solar panels anyway. Since heating water accounts for 25% of your household's energy use and energy from the sun is free, solar water heaters can significantly reduce a household's water-heating costs—savings that, in turn, can offset the higher purchase and installation costs of a solar system over a conventional water heater. I know what you're thinking. You're Canadian, what good is the sun going to do you when you want to take a shower at 6 a.m. on a cold December morning? At times like that, you're right, you'll need a backup source. And you might as well go super-efficient and get a tankless system like those from takagi.com (as long as that tankless system can vary its heat output when it meets water that's been pre-warmed by your solar system). But overall, Natural Resources Canada will tell you that you can get on average 50% of your $H_2O$ heating needs from the solar-powered devices (close to 90% in summer and 10% in winter, depending on where you live).

As a Canuck, there are really only two types of solar hot-water heaters you need to know about: year-round (a.k.a. active) and seasonal (a.k.a. passive). The Canadian Solar Industries Association has a database of dealers and manufacturers in your area (cansia.ca).

Getting Started:

- For year-round use, evacuated (a.k.a. vacuum) heat tube models are the way to go. And lucky for you, the price has really come down on these in recent years (all installed, it now costs $4,000 to $8,000, depending on the efficiency of the system and difficulty of your roof's accessibility, which direction the roof is facing, etc.).
- Seasonal cottagers might want to check out passive solar hot water types since they're not only cheaper, but easier to maintain and considered more durable. However, they are less efficient and won't do you much good when temperatures plummet.

## DIRTY ELECTRICITY GETTING YOU DOWN?

Fluorescent lights exhausting you? Computer screens giving you headaches? Electrical pollution from radio frequencies and electromagnetic waves might be the cause. According to stats from Sweden and Britain, about 2% or 3% of the population suffers from potentially debilitating electro-hypersensitivity, or EHS. Symptoms are all over the map and include nausea, headaches, chronic fatigue, chronic pain, tinnitus and rashes, to name a few. Researchers also say that many more are a little electro-sensitive and just don't know it, blaming restless nights, office brain fog and Motrin moments on everything but our electrified environment. The condition is pretty unheard of in Canada, but Sweden, with an estimated 250,000 sufferers, leads the pack by recognizing EHS as a full-on disability. Authorities there will not only electrically retrofit your home and your office, but will make a restaurant remove, say, offensive lighting if an electrically sensitive person wants to eat there but can't—kind of like Canada's policy on wheelchair ramps. Stockholm's even planning a special EHS-friendly village.

An environmental science professor at Trent University, Magda Havas works with people with MS, diabetes and other illnesses and documents how many found their symptoms improved when their environments were electrically cleaned, so to speak, by placing capacitators (filters) throughout their homes. Researchers like Columbia U cellular biophysics prof Martin Blank back the findings, arguing that electromagnetic waves and radio frequencies actually trigger stress responses in cells that exacerbate various health conditions.

Health Canada insists our exposure to all this stuff is safe. Nonetheless, until a couple years ago, Toronto Hydro's website encouraged anyone concerned about EHS to move clock radios away from their bed and to air-dry after bathing to cut down on hair-dryer time. Many people aren't waiting around for global consensus on the issue. They're unplugging their cordless phones, dimmer switches, baby monitors, even energy-saving CFL bulbs. For more info on dirty electricity solutions, check out **dirtyelectricity.ca**.

$$ Install a solar hot water system that meets CSA standards and you'll get a good $1,250 back from the feds under their eco-ENERGY Retrofit program. If you buy an Energy Star or R-2000 home in Saskatchewan, the government will give you $1,000 towards solar thermal systems. Ontario will give you a tax rebate on your system and match the federal rebate through its Home Energy Savings Program. B.C. hopes to have 100,000 roofs with solar water heating by 2020. It's offering a PST rebate, as are P.E.I. and Ontario.

For information on solar shingles, see page 234.

## PASSIVE SOLAR

Open up your home and let the sun shine in. If you build a house right, and position it just so, you can make the sun work for you, without fancy solar panels or heat pumps. With smartly designed passive buildings, well, the Canadian Solar Industries Association says it best: "A building can be more than a simple container to hold people and items—if properly designed, it can also be an engine driven by the sun to eliminate much of the external energy needs."

In fact, on sunny winter days you won't even need to turn on your furnace. To Canadian ears, that's just about as close to a miracle as you can get.

Getting Started:
- For a passive solar design to succeed, you'll need lots of thermal mass (like masonry walls and concrete or tile floors) to absorb, store and slowly release heat energy.
- The key is to have your well-insulated home facing south, with most of its high-performance, triple-glazed windows and living spaces on that south face.
- While you want to cut down on windows in the north-, east- and west-facing walls, you don't want to go overboard with big south-facing windows either—in cold climates, south-facing windows should cover no more than 7% to 12% of total floor space. If you

want more windows here, you'll need more thermal mass to store the extra heat energy.

- Come summer, well-positioned deciduous trees and overhangs should keep the sun off your windows and the insides comfortably cool.
- Fold in green power sources like a solar hot water system and you can end up close to a "net zero home" (see sidebar, page 269) that produces almost as much electricity as it consumes.

How to Do It: Any earth-conscious designer/architect should be able to help you create your passive solar dream home, but a few names that specialize in it include solares.ca, coolearth.ca, mosssund.com and bradenhomes.ca. If you can't find an architect/builder that expressly works with passive solar principles near you, don't fret. Today's architects have been schooled on passive solar in their studies, so ask some local architects if they'd be willing to give passive solar a try. Get yourself a copy of *Tap the Sun: Passive Solar Techniques and Home Designs* to learn more.

Of course, you don't need to knock your house down and start afresh to incorporate passive design principles. When Europeans want to renovate according to passive solar house principles, they just load up on **insulation**, install **triple-glazed windows**, shade the house with **window awnings** in summer, plant large **deciduous trees**, buy **extra-efficient appliances** and throw in a **solar hot water system**. Really, your typical green reno wish list.

## GEOTHERMAL HEATING AND COOLING

You don't have to journey to the centre of the earth to access the free energy simmering under the surface. All you have to do is dig a few metres under your daffodils. How does it work? Just lay a loop of pipes down below (where the temperature's always 9°C to 12°C), run a little antifreeze through them and draw those stable temps into your home with a geothermal heat pump (where condensers bring the temperature up to where you like it) to keep your abode nice and toasty in winter and cool as cucumber dip in summer. It's the only renewable energy source for homeowners that works even if the sun ain't shinin' and the wind ain't blowin'. Even those living in the far north can tap into the warmth beneath the permafrost. And doing so will mean a 40% to 70% reduction in your heating and cooling bills (it all depends on how efficient your home is to begin with and how wasteful your habits are). No wonder sales of geothermal heat pumps are booming in Canada (even with the economy lagging). And did I mention that you can also use the system to heat your showers (reducing your water heating bills by up to 70%)? So, basically, you're getting a furnace, a/c unit and water heater all in one. Pretty damn cool (or hot, depending on what temp you want your house).

> Geothermal heating and cooling is the only renewable energy source for homeowners that works even if **the sun ain't shinin' and the wind ain't blowin'**

A head's up: because geothermal systems do require electricity to run the pump as well as the built-in electric heating backup system for times when temperatures plummet to −35°C ten days in a row and the pump isn't working as well, you will experience an increase in your electricity bills. The places where geothermal makes the most financial sense are in houses that would make use of geothermal's heating and air conditioning capabilities pretty heavily, like southern Ontario and B.C. As well, they're fiscally wise in places where electricity is relatively cheap and clean, such as hydro-powered provinces like B.C., Quebec and Manitoba (the electricity used to power a heat pump is a fraction of the electricity used to, for instance, power a Montreal home running on an electric furnace; as well, these homes will save about 4 to 6 tons of greenhouse gases annually). It's also popular with households looking to use some of their geothermal-heated water for radiant floor heating in certain portions of their house, like say the bathrooms or a ductless finished basement. It's less attractive, wallet-wise, in places like Alberta where air conditioners are rare, electricity prices are some of the highest in the country, and natural gas was, until recently, heavily subsidized. Also, if you don't already have ductwork in place, building ductwork just to put a geothermal heating and cooling system in might be prohibitively costly.

SaskPower (which promotes geothermal with $25,000 loans) says if you're switching from high-efficiency natural gas to geothermal in a province that gets its electricity mostly from dirty coal, you should off-set the rise in your electricity needs by installing wind, solar, micro-hydro or another renewable-energy technology source large enough to offset the estimated increased electrical load.

If you see an unusual spike in your electrical bills, call your installer. You might have a problem with leaky vents or a jammed thermostat.

**Horizontal or Vertical:** If you've got plenty of yard space to work with, you can lay out cheaper horizontal piping just a few feet down. Got a well or lake near you? You can pipe in an "open loop" system, which basically sucks heat from, or sheds heat into, the fresh water without adding pollutants (you just have to be extremely careful to meet all the environmental requirements). With land at a premium, city dwellers will have to install piping into deep vertical boreholes. The alternative to backyard drilling is to dig up your driveway, if you've got one, and bury the loop there. Note: tricky vertical digging does get pricey, because you have to dig deep (roughly 150 feet). You're looking at $25,000 to $30,000 for a 1,800-square-foot downtown house (compared to $10,000 for open-loop and $20,000 to $25,000 for non-urbanites with more room to fan those loops out closer to the surface).

**How to Do It:**

- Do the backhoe test: Can you fit a backhoe into your yard? You don't need a mammoth outdoor plot to do geothermal, but you do need enough space to fit a backhoe and industrial drill. Also, if you've got tens of thousands invested in landscaping, be ready 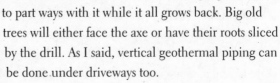 to part ways with it while it all grows back. Big old trees will either face the axe or have their roots sliced by the drill. As I said, vertical geothermal piping can be done under driveways too.

- Figure out your home's heat loss. After you've tightened up your home's envelope by adding more insulation and reducing drafts wherever possible (as you would before bringing in any renewable energy system), you'll want to ask a potential geothermal contractor for a proper F280 blower test to determine your home's heat loss (a post-reno eco audit needs to be done if you want to score federal rebates anyway). That'll help to accurately determine what size system you need. A cheaper contractor might just eyeball it or use computer modelling, but that ain't good enough.

- Suss out your soil. Your soil type will determine just how well geothermal can work for you. Why? Because some soil types are better heat conductors than others. Dry, loamy or sandy soil is a bad thing. Rocky, clay-heavy or moist soil is ideal. Of course, soil conductivity can vary from metre to metre. Your geothermal contractor will help you determine what you have a few metres down and, in turn, figure out your conductivity. The contractor will then multiply your home's heat loss by your soil's conductivity to help determine what size system you need (at minimum, Canadian standards dictate at least 70% capacity has to be met by your new system). According to Bill Eggertson at the Earth Energy Society of Canada, bad soil conditions could mean having to install four times the amount of loop to get the same heat from the earth, compared to good soil conditions.

- Choose a contractor who's been professionally accredited and trained by an organization like the Canadian GeoExchange Coalition (geo-exchange.ca), especially if your home is potentially eligible for a federal rebate (otherwise, you can also go with drillers and installers accredited by the International Ground Source Heat Pump Association (igshpa.okstate.edu). NextEnergy is a ClimateMaster distributor with accredited dealers all across the country (climatemaster.com). WaterFurnace (waterfurnace.com) is another big product manufacturer with national distribution. Carrier also makes geothermal systems now. According to insiders, they're all essentially the same; you just have to weigh which individual features and models (as well as which local contractor) you prefer by snooping around. There's a list of excellent questions to ask the contractor and the manufacturer at earthenergy.ca.

- Don't forget to do the upkeep. Not cleaning your filter out every other month can cause serious clogs in your system and may even void your warranty. Get someone in to check your fluid levels and various mechanical aspects about once a year.

- Looking for more background info? Natural Resources Canada is a great resource on this topic. (Just look up Earth Energy on the canren.gc.ca site.) Earthenergy.ca and geo-exchange.ca are other good online resources. And just think. Soon you'll be able to sleep easy at night, dreaming of how green your house is, now that it's heated and cooled with a little TLE—tender, lovin' earth.

Besides the fact that your heating and cooling bills will drop, oh, 50% to 70%, remember that you're up for a whack of cash back, including a $4,375 grant from the feds, an additional rebate in certain provinces, like a $4,375 rebate in Ontario, $1,250 in B.C., up to $2,800 in Quebec or $20,000 in financing through Manitoba's Residential

## GREEN POWER FOR THE SPATIALLY (AND CASH) STRAPPED

Just because you don't have the space and/or the funds to slather your roof with solar panels or a yard to dig up for geothermal doesn't mean you can't ease your guilt (and your environmental footprint) by buying green power from a third party:

**Bundled Green Power:** Feeling dirty about all the polluting power your place uses? Depending on which province you live in, you may be able to link your monthly power usage to a green power retailer. Now, don't expect solar panels to show up on your roof. You're actually paying for the retailer to feed the general grid with green electricity. You'll pay a little more a month, but you'll have a clear conscience and you'll be helping to clean the air. It's not available in every province, but if you live in Ontario, B.C. or Alberta you should definitely look into **Bullfrog Power**. Bullfrog has options for homeowners as well as condo or apartment dwellers without access to their own meters or hydro bills. Unlike bill payers, this won't be tied to your actual usage but runs on rough estimates (if, for example, you have a one-bedroom apartment, Bullfrog will estimate your power use at 4,500 kWh per year and charge you $13 or so a month to go "green"; **bullfrogpower.com**). Unfortunately, Nova Scotia is cancelling its green power program, and P.E.I.'s green power program is full (with no plans of expansion).

**Renewable Energy Certificates:** Just because you live in a province without a green retailer like Bullfrog doesn't mean you can't offset some of the GHG emissions created by your home. You just need to buy some carbon offsets or renewable energy certificates. Let's say your house uses 7,000 kilowatt-hours of electricity a year (like the average Canadian house does). You can buy $140 in clean, green wind, biomass and low-impact hydro certificates through the **Canadian Hydro Developers** (in $20/1000-kWh blocks) to make yourself feel better and to help support renewable energy (the certificates are certified by Environment Canada's EcoLogo Program: **canhydro.com**). SaskPower offers GreenPower for $2.50 per 100-kWh block. You can also buy offsets to compensate for your electricity and heat use through sites like **greennexxus.com**, **planetair.ca** and **carbonzero.ca**.

No, you're not literally powering your home with green energy, but think of it like this: you can get carbon offsets to compensate for the carbon dioxide emissions created by your flight to Mexico, but that doesn't mean you're going to literally be flying a solar-powered plane. Critics say that buying offsets gives people an excuse to pollute by making them feel better about their energy usage, but really, certificates should be seen as a way of funding clean energy projects when you can't afford to get your house off the grid, you live in an apartment or you just don't have the space for your own personal solar or wind farm. Note: you'll still get the same bill from your regular utility provider. There will be no added fees attached, as with bundled green power.

Earth Power Loan. (FYI, Manitoba's actually the national leader in per capita geothermal installations.) Saskatchewan, Ontario, P.E.I. and B.C. offer a tax rebate. Check geo-exchange.ca for info on financial support in your home province. By the way, one colleague with a geothermal system in his suburban home says his gas bill was down to $14 in the heart of February!

## WIND ENERGY

You know all those blustery winds that whip you in the face come November? Just imagine if you could harness that power to keep your house warm and bright. If you've got an average annual wind speed of, oh, 6 metres per second, you'll get about 300 kWh of electricity per month—enough to power a third of your home's needs. Turbines are especially useful in tandem with solar panels. On those blustery winter days when the sky's grim and solar panels are about as useful as a bikini in Yellowknife, that's when your turbine tends to come in extra handy.

Getting Started: The experts at the Canadian Wind Energy Association will tell you small wind energy (a.k.a. residential wind energy) could be right for you if:

❏ You have the room: Do you have at least half an acre of property with decent gusts? Make sure you have a spot far enough from buildings and fences (say 200 metres away if you want to avoid any noise associated with the spinning blades) and well above buildings and treetops. Basically, you'll need to hoist your turbine up on a tower to avoid wind obstructions (the higher the better and at least 10 metres above anything within 100 metres). Also, if you want a turbine big enough to power your whole home, you're looking at a 10-kilowatt system, which would have a blade diameter of, oh, 7 metres. That's no lawn ornament. Basic cabins can benefit from smaller systems, like **AirX**, the 400-watt wind generator from Canadian Tire for only $800 (plus the tower, a certified inverter, wiring, fuses, installation, etc.).

❏ You're in the clear: You've cleared your turbine plans with your municipality, checking zoning laws and seeking the necessary building permits.

❏ You're NIMBY-free: Not-In-My-Backyarders may not be happy with the idea of you hoisting a big turbine in their view. Make sure you get the clearance from neighbours unless you want icy winds blowing over social interactions.

**How to Do It:** For planning tips and helpful info on setting up your own wind turbine (including a ballpark cost calculator), as well as a directory of wind dealers and installers in Canada, check out the Canadian Wind Energy Association's Small Wind site (smallwindenergy.ca).

Check with your province to see if any rebates and incentives are offered. P.E.I., Ontario and B.C., for instance, offer provincial tax rebates.

## MICRO-HYDRO

If the term "hydro" has you picturing giant, land-flooding dams, think again. Low-impact hydro is being used by more and more utility companies, and—exciting but true—micro-hydro technology lets homeowners harness the power of water right on their own land. That is, if you're lucky enough to have the right kind of water on your property— namely a small waterfall or seasonal creek. The bigger the drop, the more power your turbine will produce, but Victoria's **WeGo Solar** says a small amount of water dropping a large distance will produce the same energy as a large amount of water dropping a short distance. You just need $3,000 or so to tap into it (see microhydropower.com, energyalternatives.ca or wegosolar.com). Of course, you'll have to look into applying for a water licence from your provincial Ministry of the Environment first.

$ Check with your province to see if any rebates and incentives are offered. P.E.I., Ontario and B.C., for instance, offer provincial tax rebates.

# MOVING

## I think a change (a change)
## will do you good

## So you've decided to change

your life's main stage. You're moving on up, or at least out, which is both exciting and plain exhausting. I find at times like these it's useful to turn to Gloria Gaynor for inspiration. That's right, get those boxes packed, honey, and walk out the door. Turn around now, you'll never see that old house any more. Maybe you're buying your first bungalow or moving into your first apartment. Maybe you're downsizing (now that the kids have left) or upsizing (to make room for a growing family). Hell, maybe you've just decided you want to taste life in a different part of the country or you're finally ready to build that dream home off the grid. Whatever your reason for moving, you'll want to make sure that your new house doesn't bring your home planet to tears.

# A SUSTAINABLE HOME

Okay, so you don't have the cash to buy a totally decked-out eco-fantasy house complete with geothermal heat pumps and reclaimed wood floors. Don't sweat it, here's a real checklist for buying a new home with some good green bones.

Location, Location, Location:
- ❏ Your home is an easy walk to decent public transportation routes.
- ❏ You can walk to food shops, schools, parks and regularly visited areas.
- ❏ You're not far from work. You can walk or take a short bus/subway/train ride to your job. (Remember, the average annual cost to own and operate a car in Canada is over $9,000. If you can drive less, drop your second car or even ditch the car altogether; that's money in the bank, and up to 5,500 kilograms of $CO_2$ saved.)
- ❏ Developers didn't pave over farmlands or green spaces to build your home.

Size Matters:
- ❏ You're not swimming in excess space. The smaller the house, the smaller your environmental footprint. And yet the average size of new homes in Canada has been growing every decade, while the number of people in those homes is shrinking. No one needs 4,000 square feet of space, and you certainly don't need five bedrooms if the kids have moved out. For every 100-square-foot reduction in your space, you save 590 kilograms of $CO_2$ per year, according to the Canada Mortgage and Housing Corporation. For a family of

The average size of new homes in Canada has been growing every decade, while the number of people in those homes is shrinking.

### No one needs 4,000 square feet of space

287

three or four, 1,700 square feet is more than plenty (definitely under 2,000 square feet). If you're a couple browsing for a condo or apartment, 900 square feet for one bedroom with an office should do you (although if you're planning on having a baby soonish, a 1,000-square-foot two-bedroom will give you a little wiggle room to grow, for now).

☐ You're open to snuggling with your neighbours. According to an urban planning report from the McGill School of Architecture, detached houses swallow 15% to 67% more energy than townhouses and accommodate 60% fewer people per net hectare than row houses. Bottom line, if you share one or more walls with your neighbours (instead of with the cold outside world), you'll automatically save money come bill time, as well as greenhouse gases.

☐ You're not hogging up lawn space. If you're not running an alpaca farm or selling veggies at the farmer's market, you don't need a massive yard. House-hunt in densely populated areas unless your work or lifestyle insists on space. I know, I know, people say they're moving to the suburbs to give their kids room to play, but come on, if you want to play, take them to a park.

Green Bonus Credentials:

☐ Lots of natural light so you don't have to rely on bulbs.
☐ New(ish) energy-efficient windows to keep drafts out.
☐ A high-efficiency furnace.
☐ Overhanging canopy trees that will shade your house come summer.
☐ Lead-pipe-free plumbing.
☐ No dodgy vermiculite or urea formaldehyde insulation.
☐ You like the house pretty much the way it is, so you're not tempted to undertake massive renovations just for aesthetics, creating unnecessary construction waste.

## REDUCE, REUSE, REMOVE: MOVING-DAY TIPS

Look, your house is full of crap you don't use—do you really want to move it all? Hold a garage sale before you jump ship. Or start a donation bin in your own home. Be ruthless—if you haven't worn that outfit in more than a year (okay, fine, two), donate it. If the dust on your bread maker is thicker than a slice of rye, donate it. Someone else could put it all to much better use—for instance, the people at Goodwill, your local women's shelter or even the avid recyclers at Freecycle (**freecycle.org**). As for the stuff you do decide to pack up and cart halfway across the country/city/street, here are a few tips:

- Avoid new cardboard boxes made with zero recycled content and either stock up on second-hand boxes from your local grocer or liquor store or sites like **Craigslist** (**craigslist.org**) or rent reusable moving crates through pioneering companies like **It's Your Move** in Vancouver (**saynotoboxes.com**). **U-Haul** has a take-a-box/leave-a-box system for used boxes.
- Wrap breakables with used newspapers.
- Stockpile bubble wrap, those horrible polystyrene peanuts and any other packing material you happen to receive in the mail for ultra-breakables (I also recommend trolling the garbage bins at your work mailroom).
- Look into alternative moving companies. Montreal-based **Transport Myette** moves furniture, appliances, boxes, construction garbage and more using a flatbed trailer pulled by a bicycle, yes, a bicycle. Fees are $25 per hour (**myette.net**). B.C.-based **Island Moving Trucks** uses propane- and bio-diesel-powered trucks (**islandmoving.com**). If they don't exist in your area, tell whatever company you do decide to rent from that you'd like to see them go green.
- Bypass the fume-inducing bleach and clean your new and old house with natural cleaners. If you're really keen on killing bacteria in your new pad, try **Nature Clean** or **Home Hardware's Natura** thyme-based disinfectants. They kill over 99.99% of bacteria, mould and fungal spores (**naturecleanliving.com**, **homehardware.ca**). That way, you can move in (or out) on a clean, green slate.

# BUYING A GREENER CONDO

Despite the sneers and jeers many utter about the mass condofication of cities like Vancouver and Toronto, you might be surprised to know that eco-heads actually support the whole skyward climb of our neighbourhoods. Better to have more of us squeezing into the downtown core than throwing more subdivisions up over farmers' fields. So, conscious condo shopper, let thee be praised for moving up, not out.

Not all such building projects should be commended, of course, since many could easily do more (like install energy-efficient lighting, for starters). And you might have noticed that renovated old buildings and factories are a hot source for lofts and condos. Enviros say cleaning up abandoned contaminated factories, be it for loft conversions or new bars, can be a green asset to the neighbourhood. Whatever place you peruse in your hunt for a permanent address, make sure to ask for a list of environmentally friendly features like the ones highlighted below. If a building you're eying up doesn't have any green credentials, tell them they're behind the times and spin around dramatically towards the door. If more buyers ask for green features and more condo owners organize to have their buildings retrofitted, the market will respond. Happy condo hunting.

Green Features to Look For:

- ❏ Energy Star appliances (which can save one ton of carbon dioxide emissions a year per unit).
- ❏ Individually controlled heating and air conditioning (which allows eco- and/or penny-conscious residents to lower their heat by a few degrees or shut off their a/c).
- ❏ Good access to transit.
- ❏ Water-saving low-flush toilets and shower heads.
- ❏ Bike parking and auto sharing.

☐ Renewable energy systems (e.g., geothermal heat pump, solar panels, deep lakewater cooling).

☐ Green finishes (low-VOC latex paints and coatings, as well as formaldehyde-free cabinetry help to keep the air in your condo pollutant-free).

☐ A green roof (at one Toronto loft, you can even buy your own rooftop garden plot!).

☐ LEED certification. Condos that have been certified via the Leadership in Energy and Environmental Design program in Canada have to meet strict environmental benchmarks. Platinum-ranked buildings, like Calgary's **Vento Residences** or Victoria's **Dockside Green** community, score the most green points, followed by Gold buildings like **Minto Roehampton** in Toronto, Silver buildings like the **Central Condominiums** in Ottawa and simply "certified" buildings like **Les Condo Wellington** in Montreal. For a list of LEED-certified and registered projects in your area, check out the database at cagbc.org. (Though note that LEED isn't a faultless system — see LEED for Homes [National], page 293).

☐ Happy neighbours. Make sure no starving artists or lower-income residents had to be ousted to build your dream condo. Otherwise, you might find you get a frigid reception from your new nabe, not to mention a condo-full of bad karma.

## GREEN HOUSING DEVELOPMENTS

Thinking of moving into a shiny new house? You're likely to consider nesting in a newly built community if a) the idea of retrofitting an old clunker of a home leaves you cold, b) you hate the cramped lifestyle of downtown living or c) your family simply can't afford a downtown-sized mortgage. Now, I'll admit, housing developments in the 'burbs haven't usually scored points with environmentalists. Cookie-cutter builders have historically paid zero attention to the mammoth environmental footprint of their creations. Instead, they've unapologetically promulgated sprawl, cleared farmland and fed our square-footage lust for bigger and grander homes with ever-expanding energy and water demands.

The good news is that there's a growing number of developers in Canada trying altogether different tactics. They're building homes that go well beyond basic building codes. Instead, they're erecting healthy, well-ventilated water- and energy-saving abodes that are much lighter on their feet (eco-footprint–wise) than those resource hogs up the block. And no, they're not just pulling random green upgrades out of thin air, they're building according to third-party standards set up by one of a number of national and regional bodies. Trouble is, there's now a zoo of green labels and certifiers out there so it can be a tad confusing, to say the least. Below is a brief breakdown of eco-conscious labels you'll spot on new housing. But listen, just because a home is Energy Star–certified or whatnot doesn't mean it's not an oversized McMansion, located far from transit, or that vital greenspace wasn't paved over to build it. You've got to use your eyes and ears and open your mouth to ask questions (like "Is there a transit route within walking distance?") to clear all the criteria on the *Ecoholic Home* sustainable home checklist (see page 287).

Just because a home is Energy Star–certified doesn't mean it's not **an oversized McMansion,** located far from transit, or that vital greenspace wasn't paved over to build it

R-2000 (National): A solid, government-backed standard that hasn't really caught on as much as other programs (maybe a more modern name is in order). Still, it's a strong standard that in many ways is better than Energy Star (for one, R-2000 calls for the use of low-VOC paints, cabinets and finishes, which Energy Star does not; some builders certify to both standards). Homes certified to R-2000 are 30% to 40% more energy-efficient than houses built to provincial building codes (typically, R-2000 homes use 30% less energy than a comparable non-R-2000 home), plus they have extra criteria for ventilation, airtightness, energy-efficient windows, insulation, water-saving devices and more. R-2000 homes must score at least an energy-efficiency rating of 80 on the EnerGuide rating scale.* For more information, see r2000.chba.ca.

**LEED for Homes (National):** The cream of the crop. Leadership in Energy and Environmental Design (LEED) is considered the toughest green-building rating system around (though it's certainly not without its critics; check out this piece on LEEDwashing sins: treehugger.com/files/2009/03/the-four-sins-of-leedwashing.php). Until very recently, the label was reserved for the V.I.G. (very important green) condo and office crowd, as well as cutting-edge schools, public housing or even churches. But as of the summer of 2009, the LEED for Homes program officially landed in Canada. It's available on new single-family homes and multi-family buildings up to three storeys. The Canadian Green Building Council (which heads up LEED in Canada) says the net cost of owning a LEED home is comparable to that of owning a conventional home once you account for lower energy and water bills. New standards are coming out for neighbourhood developments, public housing and existing buildings. For more info, see the Canadian Green Building Council's site: cagbc.org.

**Energy Star (Ontario and Saskatchewan):** Homes certified with this famous name are not only 30% more energy-efficient than houses built to paltry provincial building codes, but they're loaded with extra insulation, Energy Star–certified windows and heating and cooling systems, as well as Energy Star appliances and lighting (a natural fit, really). At the end of the day, Energy Star–qualified homes are said to churn out 2 to 3 tons fewer greenhouse gases and suck back 100,000

---

*EnerGuide for Homes is not a certifying body but a government-run system ranking a home's energy efficiency on a scale of 0 to 100. A rating of 0 represents a home with major air leakage, no insulation and extremely high energy consumption. A rating of 100 represents a house that is totally airtight, is incredibly well insulated and ventilated and requires no purchased energy (it gets whatever little energy it does need from renewable power). Many green housing labelling systems rely on the EnerGuide ranking.

## GREEN MORTGAGE$

Why get a regular old mortgage that pays zero attention to how green your home is and offers zero rewards for making energy-saving renos? Check out these cutting-edge options for financing your home.

**Citizens Bank's Green Mortgage:** The nation's first-ever green mortgage came courtesy of our favourite bank, the über-ethical Citizens Bank. With the Citizens Bank's Green Mortgage, you get a traditional Citizens Bank mortgage, plus the option of a $10,000 line of credit at prime that you can use for energy-saving renovations. You'll also score a Green Gift Package, which includes a complimentary Green$avers Home Energy Audit worth $250, coupons for energy-efficient products and services from local businesses, as well as compact fluorescent lights. The bank will also make a $100 donation to the Conservation Council of Ontario.

**TD Canada Trust Green Mortgage and the Green Home Equity Line of Credit (HELOC):** If you sign up for a green mortgage or line of credit with these guys, you'll get a reduced interest rate (a full 1% off the posted interest rate on a five-year fixed-rate mortgage or on a five-year fixed-rate portion of a HELOC) and TD Canada Trust will give you a 1% cash rebate on your mortgage or HELOC when you buy Energy Star products like, say, a dishwasher, windows and/or a furnace. So, if you have a $200,000 mortgage, you can get back up to $2,000 in cash. Plus, TD Canada Trust will donate $100 to the TD Friends of the Environment Foundation. Call 1-800-409-4424 for more info.

**Mortgage Loan Insurance Premium Refund:** The Canada Mortgage and Housing Corporation and Genworth Financial Canada offer a 10% refund on mortgage loan insurance premiums when a borrower buys or builds an energy-efficient home or makes energy-saving renovations to an existing home.

**Yukon Housing Corporation:** YHC offers mortgage financing of up to $200,000 at a reduced interest rate for homes built or upgraded to the corporation's GreenHome standard, which includes strict energy-efficiency requirements. GreenHomes must be constructed by Yukoners, and Yukon businesses must supply at least 75% of the building materials.

litres less water per year than conventionally built homes. Trouble is, Energy Star homes are currently found only in Ontario (esnewhomes.ca) and Saskatchewan (energystarsask.ca). Like other Energy Star–labelled items, this one's managed by Natural Resources Canada's Office of Energy Efficiency (oee.nrcan.gc.ca).

**Built Green (B.C. and Alberta):** This industry-initiated program was originally set up by the Canadian Home Builders' Association to promote green building practices and a third-party auditing system for green homes. A checklist is used to rate homes from Bronze to Platinum. A Bronze home has an EnerGuide rating of 72 to 74 (out of 100), a Silver home has a rating of 75 to 76, a Gold home has a rating of 77 or to 81 and a Platinum home scores 82 or higher (see footnote, page 293). For more info, see builtgreencanada.ca.

**Novoclimat (Quebec):** New single-family homes, condos, apartments and prefab homes constructed by Novoclimat-accredited builders are 25% more energy-efficient than conventional buildings, thanks to added insulation, high-efficiency heating systems, airtight doors and windows and more. The government-run program encourages the home construction industry to continually improve its building techniques, by offering training courses. Quebec's Agence de l'efficacité énergétique (AEE) offers homebuyers $2,000 in financial aid. For more info, see aee.gouv.qc.ca/en/my-home/novoclimat.

**Power Smart New Home Program (Manitoba and B.C.):** This program helps to maximize the energy efficiency of new houses by requiring extra insulation, more efficient heating, water and lighting systems and more. Its Gold Label homes have an EnerGuide rating of

80 and its Silver homes score a 77 (see footnote, page 293). The program is run through Manitoba Hydro (hydro.mb.ca/your_home) or BC Hydro (bchydro.com/powersmart).

GreenHomes (Yukon): Not only does this local-loving building standard require homes to have an EnerGuide rating of 80 or higher, but GreenHomes have to be built by Yukoners, with Yukon businesses supplying at least 75% of the building materials. Under the newer Super-Green standard, qualified homes have an impressive EnerGuide rating of at least 87, with features like a 40-centimetre-thick uninterrupted blanket of insulation in the walls. A $4,500 grant is available towards the cost of construction, and a $750 grant covers the costs of design, building permits, inspections and certification when a certified Green or SuperGreen home is built or purchased for the first time. (See housing.yk.ca for more details.)

## GREENING YOUR FIRST APARTMENT

You've moved out of your parents' house and scored your own pad. I can almost smell the freedom on you. You can finally eat what you want (cheese doodles and beer), when you want (4 a.m.), where you want (on the roof with your friends). Most run out and buy the cheapest crap they can get (hence the cheese doodles), the majority of which is loaded with chemicals and wrapped in wads of non-recyclable packaging. But don't worry, as an earth-conscious first-timer you have lots of affordable green options to choose from.

❐ Shop for second-hand coffee tables, kitchen tables and way, way more at sites like craigslist.com. As for second-hand couches, the newer the better. Lots of toxic stain repellents and flame retardants have been phased out in the last few years, so a couch that's only 4 years old would be safer than one that's 14. Unless you're going really vintage and getting some Austin Powers–esque '60s chairs. Otherwise, head to IKEA for cheap furniture that's ultra-low in formaldehyde and free of vinyl and toxic brominated flame retardants (see Decorating, page 81).

- ☐ Don't buy a cheap non-stick pan. They're made with super-persistent chemicals, so you don't want to be burning anything in these, especially if you have a pet bird (seriously, see PTFE, page 365, for more on Teflon). Best to get stainless steel or cast-iron hand-me-downs, or affordable "green pans" like EarthChef, available at Zellers for, like, $30.

- ☐ Buy everything in bulk to avoid packaging. And by "bulk" I don't mean 50 individually packaged candy bars from Costco. Hit the bulk stores and stock up on pastas, peanut butter, spices, you name it. Bring your own packaging if you have it. Of course, the bulk concept works for toilet paper (make sure to get the recycled kind, often cheaper cuz it's a teensy bit rougher) and cleaning products, too.

- ☐ Your apartment is bound to get pretty skuzzy, especially if you have lazy roommates. Don't just grab those buckets of nasty lung-irritating, potentially hormone-disrupting chemical cleaning products from the grocery store. And definitely pull out the picket signs if someone in your house wants to bring in disposable mops, toilet wands and cloths. Make your own cleaners with cheap stuff like vinegar and baking soda.

- ☐ If hair and muck have collected in your bathroom sink, stay away from super-caustic drain chemicals. Instead, pour some baking soda and vinegar down there, followed by a kettle of boiling water every week or so if you can remember. (Call your landlord to get someone to snake it if you're really plugged up.)

- ☐ Make sure everyone in your house is recycling. Put big clear labels over the recycling bins that explain what can be recycled in your hometown (check with your municipal website for info on that).

- ☐ Ban long showers. Five to eight minutes is ideal (10 minutes tops!) and ask your landlord for a cheap water-saving shower head and a $5 toilet dam you can put in the back of the tank. (It'll save your landlord money, too.)

☐ Hold green movie nights! Pop some organic popcorn and rent films with an enlightening message, everything from Woody Harrelson's *Go Further, Baraka* and *Erin Brockovich* to more hardcore teach-ins like *An Inconvenient Truth* and Leonardo DiCaprio's *The 11th Hour*.

## GREENING YOUR DORM

So let me get this straight: instead of spending all your time engineering beer bongs, you, my friend, want to shrink your residence's ecological footprint. Or maybe you want to do both. Either way, the good news is you're not alone, as the help hotlines say. Students and schools continent-wide are trying to green their residences.

• First off, if your school has a sustainability office, you should pay it a visit and see if the staff there have anything in the works you could help out with. If not, it's time to start spearheading your own campaign. Put up sign-up sheets to see if anyone wants to form an enviro team. Get reps to push different themes every month, like turning off computers and taking shorter showers.

• Sierra Student Coalition has a great campus Climate Challenge kit you could adapt to your dorm mission (**ssc.org**). It's full of ideas for stuff like holding a Do It in the Dark kick-off party where you give out flyers with the top 10 conservation tips.

• Once you've lined up support from other students, head to your campus's administrative office and book a meeting with whoever's in charge about energy-saving retrofits of light bulbs, toilets and shower heads. If you've got a creaky old rez, you might want to push for new windows and insulation, or at least some good caulking and weatherstripping. To ensure that new dorms are built in an environmentally friendly way, UBC developed its own green building assessment program, which mandates more bike storage spots, energy-efficient appliances and lights, low-VOC building materials and low-flush toilets. Talk to your admin about establishing similar standards at your school.

# GREENING YOUR COTTAGE

Come summertime, penned-in urbanites like me madly scramble to find pals like you with the mystical ability to crack open a Corona on a loon-speckled lake any weekend they please. Sure, plenty of enviros gripe that even owning a second home is bad news for the planet, especially if you have to get in your fossil-fuel wagon to get there. But I won't pretend I would turn down a charming shack nestled in the woods if it were served to me on a recycled silver platter.

The trick is keeping the whole experience as in tune with Mother Nature as possible. No beasts-by-the-lake, please. If your cottage has all the amenities of your regular house, **you're sucking way too much from the grid**. That means no clunky old dishwashers, no clothes dryers, no curling irons, no giant plasma TVs and definitely no a/c. You're in the wilds, people—embrace it. (Yes, that means you should cancel that Jacuzzi installer, too.)

**Checklist for a Green Cottage:**

- ❏ Lighten your load wherever you can: switch from 100-watt incandescents to 11-watt compact fluorescents, use a toaster oven over a real oven and use a coffee press (boiling water in an electric kettle) instead of a 900-watt coffee maker.
- ❏ Swap your old haze-emitting, draft-creating fireplace for a **high-efficiency hearth-mounted wood stove or insert** or, cooler still, a **pellet stove** (see page 251).
- ❏ Get yourself some **solar panels** (Energy Depot, for instance, has off-grid system packages for cottages from $11,099 to $20,000; energydepot.ca). Too pricey for ya? Start with a seasonal solar hot water heater for just a couple grand.
- ❏ Get rid of that old energy vampire of a fridge you have hidden in the country. A **Sun Frost** fridge, even a full-sized one, uses about 80% less energy than a regular fridge.

- Make leaky septic tanks a thing of the past. **Envirolet** (envirolet.ca) offers totally waterless **composting toilets** for peeps with and without basements. Some composting toilets can get tricky if you have lots of guests coming up to party every weekend. If that's the case, you might be better off with something like an Envirolet ultra-low-flush composting toilet that sends as little as a pint of $H_2O$ down per flush.

- If you plan on sticking with your regular loo, look into a **greywater recycling system**. **Brac** (bracsystems.com) makes some starting at $1,890 that recycle the $H_2O$ from your showers, bath or laundry (if you have one), filter it and reuse this water for the toilet tank. Or, for $32, get a quickie sink-top water catcher at envirosink.com.

- Make sure to use all-natural, highly biodegradable soaps like Nature Clean on your bod and dishes. **Dr. Bronner's Magic Pure Castile Classic Liquid Soaps** are organic and fair trade and can replace at least 18 other products (including shampoo, laundry soap and toothpaste—yep, toothpaste).

- Get yourself a big ol' **rain barrel** so you can water your roses without pulling out the hose (or just use a watering can filled from the lake for smaller jobs). And while we're on the topic of roses, leave the water-intensive flowers out from now on and stick to hardy native plants that can survive without your help.

- Resist the urge to jump on gas-guzzling, water-polluting watercrafts like jet skis. A 1998 report by Cali's Air Resources Board found that a full day of jet-skiing on a 100-horsepower craft released more polluting hydrocarbons than driving a 1998 car a jaw-dropping 100,000 kilometres. You heard me. Boats pulling water-skiers are also responsible for some serious lakefront air, water and, yes, noise pollution, not to mention all the neighbours you're pissing off.

- If your lakefront cottage is boat-access only, make sure that you're riding a cleaner four-stroke boat, instead of a seriously polluting two-stroke.
- Remember, as secluded as you feel, you don't live in a bubble. Get involved in protecting the community around you. Ask around about environmental issues weighing on the town. There's probably a dump-expansion or water-protection battle being waged nearby that could use your help.

## BUILDING SUSTAINABLE COMMUNITIES

Sure, we live in "neighbourhoods," but most of us really live in a bubble. We go home, get into our TV bubble and ignore the people sitting right next to us on the couch. The next morning, we get into our car bubbles, and forget we're not alone in the world (that's why you see drivers picking their noses like no one's watching!). Even in our public transit bubbles, we pretend there aren't six strangers pressed up against us and we never dare say hello. Well, it's time to bust out of the bubble, people, and remind ourselves that we exist in living, breathing communities.

The least talked-about part of going local is just plain connecting— to the tree out back, your neighbours, your neighbourhood, your community, your local charity. So when someone knocks on your door to tell you about a meeting to stop the incinerator, the clear-cutting or the chemical company moving into your 'hood, don't turn off the lights and hide. (They know you're in there.) Take the flyer and go to the meeting.

And remember, every local green act has a broader impact. Stopping a big box retailer from paving over wetlands will help safeguard your community from flash flooding. Starting a local organic farmers' market in a school parking lot not only supports the local economy, it shrinks everyone's ecological footprint. And fighting for a ban on lawn pesticides helps protect children from cancer-causing chemicals for generations to come.

**Link Up with a Local Cause:** Pick an issue that has you irked and look for allies. Meeting face to face with other people who worry about the same things you do is the most effective way to get movin'. Even if it's just you and three neighbours from up the road. You can also check with your regional environmental network for a list of established eco orgs in your home province (cen-rce.org/eng/networks.html).

**Start a Green Neighbourhood Watch:** If we're going to look out for our kids' safety, we should also protect their right to clean air, water and more. A green neighbourhood watch could encourage locals to note illegal tree cutting, creek dumping, retail and industrial pollution, and idling cars, as well as advocating for community gardens, rain barrels, neighbourhood carpooling and more. Nervous about confronting your neighbours face to face? Think friendly. Leave a helpful info-filled leaflet in the offender's mailbox.

**Tap Your Community's Right to Know:** Pollution comes from all kinds of sources, not just the big factory outside of town. And yet in most Canadian municipalities, it's nearly impossible to find out about the toxins being dumped by your local auto body shop or dry cleaner. Without the right to know, you might not realize that the old warehouse up the street is still storing PCB drums or that the vacant lot next door is an old toxic dumping ground. Which is why Canadians across the country have been fighting for their community right to know. Shouldn't we know what toxic chemicals are used, stored and released in our neighbhourhood? Gather up some friends and push for your community's right to know.

**Form a Green Tenant Group:** The whole greening-your-home thing is great and all, except that it can be pretty biased against us renters without a permanent stake in our humble abodes. But that doesn't mean we should just sit here and accept our wasteful fate. The truth is, there are tons of really affordable measures you can take on, even if your landlord won't (like getting a low-flow shower head, a water-saving toilet dam and a worm compost bin, as well as caulking and weatherstripping drafty windows). But what if you'd like to see bigger changes to your whole building? It might be time to form an enviro tenants group. Remember: united they stand, divided they freeze in leaky, inefficient apartments (at least in the winter). So go ahead, post signs about forming a new energy-saving, earth-conscious tenant committee—you may be surprised how many people show up. The truth is, all these changes won't just make your building more comfortable to live in, they'll also save you and your landlord money through energy and water savings.

It might be time to form an enviro tenants group. **Remember: united they stand, divided they freeze in leaky, inefficient apartments**

- ❏ Hold a "visioning session" and determine just what lean 'n' green changes tenants would like to see. Maybe you want your landlord to consider a composting program, which would reduce your waste by a whopping 30%, or you'd like to see energy-efficient appliances prioritized whenever they upgrade washing machines, dishwashers and the like (share your research on Energy Star appliances, like how certified clothes washers use 50% less power and half the water). Perhaps you're dreaming of seeing solar panels and a green roof constructed on your boring old rooftop. (The tenants at Toronto's 25-year-old Hugh Garner Housing Cooperative wanted just that, and they're fundraising to build Ontario's largest green roof as we speak.)
- ❏ Start with the easy stuff that reduces your building's energy bills almost immediately, like switching all the lighting over to compact fluorescent bulbs in all hallways. Build up to larger upgrades like moving the whole building over to low-flow toilets (hell, if a family of four can save a swimming pool of water a year by switching to low-flow, imagine how much a whole apartment complex could save!).

## SO HAPPY TOGETHER: GREEN CO-HOUSING

If the idea of co-housing elicits flashes of dorm life or *Three's Company* episodes, think again. Picture small-town/village vibes set up by forward-thinking communities that plunk eco-friendly housing down everywhere from farmlands to urban centres. Don't worry, these aren't cult-like communes. There's no wife-swapping or money-sharing involved. Everyone gets their own private house or apartment, but, according to the Canadian Cohousing Network, they do share lush courtyards, people-friendly walkways and communal buildings decked out with yoga rooms, play spaces, stages, lounges and more. Join in weekly community dinners, or not—it's up to you. These houses aren't necessarily cheap because they're made with earth-friendly building materials, but practices like carpooling and bulk purchasing bring your cost of living down. If you long for the neighbourly vibes of yore with a new green twist, browse the gorgeous locations dotting Canada at **cohousing.ca**. Note: B.C. is blessed with a ton of amazing co-housing options, but just because there aren't any in P.E.I. or Manitoba doesn't mean you can't spearhead some yourself.

- ❑ Contact municipal, provincial and federal levels of government to form a list of all the rebates and incentives available to help multi-residential buildings go green. Ontario, for instance, gives landlords rebates on solar equipment. You can even help the building manager fundraise to make some of the less essential changes your community wants to see, like a new native garden out front.
- ❑ If you've got a deadbeat landlord who ignores your pleas to fix a drafty old building, don't despair. Call the local tenants association for support.

# CUTTING-EDGE GREEN HOUSING

Daydreaming of building a green homestead from scratch? Don't get stuck with the same old energy-intensive building blocks. Think outside the box and build that dream home with truly local, natural and repurposed materials. Speaking of boxes, who said your house had to be shaped like one anyway?

**Straw-Bale Homes:** It might be time to update the tale of the big bad wolf. This time around, the clever pig with a straw-bale house would sit comfortably inside his cozy, energy-efficient home, oblivious to the strong winds outside. If anything, he'd have turbines out front to capitalize on all that huffing and puffing. That's right, kids, it turns out that tight bales of dry wheat and barley stalks make for excellent (and local sources of) insulation, though of course the western Canadians and Nebraskans who pioneered straw-bale homes well over a century ago knew that already. There are even modern stats to back it. The Canada Mortgage and Housing Corporation did a survey of straw-bale houses and concluded that they were indeed toastier come winter, using on average 21% less space heating than conventional homes (they're also comfortably cool come summer). And if you opt for a load-bearing straw-bale home design (versus the classic post and beam style), you'll be sparing a lot of trees. And don't worry, they're not fire traps. In fact, they have a lower fire risk than regular buildings. They're also inherently termite-resistant, breathable and buildable by handy DIYers with access to bales. They might cost a little more than conventional homes, due to extra labour costs, but you'll make up the difference in energy savings. Looks like the wolf is going to have to seek dinner somewhere else. For more info, see strawbalebuilding.ca and strawhomes.ca in Ontario, sustainableworks.ca in B.C. and sunandstraw.com in Alberta.

**Rammed Earth Homes:** Imagine if all you needed to build your green dream home was at your feet. With rammed earth homes, that wish comes true. This ancient building technique literally digs up soil from your building site, mixes it with gravel, sand, clay and maybe a little cement, and compresses the hell out of it all to build one of the most durable and sturdy building systems on earth. The Great Wall of China is made of this stuff, for god's sake! Did I mention it's soundproof and fireproof? The walls in a rammed earth home are 60 centimetres thick, with an insulating value twice that of most Canadian homes.

You could plaster and paint the walls if you choose to, but why would you when the walls are so gorgeously earthen? Most rammed earth homeowners let the walls' beauty speak for itself and, if anything, add a little pigmentation to the earth to give it a bit of colour. No wonder Frank Lloyd Wright designed a few houses with this stuff. Check out the North American Rammed Earth Builders Association for more info and a directory of builders in Canada (nareba.org). By the way, rammed earth homes are from the same family as cob homes (lump or rounded homes, popular in pre-13th-century England), made of clay, sand and straw, but rammed earth is considered stronger, though more expensive (the cost of the wall structure is about 20% higher than stick framing). Similar southwestern adobe structures made of clay, sand and water aren't considered suitable for colder climates.

Tire Homes: If you haven't heard of tire houses, you're probably envisioning hoboes sitting around oil-drum fires next to a stack of Goodyears. But trust me, homes made of tires can be quite comfy and, yes, even aesthetically pleasing. In fact, they don't look too different from conventional stuccoed houses—on the inside anyway. There's a whole subculture of these babies (over 1,000 around the globe), and most are affiliated with **Earthships** (designed by "biotect" Michael Reynolds). Admittedly, tire construction hasn't caught on with green builders around here yet, but in New Mexico there are real estate websites and subdivisions dedicated to these structures. And, yes, tire homes do exist in Canada.

What are they? You start with second-hand tires, ram them full of packed earth, then start stacking. Just think of them as oversized bricks and the next steps are pretty similar to your usual homebuilding process—that is, if most houses had alternative power sources, solar hot water heaters, a cistern (a.k.a. giant rain barrel) to catch rainwater, a greywater/blackwater system so you're recycling all your water . . . you get the point. You can even order a partially prefab Earthship online (earthship.net). The kit "can be adapted to any climate" and comes in any size, not to mention the garage. Yes, people with tire homes drive, too. (Hey, if you ever blow a tire, you can just save it for your next reno job.) By the way, the total cost for building an Earthship home is about $200 per square foot. A little higher than conventional homes, but with that cost you are also installing your own renewable power system.

Dome Homes: There's nothing dramatically different about a geodesic dome house. Well, other than its shape. Done right, that igloo-style surface can not only reduce your construction material needs by 30%, it can actually save you up to 50% on your heating bills since the round shape circulates air so well. Did I mention that a dome house potentially costs homeowners up to 15% less to build than a square house of the same size (though labour costs can add up)? Plus, the structure withstands earthquakes, snowstorms and other freak weather patterns like no other. Bonus: you'll look like you live in some whimsical Hobbit village. Granted, the old '60s-style domes were riddled with leak issues, but they've come a long way, baby. Just ask Canadian dome builders like **Domespirit Geodesic Domes** (domes.ca) and the **Canadian Wooden Domes Group** (cwdg.ca) if you're curious. FYI, the founders of Domespirit say their own 2,600-square-foot home is heated using the same amount of energy as a medium-size barbecue.

## TRACKING DOWN GREEN ARCHITECTS, CONTRACTORS AND MORE

Having trouble finding environmentally conscious green home specialists? It's not just you. Unfortunately, there's no easy one-stop shop for the whole country to access this info. Of course, some high-profile pros, like architects, can be tracked through their reputations alone, since their names are probably attached to media-garnering green designs in your area. Names like **Breathe Architects** in Toronto (**breathebyassociation.com**), **Acton Ostry Architects** in Vancouver (**actonostry.ca**), **Studio MMA** in Montreal (**studiomma.ca**) and **Solterre Design** in Halifax (**solterre.com**). You can tap into the directory of architects on the Royal Architectural Institute of Canada website, but they're not necessarily green (**raic.org**).

Beyond architects alone, Ontarians can click on a directory of green professionals at **greenbuildingontario.ca**, but there's only like 10 listings so far. Those lucky ducks living in B.C. have access to Light House's non-profit **Sustainable Building Centre**, which among other things offers a solid directory of eco-conscious residential service providers, from architects to realtors (**sustainablebuildingcentre.com**), as well as a directory of green building products. On a national scale, your best bet is Industry Canada's **Canadian Environmental Solutions** green buildings directory. It will put you in touch with green designers, architects, contractors, builders, ecological landscape specialists and more. It's impossible to find the directory on this federal website, so here's a direct (though lengthy) link: **ic.gc.ca/epic/site/ces-sec.nsf/en/home**. Note that's it's a pretty tough site to navigate and, as with most of these directories, those listed are self-nominated, so you'll have to do your own background checks to make sure they're truly green.

The website **erenovate.com** does screen the contractors on its site (since the founder was screwed by a window installer he found in the Yellow Pages way back when) but not for green purposes; sorry. Still, you can join the site for free and access contractor reviews and expert reno advice, plus you can post your home reno project and review responses from eRenovate-verified contractors. Its database of contractors covers six provinces.

**Green Prefabs:** Does the word "prefab" have you envisioning cramped mobile homes or those WWII-style bunkers you've seen travelling on the back of a truck on the highway? Well, think again. Today's prefabs have become showcases for the greenest and grooviest of architects. Some are assembled as micro cottages, others are dream homes for four. Since they're modular, you can build up or out, any which way you like. A well-insulated prefab will use a fraction of the energy of a conventional home. And thanks to optional solar hot water heaters and solar panels on prefabs made by companies like B.C.-based **Jenesys Buildings** (jenesysbuildings.ca), they can also be net zero homes that make as much energy as they end up using (FYI, Jenesys says its buildings finish for about $10 more per square foot than conventional buildings of the same size, but it all depends on what options you pick and your local labour costs for assembly).

Looking for something with all the amenities, proportions and transportability of a traditional trailer-sized home but with more earth-friendly pizzazz? Check out **Sustain**'s slick **MiniHome Solo** (sustain.ca; $139,000). These 36-by-8-foot units are free of things you don't want (vinyl, formaldehyde, toxic finishes) and have plenty of things you do, like certified wood, natural rubber flooring and ultra-efficient appliances that can easily be powered by a small solar/wind package. Their MiniHome design uses on averag one-tenth the materials and resources it would take to construct a typical home or cottage.

**The Aerie** by Toronto's **Breathe Architects** is more of a seasonal micro-cabin (aerieloft.ca). It's a beautiful sail-like structure that, at the end of the day, is essentially one fancy-ass tent. Made head to toe of Eastern white cedar (a lot of which is FSC-certified), this 11-by-10-foot self-contained room with sweeping 17-foot ceilings even has a second-floor loft big enough to fit a queen-sized bed. Its designer, Martin Liefhebber, says it's really a lean-to with mosquito screens. It just so happens to come with a few extra comforts, like a composting toilet, a clean-burning EPA-certified wood stove, a simple rainwater catchment system and an outdoor passive solar shower (just like the kind you get for camping). Not to mention the solar panels to power efficient lights and maybe a small appliance. You could even winterize the thing by adding windows.

Another personal fave is definitely the über-sophisticated Quebec-based **Énóvo**. These sexy structures come with a bevy of drool-worthy standard features, including a green roof, LED lighting, radiant floor heating powered by solar captors, a greywater recycling system, triple-pane low-E argon windows, **TOTO** low-flush toilets, the works. And the whole thing is designed with 100% FSC-certified wood and materials sourced within 800 kilometres of the plant in Quebec. Swoon (especially if you live anywhere near Quebec.) Better still, it arrives as fully finished modules! They can be designed to work on their own (as 48-by-16-foot modules) or they can be clipped together in various formations. And these babies are sturdy: one was dropped going full speed ahead on the Trans-Canada and the windows didn't even shatter. Sure, they might look a little southern California but this company actually started as an insulation manufacturer (it even built arctic camps) so you trust them to make it through the depths of winter, no problem. So how much do they cost? Typically, anywhere from $190,000 to $250,000 installed, excluding transportation and building the foundation (enovo.ca).

But beware: many conventional prefab home builders are trying to milk the green train by telling potential clients their homes are inherently eco because there's no on-site construction waste. That doesn't mean their homes are built with sustainable materials, so be sure to probe.

# THE ECOHOLIC DREAM HOME

If I had a pair of ruby slippers (and a bottomless bank account), I'd click them raw until a house with all of the following features fell from the sky:

- ☐ Rammed earth or straw-bale south-facing structure with full passive solar potential.
- ☐ Geothermal heat pump powered by massive solar panels (with geothermal water heating radiant floors in every room).
- ☐ Solar panels mounted over south-facing roof overhangs, which let in low-hanging winter sun but block out high-hanging summer sun.
- ☐ Solar hot water heater in tandem with drain-water heat exchangers.
- ☐ Triple-pane krypton gas–filled insulated fibreglass windows.
- ☐ Greywater recycling system that pipes shower and rainwater into toilets.
- ☐ Low-flow everything.
- ☐ Reclaimed wood ceiling, cabinetry and furniture.
- ☐ Top-of-the-line Energy Star appliances, including an induction stove.
- ☐ Backup high-efficiency wood stove (you know, in case of another Ice Storm–style blackout).
- ☐ Green roof with low-maintenance prairie grasses (if my house is in the city).
- ☐ Lush native garden complete with large shade-giving canopy trees and a big rain barrel/cistern.
- ☐ Kick-ass veggie garden.

**Top Tools For Going Green On A Dime:** Now here's a more realistic list of tools for greening your home on a tight budget:

- ❐ Caulking gun and weatherproofing for your windows and doors.
- ❐ Clothesline (to decommission your clothes dryer).
- ❐ Fans to keep you cool for cheap come summer.
- ❐ Power bars (so you can easily flick off all your electronics when you're not using them).
- ❐ Vinegar, baking soda and maybe some borax—all the cleaning ingredients you really need.
- ❐ Low-flow shower head and a cheap toilet dam.
- ❐ A programmable thermostat (to minimize your heating and cooling bills)—oh, and slippers to keep your feet warm in winter so you're not tempted to crank the heat unnecessarily.
- ❐ Packets of veggie seeds and thatch of earth or a balcony full of containers.
- ❐ A bus pass.

# RESOURCES

## DECODING GREENWASH

With so many "earth-friendly" products flooding shelves, do you ever get that feeling that the paint stripper or bug killer you're about to buy isn't as green as it claims to be? Stats prove you should trust your gut. In 2007, Terrachoice (the company that runs Environment Canada's certification program) surveyed products in six leading big box stores to see how legit green claims were, and the results were jaw-dropping. Of the 1,018 products bearing environmental claims, a whopping 99% were guilty of some sort of greenwashing sin.

Now, only a small percentage were flat-out lying; most were more discreet about their fudging. They used vague terms like "natural" or "eco-friendly." Some involved a hidden trade-off, where, say, the paper might have recycled content but is processed with toxic chemicals. Others made totally meaningless claims, like CFC-free. Hello! Everything's been CFC-free for, oh, 20 years. It's like advertising you're free of DDT. I bloody well hope you are.

By early 2009, the number of products making some sort of green claim jumped through the roof (up to a 176% increase, says Terrachoice's latest report). And virtually just as many were guilty of green sins, though a new sin had emerged: the sin of worshipping false labels. Basically, that's when marketers invent their own labels over a couple of grande lattes and make them look like official third-party seals of approval.

There is a light at the end of the greenwashed tunnel. Sort of. The Competition Bureau says there's a new sheriff in town. The revitalized agency is poised to pounce on companies that make false or misleading green claims. It has set up guidelines for terms like "recyclable," "compostable" and "non-toxic." And it's already started warning companies that they're going to have to, gasp, prove their claims—with science. Imagine that! But while it's warning businesses not to use vague wording and misleading claims, it's really just setting up a list of best practices and won't be flexing its muscles with penalties and charges unless a product makes totally fraudulent statements. Not nearly as hard-core as California, where the Attorney General has actually sued companies that don't fess up to using carcinogens. Still, it's a good start.

In the meantime, you'll have to rely on your own judgment. Here are some tips on distinguishing greenwash from the real thing.

### Green or Greenwash?

- Don't be fooled by a pretty green package. Just because it has leaves on the front and the word "nature" or "organic" in its tag line doesn't mean it's not harmful to the environment. (Benjamin Moore's Organic Comfort paint collection, for instance, isn't even low-VOC, and an Ontario gift store chain called Green Earth has so few earth-friendly products on its shelves, you'd think you'd stumbled into the wrong store.)

- Look for an ingredients list. You might not recognize the ingredients, but if, say, a cleaning company is transparent enough to list its ingredients that's a good start (though, FYI, all beauty products have had to display ingredients lists for a couple of years now). How are we expected to trust President's Choice Green cleaners if reps won't even tell you what the ingredients are when you call its consumer line?

- Search for specifics. "Contains recycled content" isn't good enough; "80% post-consumer recycled content" is much better.

- Look for third-party certification. Certified organic is a good one, but it doesn't mean much if two ingredients are certified organic and the rest are dodgy chemicals.

- Beware of poser labels. When companies can't meet third-party standards like FSC, certified organic or Green Seal, they might make up their own seal that looks super-official. Run labels by *Consumer Reports* Eco-Labels centre (greenerchoices.org/eco-labels).

- Do your homework. Scour the web for info, or easier still, check with *Ecoholic Home* before you shop!

# DECODING ECO LABELS

Where's the GPS when you need it? Shopping for products that don't traumatize the planet can leave you feeling like a drugged-out mouse in a maze. Especially if you're trying to keep your green labels straight—just snap your fingers and another dozen logos seem to manifest as major companies and retail chains take it upon themselves to invent their own eco labelling system. Thanks for the help, guys, but what we really need is a national, agreed-upon-seal (kind of like the Canada Organic label new to food aisles), one that we all know and recognize. The Competition Bureau promises to crack down on misleading green claims (see page 315) but don't expect it to stamp out weak labels. In the meantime, here's a quick rundown of some of the more revered labels on shelves. So should, you trust 'em?

 **Biodegradable:** Don't bank on products that claim to be biodegradable without coughing up third-party certification like the Scientific Certification Systems. But even that doesn't tell you a product is 100% biodegradable, it just means it will biodegrade by 70% within 28 days. Look for products with better specs like "Biodegrades 99% within 28 days according to OECD test #301D."

**CFC-Free:** Um, thanks, but everything's been free of ozone-depleting chlorofluorocarbons since like the mid-'90s (in North America, anyway). This label in no way means the chemicals used in a CFC-free product are good for the ozone layer, the planet or the people in your home. CFC replacements like HCFCs have also been found to be detrimental to the ozone layer. Although if you happen to be shopping for products while in a developing country, CFC-free is still an important logo, since developing countries have until 2010 to phase out CFCs.

 Compostable: If it's certified by the Biodegradable Products Institute/US Composting Council, you can trust this to mean that a product has been tested to biodegrade at the same rate as yard trimmings and food scraps. But it doesn't mean it can be put in your backyard composter. Some municipalities with door-to-door organic waste pick-up may mandate that certified compostable garbage bags be used, but others, like Toronto, accept any and all plastic bags (then filter them out), whether they're compostable or not (bpiworld.org).

 **Cradle to Cradle:** The cutting-edge peeps behind this label certify products as Cradle to Cradle Basic, Silver, Gold or Platinum based on the use of green chemicals and the perpetual recyclability of the materials used to make them. They pride themselves on meeting and exceeding the most hard-core environmental standards in the world. Nearly 200 products have been certified, including office chairs, textiles, surf wax and more. The end products aren't necessarily perfect (no item has received Platinum certification, for instance, and not all have upcycling infrastructure in place), but the certifiers are trying to keep the trajectory moving ahead to a brighter, greener future (mbdc.com).

 **EcoLogo/Environmental Choice:** This respected Canadian label was founded in '98 by Environment Canada. The logo can now be spotted on over 7,000 products North America–wide, from personal care and cleaning products to paint, flooring, office supplies, building materials and much more, with comprehensive set standards for each. These guys actually require independent verification of product claims, which too few do (ecologo.org). EcoLogo products should be greener than roughly 80% of the products in any given category.

**Energy Star:** The blue-and-white government Energy Star logo tells you an appliance uses 10% to 50% less energy than standard models and that an electronic item like a DVD player uses up to 75% less electricity in standby mode. In 2008, *Consumer Reports* slammed the government-led program started in the

U.S. but adopted by Canada and others. *CR* said the 17-year-old program was too lax about who gets the star and that it needed more random spot checks and independent testing to make sure products are living up to the label. Since then, politicians south of the border have vowed to at least update and tighten Energy Star standards more regularly. Even if Energy Star appliances save half of the 40 million tons of greenhouse gas emissions they claim to prevent, they're still a good label to look for (energystar.gov; oee.nrcan.gc.ca/energystar).

 **EPEAT (Electronic Product Environmental Assessment Tool):** This system helps public and private sector buyers purchase greener computers (epeat.net). The program relies on electronics makers themselves to declare themselves in compliance with the EPEAT standards, and there's no third-party certification. Products score a Bronze, Silver or Gold depending on energy use, packaging, product longevity and the reduction of toxins. All EPEAT computers meet the Energy Star standard. Still, some critics say it doesn't go far enough. For more on the debate, punch in "beyond EPEAT" at etoxics.org.

 **Fair Trade Certified:** You'll find this label mostly on food products, like sugar, tea, coffee, chocolate, etc., but it can also appear on cotton poducts or sports balls. This seal tells you workers are paid a decent wage and the premiums you fork out for that cup of joe or whatnot also fund health care and education. Dangerous pesticides are banned and organic practices are encouraged, but unless it comes with the certified organic seal, there are no guarantees. Handicrafts like those at Ten Thousand Villages aren't covered by this certification scheme (transfair.ca).

 **Forest Stewardship Council (wood/paper):** It's still considered the best wood label we have, but critics say the FSC's global monitoring of forests has major gaps and that old-growth trees aren't well protected from the axe. To avoid chopping old-growth rain forests, it's best to stick to domestic FSC lumber. FSC Pure means it's 100% certified; the FSC Mixed Sources label, on the other hand, means it contains up to 30% non-certified sources, which gets a little dodgy. Go with the pure stuff from more local sources (fsccanada.org).

**Green Seal:** An indy, non-profit org with a comprehensive certification scheme that varies depending on the product category (from cleaning products, furniture and paper to paint, hotels and more). These guys actually visit the factory floor and do annual monitoring, and they insist on independent verification of product claims (greenseal.org).

**GREENGUARD:** This logo tells you one thing and one thing only: that a product shouldn't emit too many indoor-air-polluting VOCs into your home/business/school. Insulation with this logo may have minimal formaldehyde emission, but that doesn't mean it wasn't bound with dodgy flame retardants or that it has any recycled content. GREENGUARD Indoor Air Quality Certification was started mainly for the commercial sector; the more stringent GREENGUARD Children and Schools Certification standard was developed more for schools and homes (greenguard.org).

**HCFC-Free:** Now we're getting somewhere—this label is way more relevant than CFC-free. Though hydrochlorofluorocarbons were originally brought in as a greener replacement for CFCs, HCFCs turned out to be an ozone-depleting greenhouse gas. In 2007, at a United Nations Environment Programme meeting, 200 countries agreed to phase out HCFC production by 2013.

**Hypoallergenic :** The FDA in the U.S. says it "does not know of any scientific studies that prove whether 'hypoallergenic' products produce fewer allergic reactions than products that don't have the claim." Sorry to disappoint.

**Includes Biodegradable Surfactants:** Okay, so the surfactants (wetting agents that help lift dirt and oil away) might be biodegradable, but don't be fooled into thinking this applies to the product as a whole. This claim has no real third-party monitoring.

 **Leaping Bunny:** One of the only certified "no animal testing" logos around. Unless you see this exact bunny with stars in the logo, it probably wasn't certified (most companies just stick any old rabbit image on their product and call it a day). This one's on a lot of cleaning products, as well as personal care goods, and tells you the company has officially pledged to the Coalition for Consumer Information on Cosmetics that neither it nor its suppliers conduct or commission animal testing, though they might have in the past (leapingbunny.org).

**Non-toxic:** Think someone's overseeing the use of this term? Think again. Health Canada told me this is an "industry-devised marketing term." No universal meaning, though. In fact, in California, it's not unheard of for a consumer to spot the non-toxic label on a product that also comes with California's warning system that alerts consumers that "this product contains a carcinogen."

 **NSF (National Sanitation Foundation):** This nonprofit is considered the leader in setting standards for product safety and efficacy (so that if a water filter says it filters bacteria, it actually does). They certify everything from water filters, bottled water, appliances, plumbing and faucets to pool and spa components. You can find the seal on millions of products (nsf.org).

**Oeko-Tex:** This is an international standard for textiles. Oeko-Tex Standard 100 has been around since 1992 and essentially screens for harmful chemicals like formaldehyde on the finished fabric. It tells you how "skin-friendly" a product is. Newer Oeko-Tex Standard 1000

is much more substantive. It involves auditing and certifying that a product is manufactured from start to finish in environmentally conscious facilities free of child labour. The International Oeko-Tex Association is a grouping of 14 textile and test institutes in Japan and Europe that's responsible for the independent Oeko-Tex tests (oeko-tex1000.com).

**Organic:** You'll see certified organic food and beauty products that come with the USDA seal (and now the Canada Organic seal on Canadian food), but rarely will you see an organic seal on organic curtains or sheets. The label should tell you that no chemical inputs have been used for at least three years and that the farm that grew the cotton or hemp or whatnot is focused on using natural pest control, crop rotation and boosting the soil's fertility without synthetics. You'll have to call up the company directly if you want proof that it's actually organic. Some are members of the Organic Trade Association (ota.com). Note that "organic" doesn't mean the workers were fairly paid; only "fair trade" means that.

 **Processed Chlorine Free (PCF):** Spot this logo on recycled paper and you'll know the recycled content wasn't rebleached with chlorine-containing compounds. This label is third-party certified (chlorinefreeproducts.org).

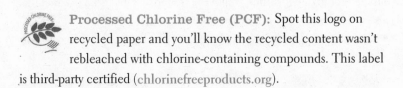 **RugMark:** No children were involved in making rugs that come with this label. Founded in 1994, the RugMark Foundation was established by a coalition of groups like UNICEF, government bodies, businesses and others to certify rugs made free of child labour. More than four million rugs have been sold with the RugMark label in North America and Europe (rugmark.org).

 **SFI (Sustainable Forestry Initiative):** This industry-run program of the American Forest and Paper Association doesn't get much R-E-S-P-E-C-T from enviros. Not only do they allow clear-cuts of up to 120 acres, but they greenlight genetic engineering and the axing of old-growth forests (sfiprogram.org).

**SmartWood (Rainforest Alliance):** This label can signal a couple of things, so it can get kind of confusing. SmartWood is the leading FSC certifier, so the SmartWood label will often mean the same thing as FSC-certified. But it could also mean that the product is made of reclaimed or rediscovered wood (see below; smartwood.org).

**SmartWood Rediscovered Wood (Rainforest Alliance):** This label tells you the wood used came from dead, fallen, diseased or nuisance urban trees, unproductive orchard trees, wood recovered from landfills or wood that was a by-product of another manufacturer. The removal of abandoned wood from underwater sources like, say, a river or ocean, should not disrupt the ecosystem from which it was taken. It also discourages the use of chemicals on these wood products and ensures that you're not pissing off any local Native groups by removing it (smartwood.org).

**Totally Chlorine Free (TCF):** When this logo appears on virgin (non-recycled) paper products, it guarantees that the pulp that went into them wasn't bleached with chlorine or chlorine-containing compounds (chlorinefreeproducts.org).

**Underwriters Laboratory:** The Underwriters Laboratory is an independent product safety certification organization that's been around for over a century. It has over 1,000 safety standards in place, and UL marks appear on 72,000 products each year (ul.com).

**VeriFlora:** A certification process for flowers that tells you your cut flowers and potted plants were picked under fair labour conditions with minimal chemical pesticides. It also requires growers to plan to convert to organic pest management, and farms must also meet significant greenhouse gas reduction and energy-conserving goals (veriflora.com).

# REBATES AND INCENTIVES GUIDE

## FEDERAL INCENTIVE$

Home Renovation Tax Credit: You can thank the recession-weary federal budget of 2009 for this "targeted stimulus"—a temporary, one-year, 15% federal tax credit to families on home renos for work performed or goods acquired between January 27, 2009, and February 1, 2010 (though hopefully this gets extended). The credit can be claimed on eligible expenditures above $1,000 but no more than $10,000; the maximum credit is $1,350. Furniture, appliances, electronics and reno tools are not covered. Look for the Home Renovation Tax Credit link on the feds' site (cra-arc.gc.ca).

ecoENERGY Retrofit for Homes: This federal program gives homeowners (including condo owners and owners of co-op housing and rental houses) up to $5,000 in grants to offset the cost of making energy-efficient improvements, from increasing insulation to upgrading a furnace. The thing is, you have to get an energy audit done before and after you do those renos (and the auditor has to be certified by Natural Resources Canada). You've got 18 months from the time of the first audit to have the renos completed if you want a cheque in the mail (ecoaction.gc.ca). The program technically ends March 2011 but grants end when the allocated money runs out, so get renos done sooner rather than later. Also keep in mind that some provinces, like Ontario and B.C., will match the federal grants dollar for dollar, or close to it (see below).

## PROVINCIAL AND TERRITORIAL REBATE$ AND INCENTIVE$

Most utility providers and municipalities also offer rebates for eco-friendly retrofits, so be sure to inquire. For more info about the rebates available in each province and territory, see ec.gc.ca/incitatifs-incentives.

And since low-income tenants tend to spend on average three times more of their income on utility bills than the rest, I've included low-income energy assistance options for each province and territory, where available.

## BRITISH COLUMBIA

Get a certified energy audit through the LiveSmart BC Energy Efficiency Program and they'll match many of the rebates offered by the feds. You'll also find PST exemptions on many green home retrofit purchases (livesmartbc.ca).

Low-Income Energy Assistance: Get a free energy-savings kit from BC Hydro that includes compact fluorescent light bulbs, weather-stripping for windows and doors, fridge and freezer thermometers and low-flow shower heads. Call 1-877-431-9463 to apply (bchydro.com/powersmart/residential/energy_saving_kits.html).

## ALBERTA

Alberta finally started a reno rebate program in early 2009. They'll give you $400 to $600 for a high-efficiency heating system, up to $3,150 for insulation, $100 for an Energy Star clothes washer, up to $300 for a new water heater, and $200 towards the home energy audit needed to qualify for the feds' ecoENERGY Retrofit rebates. Any Albertan who buys a detached or semi-detached home with an EnerGuide rating above 80 can also score some cash. The provincial rebate program is administered by Climate Change Central (climatechangecentral.com).

## SASKATCHEWAN

Saskatchewan residents who build or purchase a newly constructed Energy Star–qualified or R-2000-certified home can get up to $2,400 in rebates. The province also offers up to $5,000 in rebates for making energy-efficient upgrades in your home, and there is a PST exemption for all Energy Star–certified boilers, furnaces and ground- and air-source heat pumps, as well as an Energy Star loan program that will help you finance the installation of a qualified boiler or furnace. The installation of a programmable thermostat will score you a rebate of $15 (saskenergy.com/Saving_Energy/specialoffers.asp).

**Low-Income Energy Assistance:** The Saskatchewan Home Energy Improvement Program (SHEIP) for low and moderate income households offers financial assistance to help homeowners with the cost of making energy-efficient improvements to their homes. Call 1-866-388-8433 for more info. SaskEnergy's Share the Warmth Home Energy Efficiency Project helps Saskatchewan families lower their energy costs (saskenergy.com/Saving_Energy/specialoffers.asp).

## MANITOBA

The provincial energy-efficiency rebate for new homes starts at $1,000 with the purchase of an Energy Star–qualified or R-2000-certified home and moves up to a maximum of $2,400. Manitobans can also receive up to $3,000 in incentives, including a refundable Green Energy Equipment tax credit worth about $2,000 and a $1,000 grant for the installation of geothermal heat pumps in homes located in areas with natural gas service (gov.mb.ca/stem/energy/geothermal/incentives.html).

The province also offers a $50 rebate, introduced on February 12, 2009, for the installation of a dual-flush toilet. Manitoba Hydro offers rebates of $245 for an Energy Star furnace; as well it offers loans for solar and geothermal power. (hydro.mb.ca).

**Low-Income Energy Assistance:** Qualified lower-income households are eligible for free home evaluations, low-flow shower heads, compact fluorescent light bulbs and faucet aerators. Free or low-cost insulation upgrades are also available, as well as a rebate of $2,500 for natural gas boilers and furnaces at a cost of $19 per month for five years (energy savings for the upgrade will more than cover the monthly payments; hydro.mb.ca/your_home/lower_income.shtml).

## ONTARIO

Through the Home Energy Audit Program, the government of Ontario offers to pay 50% of your first home energy audit (up to $150). Under the Home Energy Retrofit Program, you can get up to $5,000 from the government of Ontario, basically matching the federal rebates dollar for dollar (homeenergyontario.ca).

Ontario Power Authority offers up to $550 in rebates to homeowners who replace their heating and cooling system with an Energy Star–qualified model (everykilowattcounts.ca).

Enbridge offers a $15 rebate on programmable thermostats, a $50 natural gas water heater rebate offer (for new customers only) and a $100 rebate for Energy Star–qualified natural gas heating system upgrades.

Low-Income Energy Assistance: The Enbridge Home Weatherization Retrofit program provides eligible participants with a free home energy assessment and weatherization upgrades at no cost, to improve the energy efficiency of their home. Enbridge will also install programmable thermostats and low-flow shower heads for low-income households. Check with your local utility provider for comparable programs in your area.

## QUEBEC

The Agence de l'efficacité énergétique (AEE)'s Renoclimat program offers financial assistance for home energy audits (valued at $300) and links you to grants from energy distributors like Hydro-Québec and Gaz Métro (aee.gouv.qc.ca/en/my-home/renoclimat/financial-assistance).

Low-Income Energy Assistance: L'Agence de l'efficacité énergétique's EconoLogis program offers modest energy-efficient upgrades and a programmable thermostat to low-income residents (aee.gouv.qc.ca/mon-habitation/econologis).

## NEW BRUNSWICK

The Efficiency New Brunswick program will subsidize the cost of Natural Resources Canada's residential energy audit by $400, then they'll give a grant of up to $2,000 or an interest-free loan of up to $10,000 to eligible New Brunswick homeowners who make energy-efficiency upgrades to their home (efficiencynb.ca).

Low-Income Energy Assistance: The Department of Social Development, in partnership with Efficiency New Brunswick, aims to help low-income households improve their energy efficiency through financial assistance of up to $4,500 for upgrades to insulation, windows, ventilation systems, air sealing and heating systems. For further info, contact a regional office of the Department of Social Development.

## NOVA SCOTIA

In tandem with the federal rebate program, Nova Scotia's EnerGuide for Houses Program offers up to $1,500 in rebates for energy-saving retrofits. For new houses, homeowners will receive a rebate of $175 towards their energy audit. If they score an EnerGuide rating of 77 or more, they'll receive a rebate of $350. They're also offering a 15% rebate on the cost of solar water-heating systems (conservens.ca).

Low-Income Energy Assistance: Low- to modest-income Nova Scotians with a net family income of less than $40,000 could get a grant of up to $400 and will also be reimbursed for the cost of a home energy evaluation through the EnerGuide for Houses Assistance Program. If you're a homeowner with a single income of less than $25,000 or a net family income of less than $40,000, you may qualify (conservens.ca).

## PRINCE EDWARD ISLAND

Through the ecoENERGY Audit Assistance Program, you can get a home audit at a reduced governmental rate starting at $100. The P.E.I. Energy Efficiency Grant Program will pay out up to $1,500 towards green retrofits, and $30 for each Energy Star–qualified window or door.

Also, the Office of Energy Efficiency will provide a $300 incentive on high-efficiency oil-fired heating systems (gov.pe.ca/oee). The P.E.I. Petroleum Marketer's Association also offers a direct subsidy of $200 (but only if the system is installed and purchased by one of the association's member dealers, listed on the website).

Low-Income Energy Assistance: Low-income households ($30,000 or less) can have their energy audit bill covered under the P.E.I. Home Energy Low-Income Program. The program also includes the free installation of a low-flow shower head, a programmable thermostat and an $80 voucher for furnace cleaning (gov.pe.ca/oee).

## NEWFOUNDLAND

The Newfoundland and Labrador EnerGuide for Houses Program will match federal ecoENERGY rebates for amounts up to $1,500 (ecoenergyatlantic.ca). Newfoundland Power is offering up to $10,000 in financing to cover the cost difference between a conventionally constructed home built to code and the same house built as a high-efficiency R-2000-certified home. Loan payments are made through monthly electric bills. They'll also let anyone with electric heat borrow up to $2,500 to upgrade their insulation and repay it in the same fashion.

Low-Income Energy Assistance: Through the Home Heating Rebate Program, households with an income up to $35,000 can get up to $300 back if the primary source of heat is heating oil, stove oil or propane, $200 for other sources such as electricity, wood or wood products, and $500 for anyone living in coastal Labrador. If your household earns between $35,000 and $40,000, you can get $100 back (gov.nl.ca/fin/homeheating; newfoundlandpower.com).

## YUKON

The Home Repair Program provides homeowners with an opportunity to borrow up to $35,000 to retrofit their homes to be more energy-efficient and environmentally friendly. A technical officer will assess your home and provide you with a comprehensive list of eligible repair and upgrade options. Loans under this program are amortized up to 12 years at a reduced interest rate (housing.yk.ca). The government's Energy Solution Centre offers rebates for Energy Star appliances and heating systems (esc.gov.yk.ca/programs.html).

**Low-Income Energy Assistance:** Actually, the Yukon's energy assistance program isn't strictly for low-income residents but for all seniors over 65. They get close to $1,000 a year towards heating bills.

## NORTHWEST TERRITORIES

The Arctic Energy Alliance offers several rebates through the Energy Efficiency Incentive Program (EEIP), for everything from freezers and washers to furnaces, ventilators and outdoor motors. A complete list of products and rebates is available at aea.nt.ca/ee_initiative.aspx (click on Program Guidelines). Rebates will be offered for as long as funds are still available through the program.

**Low-Income Energy Assistance:** The Northwest Territories offer a Senior Home Heating Subsidy to low-income seniors over 60 (hlthss.gov.nt.ca/seniors/default.asp).

## NUNAVUT

Nunavut's Home Renovation Program offers up to $50,000 in loans to homeowners who do major renos and repairs, with an additional $15,000 for upgrades that specifically boost energy efficiency. The Homeowner Energy Efficiency Rebate Program doles out up to $1,000 in grants for appliances, insulation, etc. (nunavuthousing.ca).

# PLASTICS GUIDE

One day far in the future, archeologists are going to look back at the remnants of today's culture and call us the Great Plastic Civilization. Look around. We've managed to envelop every inch of the planet with the stuff—including the ocean. In fact, the United Nations Environment Programme estimates that every square mile of ocean contains, oh, 46,000 tiny pieces of floating plastic. There's even a giant floating garbage patch twice the size of Texas swirling in the Pacific (it's called the Great Pacific Garbage Patch, in case you want to look it up).

No matter how planet-conscious you are, sometimes you just can't get away from using plastic, so it's best to size up which type causes the least harm.

But even safer plastics can't be blindly trusted. The *Milwaukee Journal Sentinel* had, in the fall of 2008, 10 plastic food containers lab-tested for microwave leaching, and found that even plastics Nos. 1, 2 and 5 had hormone-disrupting bisphenol A (BPA) leaching from them, including frozen food trays, microwaveable soup containers and plastic baby food packaging. Wait—isn't bisphenol A only in No. 7 polycarbonate plastic? Guess not. Stay safe and read up on the ins and outs of your plastics.

By the way, I know many of you well-meaning recyclers just toss all your plastics in the recycling bin, but if, for instance, your city takes only plastic No. 1 and No. 2, the rest of the plastic you so diligently recycled will end up in a landfill. Best to call your municipality (or head to its website) and find out which plastics belong in your recycling bin.

Know your numbers. (Those little triangular recycling logos are there for a reason.)

**Polyethylene Terephthalate (PET):** Soda bottles, shampoo bottles and water bottles. Probably the most commonly recycled plastic. Contains UV stabilizers and flame retardants, but has fewer harmful additives that will leach into landfills and your meal. PET disposable water bottles have been known to leach antimony, however. In 2008, a *Milwaukee Journal Sentinel* investigation found that even some No. 1 containers leached bisphenol A in the microwave. The news didn't spread.

**High-Density Polyethylene (HDPE):** Milk jugs, cleaning-product bottles, shopping bags (which aren't necessarily recycled in municipalities that recycle No. 2 plastic—best to check). Most municipalities accept narrow-nose containers, but not all take wide-lipped ones such as margarine tubs, even if they're No. 2s (again, best to ask). HDPE is not a bad plastic, compared to the others. Though the 2008 *Milwaukee Journal Sentinel* investigation found that even some No. 2 containers leached bisphenol A in the microwave.

**Polyvinyl Chloride (PVC):** Greenpeace ranks this one as the biggest eco-villain of all plastics. This is the plastic wrapped up in all the toy recalls, as well as shower curtain scares. PVC, or vinyl, is made with vinyl chloride, a known human carcinogen. It's said to emit persistent dioxins in both its manufacture and incineration (especially in crappy municipal incinerators). Hormone-disrupting phthalates added to soften it have been found to off-gas from the plastic. Lead and cadmium are commonly used as stabilizers and have also been found to migrate from the plastic (think lead in toys or Venetian blinds). Though it's used mostly by the construction biz (yes, your pipes just might be PVC), it's also the basis of vinyl records, old car seats and fake leather couches. If your plastic bottle has the number 3 or a V on the bottom, it's PVC. Rarely recycled.

**Low-Density Polyethylene (LDPE):** Like its high-density sibling, No. 4 plastic isn't as toxic to manufacture as other plastics are, but it's less commonly recycled.

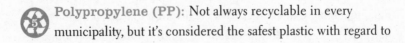

**Polypropylene (PP):** Not always recyclable in every municipality, but it's considered the safest plastic with regard to leaching potential. Shocker of all shockers, in a *Milwaukee Journal Sentinel* investigation, some No. 5 containers were also found to leach bisphenol A when microwaved.

**Polystyrene (PS):** A category best known by the trade name Styrofoam, which is often used to generically refer to the whole PS category, though Styrofoam specifically applies to one type of PS, namely extruded polystyrene. Either way, PS is tied with polyurethane for second-worst plastic, because making the stuff involves carcinogenic benzene; plus, it's very rarely recycled.

**Mixed Bag:** Basically any plastic other than Nos. 1 to 6. Not readily recyclable. Under this broad umbrella sits polycarbonate (the hard plastic used for refillable baby and water bottles), which used to be marketed as nonleaching, not to mention indestructible—perfect for outdoorsy types. Turns out it does leach the hormone-disrupting chemical bisphenol A (found in the lining of food and beverage cans and polycarbonate bottles, including baby versions). For more on the controversy, see bisphenol A, page 350. Polyurethane is also a No. 7, and though considered greener than PVC, it still emits toxins like methylene chloride during production.

## GREEN PLASTICS GUIDE

There's a maze of "green" plastics on the market today. Are they really as earth-friendly as they claim to be? Here's a breakdown of some of the plastic labels you may come across. By the way, (almost) none of these should be placed in conventional recycling bins—they're considered a contaminant that could damage the durability of, say, a recycled plastic carpet or a recycled plastic car part.

**Bioplastic:** Made from plant-based oils, starches or fibres. Could come from genetically engineered crops, so it's always best to ask.

**Biodegradable Plastic:** Biodegradable plastic is generally made of some sort of plant-based materials like cornstarch, potato starch or sugar cane (though scientists have tinkered around with plastics made from garbage like orange peels and chicken feathers, too). It needs only naturally present bacteria to dissolve back into natural elements (carbon dioxide, water, etc.). Some municipal composters, like those in Halifax, do accept biodegradable/compostable plastics, but others, like Toronto, filter any and all plastics out. If it ends up in dark, airless landfills, it's unlikely to fully break down, given that decades-old hot dogs can still be found in dumps. For that reason, as well as the possibility that biodegradable plastics could be made with genetically modified ingredients, many feel these plastics do not deserve the green hype they get. Critics also charge that food crops should be left for hungry bellies and shouldn't feed our appetite for disposable plastic products. One company makes an additive called Bio-Batch that is said to make regular plastic biodegradable *and* recyclable. To ensure a plastic is legitimately biodegradable make sure it's certified by a third party (see Decoding Eco Labels, page 317).

**Compostable Plastic:** These are similar to biodegradable plastic, but compostable plastics are considered greener since they biodegrade much more readily (the plastic is often flimsier as a result). They are often certified to break down in a municipal composter as fast as other compostable goods, with no toxic residue. They may or may not break down in your backyard composter, so read the fine print. Look for the certified compostable seal (see Decoding Eco Labels, page 317).

**Degradable or Oxo-degradable Plastic:** These plastics are often petroleum-based. They're designed to decompose when exposed to UV light or oxygen, both of which are rarely found in landfills. You'll find oxo-degradable plastic bags comparing themselves to a fallen leaf that will disappear in time. Pu-leeze! Fallen leaves these petrol-bags are not. Still, advocates say it's better than stealing corn from the mouths of babes to make biodegradable plastics. They also say oxo-degradable plastics can go in the recycling bin, unlike biodegradable and compostable plastics.

# HOUSEHOLD HAZARDOUS WASTE DISPOSAL GUIDE

Millions of Canadian households are saddled with hazardous waste without a clue as to how to get rid of it. According to Statistics Canada, only one-quarter of us use designated depots to return batteries. Less than half return expired drugs to a pharmacy. And 38% of us have old paint sitting around gathering dust. No wonder, when hazardous waste depots are often tough to access. The ones in Toronto are deep in industrial zones with crazily restricted hours. Hardly conducive to public drop-offs. But to be fair, Toronto does offer free "Toxics Taxi" pick-up services to residents with over 10 litres of household hazardous waste (HHW) as well as rotating community environment day events where residents can drop off hazardous waste in their ward one day a year. Plus, a new website (dowhatyoucan.ca) allows Ontario residents to track down haz waste drop centres near them. Luckily, many provinces have partnered up with local retailers so that residents can drop off old paint cans and such at shops instead of schlepping to waste depots. Make sure you inquire about all the HHW drop-off options near you.

What should you return to municipal hazardous waste depots?
- Anything with a corrosive symbol (e.g., drain cleaner)
- Anything with a flammable symbol (e.g., turpentine)
- Anything with a poison/explosive symbol (e.g., aerosol)
- Paint (latex and oil-based)/sealants
- Pesticides/fertilizer
- Used motor oil
- Harsh chemical cleaners (e.g., half-empty bottles of drain or oven cleaners)
- Fluorescent light tubes and compact fluorescent bulbs
- Pool chemicals
- Rechargeable batteries (many municipalities will tell you to put single-use batteries in the trash, though the wiser ones consider both rechargeable and nonrechargable HHW—check with your municipality)

## TAKE IT BACK TO WHERE YOU BOUGHT IT

Picture it: town dump, turn of the 19th century. When municipalities finally started caving in to citizens' calls to rid laneways and back alleys of festering trash, cities were mostly hauling away buckets of sewage and coal ash from stoves. Fast-forward to today, when the Product Policy Institute says a whopping 75% of municipal solid waste is manufactured goods, from mattresses to polystyrene cups. No one really questions the fact that, while industry is responsible for spitting that mess off assembly lines, our discards are dutifully picked up from our curbs on the city's (a.k.a. the taxpayers') tab. Kind of like welfare for waste. We shouldn't be surprised that repair shops are vanishing when products are effectively designed for the dump. Zero-wasters want producers to take responsibility for the products they put out there. The concept is called extended producer responsibility and it's huge in Europe. The good news is that a growing number of Canadian companies (and provinces) seem to be listening.

Here are a few examples of retailers that will take back your HHW and more:

- RONA, Home Depot and IKEA will take back **old compact fluorescent lights**.
- Punch in your postal code at **rbrc.org** to find the retailer nearest you that takes back rechargeable batteries.
- Shoppers Drug Mart will take your **old pharmaceuticals** and **insulin needles** (bring them in a plastic bag). Ask your local pharmacy if they will too.
- Some grocers, including certain Metro and Loblaws locations, have **plastic bag** drop boxes.
- Some home improvement stores act as depots for used motor oil, old tires, paint, etc.; for instance, Home Depot and RONA locations in Ontario and Alberta will take old paint, and Jiffy Lube will take antifreeze and motor oil. Canadian Tire in Red Deer, Alberta, will take your old motor oil. Check with your local home improvement stores for details.
- All of the most responsible electronics companies have e-waste recycling programs now, so check with whoever made your computer, TV, etc.

# GREEN HOME STOREFRONTS

*If you know of any great green home storefronts that we didn't include in the list, please email the details to* eco@ecoholic.ca.

## NATIONAL

While there's no real national chain of totally green storefronts (well, except ReStores), here are some major national retailers that offer a selection of green products. I can't, however, guarantee that there are no greenwashed products on the shelves.

Canadian Tire: New Blue Planet line of products are accredited by either Energy Star or EcoLogo (a.k.a. Environmental Choice) and focus on water conservation, waste reduction, energy conservation and healthy homes and gardens (canadiantire.ca).

Habitat for Humanity ReStores: Green through and through. Best national source of used and surplus building materials that are sold at a fraction of normal prices. Proceeds from ReStores help local affiliates fund the construction of Habitat for Humanity houses within the community. Over 60 storefronts, located in every province but Newfoundland (habitat.org).

Home Depot: The world's largest home-improvement retailer has thousands of greener products (from front-load washing machines and FSC-certified wood to cellulose insulation and compact fluorescent bulbs) under its Eco Options label. Products pass certain internal screens, but I've seen some pretty toxic skull-and-crossbones-type "natural" pesticides in stores that come with the Eco Options label (homedepot.ca).

Home Hardware: Its EarthCare logo identifies products that are energy-efficient, biodegradable, recyclable, reusable, non-toxic or organic; are manufactured from recycled material; or help to conserve water (homehardware.ca).

**IKEA:** These guys don't really have a green line of products, but all their goods are free of PVC and brominated fire retardants, and their pressed woods are ultra-low in formaldehyde. About 7% of their wood products are FSC-certified and overall they have pretty decent forestry policies (ikea.ca).

**RONA:** Most of the products in the RONA ECO line at this home improvement chain are also certified by Energy Star, the Forest Stewardship Council (FSC), EcoLogo, Watersense, Green Seal or, less impressively, Sustainable Forestry Initiative (SFI). RONA says 100% of the company's lumber will come from eco-certified sources by the end of 2010, and their goal is that 25% of that lumber will be FSC-certified by 2012 (rona.ca).

## REGIONAL

Here's a cross-Canada list of independent green storefronts that sell a wide range of home-related products under one roof, from bedding to paint. Some specialize in building/reno supplies, and most are stuffed to the rafters with smaller home goods like linens and kitchenware. To help you get a clearer picture of what's in store, I've included a mini product listing for each. FYI, you can also try finding earth-conscious reno products through eco-friendly renovators like **Equinox Home Innovations** in Saskatoon (equinoxhomes.ca).

### BRITISH COLUMBIA

All Things Being Eco (discount organics store: linens, decor, glassware, dishware, office supplies, kitchen supplies)
105-7388 Vedder Road
Chilliwack, BC
V2R 4E4
Tel: 604-824-9442
allthingsbeingeco.ca

**CBR Products—Canadian Building Restoration Products Inc.** (coatings, exterior and interior finishes, paints, cleaners)
102-876 Cordova Street Diversion
Vancouver, BC
V6A 3R3
Tel: 1-888-311-5339
cbrproducts.com

**Eclectrix** (countertops, flooring, lighting, paint, mattresses, linens, textiles, window coverings, cribs)
7A-15223 Pacific Avenue
White Rock, BC
V4B 1P8
Tel: 778-292-0277
eclectrix.com

**Elements Home Design** (bedding, drapery, furniture fabrics, linens, beds, paint, carpets, floors, heating and lighting, textiles, window coverings, baby supplies)
102 Seaview Avenue
Salt Spring Island, BC
V8K 2V8
Tel: 250-537-2344
elementshomedesign.ca

**Gecko Green Living** (bedding, kitchenware, glassware, linens, baby supplies, office supplies, gardening supplies, cleaning products)
364 Lower Ganges Road
Salt Spring Island, BC
V8K 2V7
Tel: 250-537-1151
geckogreenliving.com

**The Good Planet Company** (mattresses, futons, bedding, towels, alternative-power electronics)
764 Fort Street
Victoria, BC
V8W 1H2
Tel: 250-590-3500
goodplanet.com

**Green Paint Eco Friendly Products** (interior paint, exterior paint, swatch kits, primer)
Unit 103, 1075 West 1st Avenue
North Vancouver, BC
V7P 3T4
Tel: 604-986-1224
greenpaint.ca

**GreenWorks Building Supply** (lumber, flooring, countertops, roofing, insulation, plumbing)
386 West 8th Avenue
Vancouver, BC
V5Y 3X2
Tel: 604-685-3611
greenworksbuildingsupply.com

**m-smart design** (wallpaper, fabrics, dining, bedding, bath, furniture, pillows, mattresses, accessories)
Unit H5, 925 Main Street
Park Royal South
West Vancouver, BC
Tel: 778-280-3610
m-smartdesign.com

## YUKON

**Any-Avenue Design** (countertops, paint, flooring)
Suite #1
1114 First Ave
Whitehorse, YT
Tel: 867-668-2008

## ALBERTA

**Carbon Environmental Boutique** (FSC furniture, flooring, paint, countertops, bedding, mattresses, decor, lighting, renewable energy electronics, air and water purifiers)
10184-104 Street
Edmonton, AB
T5J 1A7
Tel: 780-498-1900
carbonboutique.com

**Earth's General Store** (bedding, kitchenware, lighting and heating products, cleaning products, baby products)
201-10832 Whyte Avenue
Edmonton, AB
T6E 2B3
Tel: 780-439-8725
egs.ca

**The EcoStore** (kitchen supplies, baby products, household supplies, recycling and compost, hemp products, paper and office supplies)
809 4th Avenue SW
Calgary, AB
T2P 0K5
Tel: 403-230-1443, ext. 222
cleancalgary.org

Riva's The Eco Store (linens, mattresses, countertops, flooring, air and water filters, paint, insulation)
1534 17th Avenue SW
Calgary, AB
T2T 0C8
Tel: 403-452-1001
rivasecostore.com

## SASKATCHEWAN

The Better Good (mattresses, home decor, linens, kitchenware, garden supplies)
640 Broadway Ave.
Saskatoon, SK
S7N 1A9
Tel: 306-242-4663
thebettergood.com

## MANITOBA

Humboldt's Legacy (linens, bedding, kitchenware, decor, outdoor furniture, gardening supplies)
887 Westminster Avenue
Winnipeg, MB
R3G 1B4
Tel: 204-772-1404

## ONTARIO

Arbour Environmental Shoppe (bedding, gardening, cleaning products, lighting, alternative energy products, rain barrels)
800 Bank Street
Ottawa, ON
K1S 3V8
Tel: 613-567-3168
arbourshop.com

**Eco Building Resource** (flooring, paint, LED lighting, insulation, fencing)
Unit 5, 136 Wellington Street East
Aurora, ON
L4G 1J1
Tel: 905-841-3535
eco-building.ca

**Ecoexistence** (green cookware, custom reclaimed furniture, decor, linens, lamps, baby products)
Unit 103, 21 Vaughan Road
Toronto, ON
M6G 2N2
Tel: 416-652-0808
ecoexistence.ca

**Ecoinhabit** (building materials, countertops, roofing, flooring, paint, furniture, fixtures, mattresses, beds, bedding)
121 Old Highway 26
Meaford, ON
N4L 1W7
Tel: 888-538-0777
ecoinhabit.com

**Grassroots Environmental Products** (linens, mattresses, decor, natural cleaners, office supplies, air and water filters, alternative-energy supplies, gardening supplies)
372 Danforth Avenue
Toronto, ON
M4K 1N8
Tel: 416-466-2841

*and*
408 Bloor Street West
Toronto, ON
M5S 1X5
Tel: 416-944-1993
grassrootsstore.com

**Green Design Studio** (furniture, reno materials,
countertops, lighting, textiles, decor, custom-built furniture/kitchens/
installations)
Unit 104, 171 East Liberty Street
Toronto, ON
M6K 3P6
Tel: 416-538-0326
greendesignstudio.ca

**The Healthiest Home** (flooring, cabinetry, countertops, design,
installations and removals)
135 Holland Avenue
Ottawa, ON
K1Y 0Y2
Tel: 613-715-9014
Toll-free: 1-877-ECO-4211
thehealthiesthome.com
homesteadhouse.ca

**Homestead House Paint Company** (VOC-free paint, milk paint,
hemp oil, beeswax finish)
95 Niagara Street
Toronto, ON
M5V 1C3
Tel: 416-504-9984

**Organic Lifestyle** (linens, mattresses, flooring, paint, reclaimed furniture, baby bedding, shower curtains)
Check website for locations of partner retailers.
Tel: 416-921-7317
Toll-free: 1-800-864-5690
organiclifestyle.ca

**Pistachio** (glassware, kitchenware, decor, throw pillows, dishware, office supplies)
2433 Yonge Street
Toronto, ON
M4P 2E7
Tel: 416-322-9451
*and*
Yorkdale Shopping Centre
Unit 240, 3401 Dufferin Street
North York, ON
M6A 2T9
Tel: 416-256-3845
epistachio.net

**P'lovers** (linens, decor, rugs, cleaning products, office and garden supplies)
180 Queen Street
Port Perry, ON
L9L 1B8
Tel: 905-982-0660
*and*
56 Ontario Street
Stratford, ON
N5A 3G8
Tel: 519-271-3883

*and*
11 Main Street
Bayfield, ON
N0M 1G0
Tel: 519-565-5161
plovers.ca

**ShopEco** (household items, gifts, blankets, wall art, cleaning supplies)
Unit 104, 640 Chilver Road
Windsor, ON
N8Y 2K1
Tel: 519-735-7997
shopeco.ca

**Sustain** (flooring, paint, countertops, mattresses, bedding, decor, furniture, baby stuff)
8 Crescent Road, Unit B-2
Huntsville, ON
P1H 0B3
Tel: 705-787-0326
sustainmuskoka.com

**The Zero Point** (paint, wallpaper, counters, flooring, upholstered furniture, bedding, kitchenware, mattresses, cleaners)
1590 Queen Street East
Toronto, ON
M4L 1G1
Tel: 416-602-6586
thezeropoint.ca

## QUEBEC

**Coop La Maison Verte** (cleaning supplies, office supplies, gardening supplies, air and water filters, composting toilets, toilet dams)
5785 Sherbrooke Street West
Montreal, QC
H4A 1X2
Tel: 514-489-8000
cooplamaisonverte.com

**Cooperative Du Grand Orme** (cleaning supplies, water filters, decor)
99 rue Ste-Anne
Sainte-Anne-de-Bellevue
Montreal, QC
H9X 1L9
Tel: 514-457-0858
coopdugrandorme.ca

**Éco-Reno** (recycled paint, used cabinetry, woodworks, windows, mouldings, doors, tubs, taps)
6631 Papineau Avenue
Montreal, QC
H2G 2X3
Tel: 514-725-9990
ecoreno.com

**Maréka** (cleaning products, rain barrels, composters)
535 Lakeshore Dr.
Dorval, QC
H9S 2B1
Tel: 514-403-0602
mareka.ca

Noyma (bedding, mattresses, bath accessories, baby products)
Unit 101, 2500 rue des Nations
Montreal, QC
H4R 3J9
Tel: 514-333-3233
noyma.ca

## NOVA SCOTIA

P'lovers (linens, decor, rugs, cleaning products, office and garden
supplies)
5657 Spring Garden Road, Box 224
Halifax, NS
B3J 3R4
Tel: 902-422-6060
Toll-free: 1-800-565-2998
*and*
The Old Station, 3 Edgewater
Mahone Bay, NS
B0J 2E0
Tel: 902-624-1421
plovers.net

## GOOD GREEN HOME WEBSITES

Canada Mortgage Housing Corporation: The CMHC site has
tons of useful info on all things home-related, including buying, rent-
ing, maintaining and reno-ing a home, as well as green mortgage loan
insurance and financial assistance. cmhc-schl.gc.ca/en/co

Care2 Make a Difference: Goes by Care2. It's got a news section
and a petition section, but the Healthy Living section, crammed with
DIY tips on everything, is the most handy part. care2.com

**Environmental Health News:** Okay, so this one isn't specifically home-related, but just like you'd get a newspaper delivered to your door, check EHN every day to stay on top of extensive enviro news coverage from around the globe. environmentalhealthnews.org

**The Green Guide:** These guys have been taken over by *National Geographic* and still put out an excellent website full of helpful tips and product reports for the home and much more. Full of practical reports on green problems and solutions for everyday things. thegreenguide.com

**Green Your Decor:** The name says it all. This blog basically showcases new green design finds. Best part: "Green Steal of the Week" and electronic coupons. greenyourdecor.com

**Inhabitat:** A weblog devoted to the future of design, tracking the innovations that are pushing architecture and home design towards a smarter and more sustainable future. inhabitat.com

**Re-Nest:** Its slogan is "abundant design for green homes." Beyond highlighting funky green designs and homes, this site offers DIY posts on making your own coffee table from reclaimed wood or using glass jars as photo frames; green product reviews; and a green home shopping directory (mostly American). re-nest.com

**Treehugger:** This green consumer blog/"green CNN" features, amongst other things, all the latest on design and architecture as well as great green buying guides. treehugger.com

(For a listing of strictly green home reno websites, see page 189.)

# GLOSSARY

**1,4-dioxane:** A petroleum-derived contaminant considered a probable human carcinogen by the U.S. Environmental Protection Agency (EPA), and a definite animal carcinogen. It's a by-product of chemical processing found in many sudsy products, like shampoo, bubble bath and dish soap. Potentially contaminated chemicals include polyethylene, polyethylene glycol (PEG), polyoxyethylene, polyethoxyethylene and polyoxynolethylene.

**bioaccumulation:** The build-up of chemicals in the tissues of a living thing, whether human, wildlife or plant. (Chemicals enter our bodies through the food we eat, the air we breathe and the water we drink.) Bioaccumulation explains why larger, older fish have higher levels of mercury, for instance, than do smaller, younger ones.

**biodegradable:** The insinuation is that whatever you purchased will fully break down and return to nature (hopefully in the form of $CO_2$ and $H_2O$), but the label isn't policed. Be your own sheriff. Read labels carefully. Look for certification symbols and details about biodegradability testing standards, and do your research. If a product sports the word "biodegradable," call the company and ask what it means. Has the product passed any particular third-party tests? Under what conditions does the product degrade (only in full sun or also in dark, airless landfill piles)? And just how long does it take to return to nature?

**bisphenol A (BPA):** Found in polycarbonate plastic bottles (the ones with the little No. 7 on the bottom), ceramic dental fillings, paper products, and food and beverage can linings. It is an estrogen-mimicking hormone disrupter found to leach from products. Numerous studies have tied low exposure levels to birth defects, breast and prostate cancer, and more (a study released in 2008 by the *Journal of the American Medical Association* said that adults exposed to higher amounts of the chemical were three times as likely to suffer from heart disease and 2.4 times as likely to have type 2 diabetes). Manufacturers argue that the levels are so low they're not a health risk, but in 2008 Nalgene stopped using the plastic and many retailers, like Toys "R" Us, pulled polycarbonate baby bottles from shelves. Health Canada deemed the compound dangerous in 2008 and promised to remove it from kids' products.

**brominated fire retardants (BFRs):** These babies might make your mattress, couch and electronics less likely to erupt in flames, but they're part of a family of chemicals that are incredibly persistent and tend to accumulate in human and animal tissue. The most famous members of the brominated family are polybrominated diphenyl ethers (PBDEs). *See also* PBDEs, page 362.

**BuildingGreen:** This highly revered independent company is turned to by the eco-conscious building sector for its unbiased assessments of green building products. It's responsible for publications that include *Environmental Building News* and *GreenSpec*, a green building product directory. BuildingGreen also has interesting side projects up its sleeve, like maintaining the U.S. Department of Energy's database of high-performance buildings and overseeing curriculum for Boston Architectural College's online sustainable design program.

**cadmium:** A metallic element that is considered a probable human carcinogen.

**carbon footprint:** Nothing to do with your foot size. This has to do with the total greenhouse gas emissions directly and indirectly caused by a product, your house, your car, your vacation, you name it.

**carbon neutral:** Essentially this means you have a carbon footprint of zero—for instance, a carbon-neutral house should create as much green, renewable energy as it uses. But the term is more widely associated with buying outside carbon credits, or offsets (*see* carbon offset, page 352), that in effect neutralize your emissions. So even if your house isn't powered by windmills, you can still pay someone to produce enough wind energy somewhere else in the grid to offset the greenhouse gases your home creates through its gas furnace, electricity use and so on. Some companies are going "carbon negative," which means they are supporting enough greenhouse gas–abating projects that they can claim to have a carbon footprint of less than zero.

carbon offset: For every ton of greenhouse gases produced by an activity or object, you can mitigate that pollution by supporting a greenhouse gas–saving project (like a wind farm or a tree farm). So let's say your car puts out 10 tons of greenhouse gases and you feel guilty about it, you can then decide to buy wind energy credits/offsets that result in less carbon dioxide or other greenhouse gases in the atmosphere than would otherwise occur.

carcinogen: Anything that may cause cancer.

chemical sensitivities (a.k.a. multiple chemical sensitivities): A chronic syndrome caused by a person's intolerance to chemicals. Even low doses of the offending chemicals can stimulate a negative reaction. Symptoms vary but can include headaches, a runny nose, aching joints, confusion, fatigue and sore throat. Symptoms generally improve or disappear when the chemicals are removed. A team of researchers recently found that people with multiple chemical sensitivities are missing certain enzymes that help metabolize chemicals.

chlorinated tris: A carcinogenic fire retardant banned from children's PJs 30 years ago but still used on furniture foam. Deemed a health hazard by the World Health Organization, the National Cancer Institute and the National Research Council.

chloromethane (a.k.a. methyl chloride): A potent neurotoxin and possible human carcinogen found in air, water (including ground- and drinking water) and soil samples. Sources include burning PVC and silicone rubber, as well as cigarettes, chlorinated pools and polystyrene insulation.

chromated copper arsenate (CCA): Lumber intended for outdoor use (known as pressure-treated wood) is often treated with this stuff, which is heavy in chromium and arsenic. Several towns have ripped out playgrounds built with this kind of wood after realizing that it leaches quite readily into surrounding soil (especially sandy soil, and especially when exposed to sunlight, which is, like, all the time). If your flower beds are framed with arsenic-laced pressure-treated wood, the toxins could make their way into your veggie patch too. (If you decide to toss your old wood, make sure to bring it to your local hazardous waste depot. Call your municipality for details.)

closed-cell: Used in reference to plastics found in products like yoga mats, as in "100% closed-cell PVC mat." The term may imply that the product doesn't off-gas, but all it really means is that its plastic cells are sealed within their own little bubble, making it highly water-resistant.

Competition Bureau: The Competition Bureau is an independent Canadian law enforcement agency set up by the government of Canada. It investigates consumer complaints about false advertising and unfair pricing.

Cradle to Cradle: *See* Resources: Decoding Eco Labels, page 317.

cyanobacteria: Often called "blue-green algae," cyanobacteria are a type of aquatic bacteria found in freshwater lakes. In a balanced state, cyanobacteria in tropical lakes can provide nourishment to soil and rice paddies, but they can turn poisonous in Canadian lakes and ponds. Just swimming in a lake with blue-green algae scum can bring on a rash, nausea and/or diarrhea. Too many phosphates (found in fertilizers and dish detergent), as well as too much nitrogen (again found in fertilizers), can lead to massive blue-green algae blooms. If animals drink tainted water, they can become paralyzed and die. No joke. Quebec has been hit especially hard by such blooms, with warnings being issued on over 50 lakes in the summer of 2007. The federal government has finally followed Quebec and Manitoba's lead by banning phosphates from dish and laundry soap by 2010.

decaBDE: *See* PBDEs, page 362.

DEGME (2-[2-Methoxyethoxy] ethanol): This endocrine-disrupting jet-fuel additive can be found in floor cleaners, degreasers, paint, paint strippers and pest control products, as well as some skin creams. In early 2009, the feds noted DEGME's ability to impair fertility and harm the development of fetuses. Good thing the federal government's Chemical Management Plan just declared it toxic, paving the way for it to be banned in cosmetics, anyway. DEGME is also sometimes listed as methoxydiglycol on a product label.

DEHP: *See* phthalates, page 364.

dimethyl ditallow ammonium chloride: Found in anti-static products, fabric dyes, fertilizers and lubricating oil. Made from animal fat, it is toxic to fish and algae, and it isn't readily biodegradable.

dioxins (a.k.a. furans): Carcinogenic, endocrine-disrupting neurotoxins. There are lots of different types of dioxins, but they all contain chlorine, and they're all bad. The largest source of dioxins in Canada is the burning of municipal and medical waste (mainly from burning PVC products). Burning plastics in your backyard releases dioxins too, as does burning chemically treated wood. Dioxins build up in animal tissues, which explains why the main way humans ingest dioxins is by eating meat, milk products and fish. The pulp and paper processing biz was historically also a big source of dioxins, but the industry says it has seriously reduced dioxin pollution.

EcoLogo: *See* Resources: Decoding Eco Labels, 317.

EcologyAction: A California-based non-profit environmental consultancy on conservation and pollution-preventing initiatives for business, schools, government and individuals (ecoact.org).

embodied energy: Basically, this just refers to the energy it took to manufacture a product like insulation or flooring from start to finish (including sourcing the materials needed to make the product).

EMF (electromagnetic field): Electric and magnetic fields are invisible lines of energy created by the production and transmission of electricity. Electric fields are kick-started whenever an electronic object is plugged into a socket (even if it's not turned on). Magnetic fields are created when that device is flicked on. The closer you are to the source, the stronger the EMFs. EMFs are given off by everything from household wiring and lighting to anything plugged into a wall. In those with electro-hypersensitivity (EHS), EMFs can trigger nausea, headaches, chronic fatigue, chronic pain, tinnitus, rashes and more. Health Canada says, "There is no conclusive evidence of any harm caused by exposures at levels normally found in Canadian living and working environments." Sweden, with an estimated 250,000 EHS sufferers, leads the pack by recognizing EHS as a full-on disability.

endocrine disrupters: Chemicals that interfere with the endocrine system, which secretes development-guiding and reproductive hormones. *See also* hormone disrupters, page 358.

EnerGuide: An official federal government labelling system in which appliances, homes and cars are scored on their energy (or fuel) consumption on a scale of 1 to 100.

Energy Factor (EF): Energy Factor is an energy performance measurement of both the federal EnerGuide standard and the Energy

Star program. The higher the Energy Factor, the more efficient the dishwasher, hot water tank, etc.

**Energy Star:** A voluntary labelling system started as a joint program of the U.S. Environmental Protection Agency and the U.S. Department of Energy in 1992. The program has been adopted globally by Australia, Japan and, yes, Canada. The label is administered by Natural Resources Canada's Office of Energy Efficiency (OEE). According to them, products have to meet or exceed Canadian federal energy-efficiency standards, but to be honest, even the OEE website admits that most products that qualify in the U.S. automatically get the little blue-and-white star here, no questions asked. In 2008, *Consumer Reports* came out with a major dig against the government-led program, saying it's too lax about what gets the star of approval, with too few spot checks and too little independent testing. However, in 2009 U.S. President Barack Obama ordered Energy Star to toughen up its standards.

**Environment Canada:** The federal government department in charge of conserving natural resources, protecting water resources, predicting the weather and coordinating environmental policies and programs.

**Environmental Working Group (EWG):** Founded in 1993, this non-profit D.C.-based group is responsible for extensive research and advocacy on toxic chemicals in consumer products and farming as they relate to health, food and water pollution and more. Lately, they're best known for their extensive product testing and research (ewg.org).

**EPA (Environmental Protection Agency):** The American equivalent of Environment Canada. The EPA develops and enforces environmental regulations, gives grants to state and non-profit enviro programs, researches environmental issues and educates the public on green subjects. It also runs the Energy Star program in the U.S. with the U.S. Department of Energy.

EPEAT: *See* Resources: Decoding Eco Labels, 317.

estrogen-mimicking: Describes a chemical or ingredient that mimics the female hormone estrogen. Estrogen mimickers can also interfere with the normal metabolism of estrogen in the body. They have been known to spawn intersex fish. In addition, they've been linked to decreased sperm counts in men and elevated endometriosis and breast cancer rates in women.

Forest Stewardship Council: *See* Resources: Decoding Eco Labels, page 317.

formaldehyde: Commonly found in pressed woods (particleboard and medium-density fiberboard), permanent-press fabric (clothing and curtains) and insulation. Urea formaldehyde releases volatile formaldehyde gas; phenol formaldehyde tends to off-gas less, according to the National Safety Council. Formaldehyde may cause cancer in humans (it's classified as a known human carcinogen by the International Agency for Research on Cancer and as a probable human carcinogen by the U.S. EPA), as well as wheezing, fatigue, rashes, and eye, nose and throat irritations. Some people are especially sensitive to it. It's also a major component of smog.

furans: *See* dioxins, page 354. (Though not exactly the same, these two are usually lumped together and are often given the same description.)

grandfathered: Exempt from a new regulation.

Green Seal: *See* Resources: Decoding Eco Labels, page 317.

GREENGUARD: *See* Resources: Decoding Eco Labels, page 317.

HCFC: When ozone-depleting CFCs were phased out in the mid-1990s, HCFCs (hydrochlorofluorocarbons) were brought in as their greener alternative. We soon realized that HCFCs (refrigerants used by the air-conditioner and fridge sector) are also ozone-depleting substances, as well as greenhouse gases. The most common HCFC is R-22. By January 1, 2010, 65% of HCFCs imported into and manufactured in Canada will be phased out.

**HFC:** This refrigerant is considered the relatively greener alternative to HCFCs, since it doesn't affect the ozone layer, but it's still an extremely potent greenhouse gas. And this stuff is used not only in air conditioners, but also as a foam blowing agent, aerosol propellant and solvent. Since the '90s, Greenpeace International has been trying to convince companies to avoid HFCs and to use natural gases instead. In 2000, a large pre–Sydney Olympic Games campaign pressured Coca-Cola, Unilever and McDonald's to phase out HFC.

**high-density polyethylene (HDPE):** *See* Resources: Plastics Guide, page 331.

**hormone disrupters:** Chemicals that mimic or block hormones, potentially throwing off normal body functions and triggering behavioural, reproductive and developmental problems. *See also* endocrine disrupters, page 355.

**Integrated Pest Management (IPM):** IPM is considered a more environmentally sensitive approach to controlling pests on farms as well as in backyard gardens. The first line of defence is preventing an outbreak by, for instance, rotating crops. IPM encourages the use of less risky pesticides first, including releasing predators or using pheromones to disrupt pest mating or to trap pests. Chemical pesticides are a last resort.

**leaching:** The process by which a chemical or toxin is transferred from one surface to another. For instance, cooking high-acid foods like tomatoes in an aluminum pan can cause the aluminum to be transferred to the tomatoes.

**LED (Light-Emitting Diode):** Early LED lights (in the 1960s) were all a shade of red, but today's LEDs come in every colour you can imagine, including good old-fashioned white light. Plus, they beat out compact fluorescent bulbs for being ultra-energy-efficient (they're 90% more efficient than incandescent), are quick to turn on and don't contain mercury. So far they're too expensive to produce to be popular with the masses, but their time is coming. Scientists have discovered a new way of making affordable LEDs that last, oh, 100,000 hours.

**low-density polyethylene (LDPE):** *See* Resources: Plastics Guide, page 331.

**mercury:** The shiny stuff in old thermometers and the only metal that's liquid at room temperature. Mercury is used in dental fillings and batteries and as a preservative in some vaccines. Most of the mercury in landfill comes from the mercury switches found in cars (the switches have been used to activate trunk and hood lights). Most human exposure to the potent neurotoxin comes from eating mercury-contaminated fish, according to the U.S. EPA. Developing fetuses are most at risk and can develop severe disabilities from exposure—hence the 2004 EPA warning to women who want to become pregnant, pregnant or nursing moms, and young children to curb their tuna intake (enviros say to ditch it altogether). The EPA estimates that 300,000 newborns each year have an increased risk of learning disabilities thanks to exposure to mercury in the womb. How do fish get so full of mercury to begin with? Emissions from coal plants and other factories send mercury up into the air, where it can travel great distances on wind currents and come down as rain or snow over bodies of water. It then collects in the bodies of aquatic animals and moves up the food chain. *See also* bioaccumulation, page 350.

**methyl chloride:** *See* chloromethane, page 352.

**methylene chloride:** Emitted in polyurethane production and found in paint thinners and strippers, shoe polish, fabric protectors and pesticides—and, oh yes, used in the production of decaf coffee and tea. The EPA classifies it as a probable carcinogen. It doesn't dissolve well in water and can be found in drinking water.

multiple chemical sensitivities: *See* chemical sensitivities, page 352.

nanotechnology: Nanotechnology essentially creates and manipulates molecules or atoms that are one-billionth of a metre in size (that's 100,000 times smaller than the width of a human hair follicle). Industry swears nano-mania will soon revolutionize everything from make-up to electronics, but critics say it's the next GMO (genetically modified organism), and cautionary lessons should be learned from our experience with genetically engineered seeds. Some aspects of nanotechnology, like making solar cells 100 times thinner and 100 times faster or using nanotech in sensors that detect harmful contaminants, are more welcome by environmentalists, but greenies consider others, like embedding nano particles of antibacterial silver ions into socks and plastic food containers, to be gross abuses of the tech. Health Canada says it's evaluating the potential risks and benefits of nanotechnology, and Environment Canada says new nanotech must undergo a risk assessment of its potential effects on the environment and human health.

National Research Council of Canada: This federal research and development org has been around since 1916. Beyond undertaking research in IT, biotech, aerospace, engineering and more, it runs the national science library, publishes scientific and technical info and certifies scientific instruments and materials.

Natural Resources Defence Council: One of America's most powerful environmental orgs. Founded in 1970 by a bunch of law students and lawyers, today it has 1.2 million members. Their priorities are climate change, clean energy, revitalizing the oceans and more.

**net zero:** If your home's renewable energy systems are capable of producing as much (or as little) energy as you consume over the course of the year, you can proudly call yourself a net zero house. Realistically, this concept is more feasible in new homes designed to be highly energy-efficient. Canada's Net-Zero Energy Home Coalition is a multi-stakeholder organization that champions energy-efficient residential building products, as well as the use of renewable technologies.

**neurotoxin:** A toxin that affects the central nervous system, harming neural tissue.

**nickel-metal hydride (NiMH):** A type of rechargeable battery similar to old-school nickel cadmium rechargeable batteries, but made with much less toxic materials. They don't hold a charge as long and they release their charge even when not in use more readily than nickel cadmium, but that's the price you pay for reducing toxins in the environment. Besides their use in handheld electronics, NiMH batteries are also used in electric cars like the Prius.

**OECD (Organization for Economic Cooperation and Development):** An international organization of 30 free-market, democratic countries. OECD countries swap info on policy experiences and good practices, and coordinate domestic and international policies.

**Oeko-Tex:** *See* Resources: Decoding Eco Labels, page 317.

**off-gassing:** Not a bodily function, but the release of chemicals like phthalates and volatile organic compounds (VOCs) into the air. VOCs become a gas at room temperature, so, for instance, products made with the VOC formaldehyde will often release formaldehyde gas into the air for weeks, months or years after you purchase a product. VOCs can off-gas for a period of time from cabinets, carpets and mattresses, as well as from paint, glues and sealants, even after they have dried.

361

**Organic Consumers Association:** This grassroots public interest org aggressively battles to maintain and elevate the integrity of organics. They have ongoing campaigns about food safety, genetic engineering, fair-trade issues and much more (organicconsumers.org).

**parabens:** All types of parabens (methyl-, ethyl-, etc.) have been found to be estrogenic — meaning they mimic female hormones. They have been found in breast tumour samples but haven't been conclusively linked to cancer.

**PBDEs:** A family of flame retardants used for decades in a broad range of consumer goods. Skyrocketing levels of these have been found in everything from arctic animals, lake trout, whales and waterbirds to human breast milk. PentaBDE and octaBDE production in North America ceased at the end of 2004, but they might still be found in imported products. Canada now says decaBDEs are so dangerous that it won't let companies manufacture them here, but deca is still common in consumer electronics, wire insulation, draperies and upholstery on both sides of the border.

**PCB (polychlorinated biphenyl):** An extremely persistent environmental contaminant. This industrial chemical was introduced in 1929 and used in the making of electronic equipment. The U.S. banned the substance in 1979, but it's still turning up in human tissue and farmed salmon.

**persistent:** Referring to a chemical that does not readily biodegrade but instead accumulates in the environment and living tissues. *See also* bioaccumulation, page 350.

**petrochemical:** Any chemical derived from petroleum, coal or natural gas. Petrochemicals are used to make plastic, fertilizers, paint, cleaning products, asphalt and synthetic fabrics such as polyester. All of the ecological problems that arise from fossil fuel excavation, processing and shipping are also associated with its offshoots, plus the extra pollution created by refining and manufacturing each chemical.

**PFCs (perfluorated chemicals/compounds a.k.a. perfluorochemicals):** A family of lab-made chemicals composed of fluorine and carbon responsible for making pans non-stick, raincoats waterproof and carpets stain-resistant. PFCs have been found to be extremely persistent in the environment around the globe and many have been tied to serious health problems. Brand name incarnations of PFCs include Teflon, Gore-Tex, Stainmaster and Scotchgard. For a shopper's guide to what products contain PFCs and detailed reports on the topic, check out ewg.org.

**PFOA:** An ingredient used to make non-stick surfaces on cookware, microwave popcorn bags, candy wrappers, fast-food french-fry containers, cardboard pizza trays and burger wrappers. It does not break down in the wild (even DDT breaks down eventually) and has reportedly accumulated in 95% of Americans' tissues and in high levels in wildlife, including polar bears. In early 2006, the EPA announced that it had reached an agreement with DuPont and seven other major manufacturers to cut their emissions and PFOA-containing products by 95% by 2010 and to eliminate PFOA altogether by 2015. (EPA documents show that DuPont has known about PFOA's persistence in the broader population since 1976.) PFOA is part of a slippery and persistent class of chemicals called PFCs (perfluorinated chemicals) that keep your eggs from sticking, repel stains and make rain bead off your jacket.

**PFOS (perfluorooctanesulfonate):** A chemical commonly found on older stain-repellent carpets, furniture and clothing. PFOS was the basis of Scotchgard's and Stainmaster's original formulation until 3M stopped production of the chemical in 2002 after the EPA threatened it with regulatory action. Studies found that PFOS was turning up everywhere in the environment and that it killed some rat pups even though it was their mothers that had been exposed while the pups were in the womb, not the pups themselves. Like PFOA, it was also used as a grease-repellent surface in fast-food wrappers, popcorn bags, candy bars and beverage containers. PFOS use has been phased out in Canada. PFOS is part of the persistent PFC (perfluorinated chemicals) family.

**phenols:** A broad class of chemical compounds that include hormone-disrupting bisphenol A and the estradiol in birth control pills. Phenols are used in slime-fighting chemicals, disinfectants, mouthwash, lozenges and more. And according to the U.S. Agency for Toxic Substances and Disease Registry, short-term exposure to phenol in the air can cause respiratory irritation, headaches and burning eyes. High skin exposure can cause skin burns, liver damage and worse. Some phenols are also naturally occurring in plants.

**phosphates:** Too many phosphates (found in fertilizers and dish detergent), as well as too much nitrogen (again found in fertilizers), can lead to massive blue-green algae blooms. If animals drink water tainted with blue-green algae, they can become paralyzed and die. Quebec has been hit especially hard by such blooms, with warnings being issued on over 50 lakes in the summer of 2007. The federal government has finally followed Quebec and Manitoba's lead by banning phosphates from dish and laundry soap by 2010.

**phthalates:** Chemicals often added to PVC plastic as softeners, found in everything from kids' toys to sex toys, as well as all sorts of personal-care products and perfumes. The industry insists they're safe, but the Americans have now banned six types of phthalates from baby toys and Canada is following suit. One type of phthalate in particular, DEHP, has been found to cause birth defects in lab animals and is classified as a probable human carcinogen. Harvard researchers found that another, DEP, can cause DNA damage in the sperm of adult men. Many toy companies have already phased them out in toys intended for younger children. Phthalates are also found in water, household dust, breast milk and wildlife—clearly showing that they migrate from their source.

**polybrominated diphenyl ethers:** *See* brominated fire retardants, page 351.

**polycarbonate plastic:** *See* Resources: Plastics Guide, page 331.

**polyethylene:** Without getting into lots of scientific mumbo-jumbo, polyethylene is a polymer that contains carbon and hydrogen. It forms the basis of PET (*see* polyethylene terephthalate, below), HDPE (*see* high density polyethylene, page 358) and LDPE (*see* low density polyethylene, page 359).

**polyethylene terephthalate (PET):** *See* Resources: Plastics Guide, page 331.

**polypropylene (PP):** *See* Resources: Plastics Guide, page 331.

**polystyrene (PS):** *See* Resources: Plastics Guide, page 331.

**polyvinyl chloride (PVC):** *See* PVC, page 366.

**polyvinylidene chloride (PVDC):** Used to make some plastic wrap. Ten percent of PVDC wrap can be made up of potentially hormone-disrupting, liver-damaging phthalates, which have been found to drift into food.

**proprietary:** Something that's privately owned and operated. Proprietary information is often a reference to trade secrets, as in: "We own the formula, so we don't have to share it with you people."

**PTFE:** Generally considered a PFC (perfluorinated chemical), though a chemist might argue the point and say it's in the fluoroplastic family. The trade name for PTFE, owned by DuPont, is Teflon. Gore-Tex products are basically PTFE with micropores. Gore-Tex swears its gear is so stable it'll never break down, but you wouldn't want to, say, accidentally throw your rain gear in a fire. A few groups of scientists found that using PTFE-coated heat lamps to warm chicks and duck-lings killed up to 52% of them within three to five days. It's considered to be the compound in non-stick pans that may kill pet birds if a pan is heated to extremely high temperatures in their vicinity.

**PVC (polyvinyl chloride, a.k.a. vinyl):** Found in pipes, win-dows, toys, flip-flops, garden furniture, flooring, plastic bottles (check the bottom for recycling symbol No. 3), venetian blinds, umbrellas, fake leather couches and even the puffy 3-D cartoon on your kid's T-shirt. Just the additives—phthalates, lead and cadmium—are supercontroversial. In the late '90s, after two years of investigation, Greenpeace concluded that vinyl is the absolute worst plastic for the environment. The build-ing block of PVC, vinyl chloride, is not only a known carcinogen, but creates dangerous dioxins in the manufacturing process and when incinerated. The industry, of course, says vinyl is completely safe and claims it has cleaned up its practices since its dirtier days and now emits very few dioxins and furans. Even so, many companies, such as Adidas, Reebok, Puma, Nike, Microsoft, Hewlett-Packard, Toyota and Honda, are committed to reducing or eliminating the plastic. IKEA outlaws the substance altogether, and several municipalities have been making moves to do the same. *See also* Resources: Plastics Guide, page 331.

**Rainforest Relief:** This New York–based organization was founded in 1989 and has since been fighting to end the import and use of unsustainable tropical woods in the United States. It has worked to stop cities and stores, including Home Depot, from pur-chasing tropical wood. (Note: Rainforest Relief is not the same organi-zation as Rainforest Alliance.)

**RoHS (Restriction of Hazardous Substance) Directive:**
This European Union–wide directive restricts the use of six toxins (including lead, mercury, PBDE and cadmium) in the manufacture of electronics. Batteries are excluded. It took effect in 2006.

**RugMark:** *See* Resources: Decoding Eco Labels, page 317.

**R-value:** A measure of thermal resistance that tells you how well a building material prevents heat from escaping. The higher the R-value, the more insulating it is.

**Scientific Certification System (SCS):** Founded in 1984 as a third-party certification system based in California, SCS provides environmental, sustainability and food-quality certification, auditing, testing and standards development.

**SFI (Sustainable Forestry Initiative):** See Resources: Decoding Eco Labels, page 317.

**sodium laureth sulphate (a.k.a. sodium laurel ether sulfate, or SLES):** Similar to sodium lauryl sulphate (see below), but somewhat gentler. Still, it's maligned for the same reasons. Processing could create harmful 1,4-dioxanes, by-products found in many products.

**sodium lauryl sulphate (SLS):** A sudsing surfactant found in shampoos, soaps and toothpaste, and a known skin and eye irritant that may aggravate dandruff and mouth ulcers. Rumours of it being a carcinogen are considered urban myths. Health food products often contain SLS made from coconut oil.

**solar heat gain:** This basically refers to the increase in temperature as a result of sun rays hitting a surface, space or structure. Depending on the design, you might be trying to boost solar gain (to increase heat) or reduce solar gain (to decrease heat).

surfactant: A type of chemical found in cleaning products, dish and laundry detergents, shampoos and body washes. Surfactants make these products lather, spread and penetrate well. Hundreds of surfactants are in existence, many petroleum-based. Most surfactants biodegrade in sewage treatment plants, but some, like nonylphenol ethoxylates (NPEs), are of environmental concern because they don't really biodegrade, are toxic to algae and aquatic life, and have been associated with hormone-disrupting effects.

sustainable: Capable of being sustained. If it's sustainable, you can keep doing it again and again without messing up the planet for future generations. Simple as that.

sweatshop: A factory where workers put in long hours at abusively low wages, often under oppressive conditions. Avoid these like the plague by supporting fair-trade-certified products.

Teflon: See PTFE, page 365, and PFOA, page 363.

toluene: A common solvent used in paints, glues, disinfectants and rubber, as well as in tanning leather and manufacturing polyurethane foam. Inhaling toluene regularly over time can lead to brain and kidney damage. Even low doses can cause confusion, as well as memory, hearing and vision loss. Pregnant women should minimize exposure. Toluene is a petroleum by-product.

triclocarbon: A chemical disinfectant found in some antibacterial soaps, though it's less common than triclosan. Triclocarbon is persistent and has been known to survive the sewage treatment process and turn up in lakes, rivers and streams.

triclosan: The active ingredient in many antibacterial soaps, deodorants and toothpastes. Beyond accumulating in fatty tissues (it's been found in fish and in breast milk), it has made its way into lakes, rivers and streams (the U.S. Geological Survey found triclosan to be one of the top 10 stream contaminants). Researchers at the University of Minnesota found that when these chemicals are exposed to sunlight in water, they create a mild dioxin (a carcinogenic hormone disrupter that accumulates in the food chain, even at low levels). And when you throw chlorinated water into the mix, it could turn into a much nastier dioxin. Research from the University of Victoria says it also acts as a harmful endocrine disrupter in aquatic life, particularly frogs. As well, research from Tufts University found that *E. coli* that survived being treated with triclosan became resistant to 7 of 12 antibiotics. If your municipality is spreading its sewage sludge on farmers' fields, as many are, triclosan and triclocarbon are essentially fertilizing the crops in your area. Indeed, Johns Hopkins researchers estimate that about 200 tons of the compounds are spread on farms every year. Triclosan has been voluntarily banned by British food sellers like Marks & Spencer since 2003.

**U.S. EPA:** *See* EPA, page 356.

**VeriFlora:** *See* Resources: Decoding Eco Labels, page 317.

**vinyl:** *See* PVC, page 366.

**volatile organic compounds (VOCs):** Found in paint, glue, gasoline, cleaning products, ink, permanent markers, correction fluid, pesticides and air fresheners. Don't be fooled by the word "organic" in the name—VOCs aren't good for us. They're carbon-containing gases and vapours that evaporate readily into the air, contributing to air pollution. VOCs can even off-gas from non-liquid sources, such as office furniture, that contain formaldehyde, causing serious indoor air pollution. Exposure can cause dizziness, headaches and nausea. Some VOCs are more toxic than others and are tied to cancer and kidney and liver damage. Some react with nitrogen oxide to form smog-inducing compounds.

# INDEX

# ACKNOWLEDGEMENTS

They say home is where the heart is, and the heart of *Ecoholic Home* definitely lies in the affection, support and belly laughs I get every day from my beloved tribe of family and friends. From my personal abode, I have to give thanks to my true love/personal chef and joyriding partner in crime, Brad, as well as my muse, a.k.a. The Mews, for purring loudly when I returned to my writing desk. A big thank-you hug to my parents and loved ones across Canada (including Sierra, Manon, Mark, Lisa) who helped me round up green products (and put them to the test). Big up to my enthusiastic researchers, Eric and Julie, for fishing out facts in record time, and all the refreshingly forthcoming green insiders (you know who you are) who shared their insights. I also have to thank my Vintage Canada editor, Kendall, for bettering yet another *Ecoholic* edition, Kelly for designing one beauty of a book, as well as Graham, Amanda, Marion and my fabulous publicist, Sharon, for helping me bring *Ecoholic Home* to the world. Of course, I have to credit my family at NOW for supporting yet another *Ecoholic* offshoot and my agent, Denise, for having my back. I can't forget Dustin for, once again, going beyond the call of duty and graciously sharing your kick-ass photography skills. And Clayton, thank you for taking Stephen's beautiful web work to the next level, seamlessly folding in the expanding *Ecoholic* family.

And finally, I have to give props to Ecoholics nationwide for standing up for everyone's home base—the earth. Hopefully this book gives you a few more ideas on how to do just that.

**Corrections and Additions:** If you have found an error in *Ecoholic Home* or if you are a producer or retailer who would like to be considered for upcoming editions of this indispensable guide, please contact the author at her website—www.ecoholic.ca.

For Adria's podcasts, *Ecoholic* TV web episodes and weekly column, as well as book updates, event listings and more, please visit www.ecoholic.ca.

Also, be sure to join the official Ecoholic fan site on Facebook.

Adria Vasil is the acclaimed and bestselling author of *Ecoholic: Your Guide to the Most Environmentally Friendly Information, Products and Services in Canada*. She has been writing the "Ecoholic" column in *NOW Magazine* for over five years. She has appeared on television, radio and in print nation-wide and is a well-known advocate for green living. Please visit her website at www.ecoholic.ca.